P9-DCW-804

With best wishes,

[signature]

2004

ROUGH EDGES

10 ReganBooks
Celebrating Ten Bestselling Years
An Imprint of HarperCollins*Publishers*

CONGRESSMAN

JAMES E. ROGAN

ROUGHEDGES

MY UNLIKELY ROAD FROM WELFARE TO WASHINGTON

All photographs appear courtesy of the author except: insert page 2 (lower left), courtesy of Sandy Rudd; and insert page 9, courtesy of Ray Watt/Glendale News Press.

ROUGH EDGES. Copyright © 2004 by James E. Rogan. All rights reserved. Printed in the United States of America. No part of this book may be used or reproduced in any manner whatsoever without written permission except in the case of brief quotations embodied in critical articles and reviews. For information please address HarperCollins Publishers Inc., 10 East 53rd Street, New York, NY 10022.

HarperCollins books may be purchased for educational, business, or sales promotional use. For information please write: Special Markets Department, HarperCollins Publishers Inc., 10 East 53rd Street, New York, NY 10022.

FIRST EDITION

Designed by Erin Benach

Printed on acid-free paper

Library of Congress Cataloging-in-Publication Data

Rogan, James.
   Rough edges : my unlikely road from welfare to Washington / James E. Rogan.—1st ed.
      p. cm.
   ISBN 0-06-058059-3
   1. Rogan, James. 2. Legislators—United States—Biography. 3. United States. Congress. House—Biography. 4. United States—Politics and government—1989– 5. Republican Party (U.S. : 1854–)—Biography. 6. Mission District (San Francisco, Calif.)—Biography. 7. San Francisco (Calif.)—Biography. I. Title.

E840.8.R594A3 2004
324.2734'092—dc22
[B]
                                                                    2004046772

04 05 06 07 08 WBC/QW 10 9 8 7 6 5 4 3 2 1

To Christine, who said yes despite the rough edges

CONTENTS

Prologue

MEMPHIS AND
THE MARBLE ROOM

It wasn't the first time unwelcome guests had invaded the Marble Room.

A hideaway lounge next to the United States Senate chamber, the Marble Room has a "Senators Only" rule that is considered sacred. Through the 1800s, senators allowed pages and clerks to enter only to shoo out bats. During the Civil War, Union troops camped inside the Capitol building; the Massachusetts Sixth Regiment seized the Marble Room and used it as a meat locker, covering the cold floors with smelly ham and bacon slabs while a Senate doorkeeper begged them tearfully not to grease up the walls and furniture. Aside from these occasional nuisances—flying parasites, national rebellions, and the like—the Marble Room remained the senators' exclusive domain . . . until we showed up.

In 1999, the senators grudgingly relinquished their beloved sanctuary to the thirteen managers selected by the United States House of Representatives to prosecute the impeachment trial of President Bill Clinton. For almost six weeks, it became the impeachment managers' war room; I'm sure the grumpy senators would have preferred a return of the bats. Only Connecticut Senator Joe Lieberman was a good sport, complaining playfully to me that we'd taken away his place to do push-ups between votes.

Regrettably, there was nothing playful about our occupation. For the first time in American history, the House had impeached a popularly elected president. The United States Senate would determine his fate in a live, worldwide-televised trial. As a freshman congressman, my House colleagues chose me to be one of the thirteen prosecutors arguing for Clinton's conviction and removal from office.

On January 14, 1999, I sat in the Senate chamber as the trial began. Every poll showed (and every pundit expected) two foreordained results. First, the president would prevail easily; that outcome never was in doubt.[1] Second, polls showed there was a likely political casualty:

Me.

Calling impeachment unpopular back home in California is an understatement. Most voters in my Los Angeles–based district (home to many Hollywood studios) loved President Clinton. As a Republican representing a Democratic district, I was on thin ice already, winning each of my two elections to Congress by a razor-thin 50 percent margin. As the impeachment vote loomed, polls showed 75 percent of my constituents wouldn't vote for me again if I stood against the president.

Satisfied that there were enough votes to pass impeachment without my help, Republican leaders urged me to vote "no" and avoid a constituent backlash. But for me, as a former gang-murder prosecutor and state court judge, "throwing" my vote wasn't an option. This was a matter of grave constitutional importance. If my options were defending the law or defending my political hide, I'd defend the law, vote my conscience, and take my chances.

On the opening day of trial, as the time for my two-hour opening statement approached, I slipped out to grab a few silent moments in the Marble Room. Sinking into a big chair, I closed my eyes and listened to the piped-in speech of my colleague, Congressman Asa Hutchinson, as he outlined the history of Clinton's obstruction of justice. When Asa's

---

[1]For an overview of the Senate's behind-the-scenes impeachment maneuvering, see David P. Schippers and Alan P. Henry's book *Sellout: The Inside Story of President Clinton's Impeachment* (New York: Regnery Publishing, 2000).

presentation ended, it would be my turn to argue the evidence of presidential perjury. I couldn't help but reflect on the irony: Bill Clinton and I had both spent our lives trying to get to Washington. After committing perjury and obstructing justice, the president expected to salvage his job; for arguing that those offenses violated his constitutional oath of office, I expected to lose mine.

Feeling weary from late nights of preparation and little sleep, I closed my eyes and rested my head in my hands. Soon Asa's voice faded as my mind drifted to many things, but mostly to memories of Memphis.

MEMPHIS, TENNESSEE, DECEMBER 1978

As a college kid applying to law schools, I was a longtime political junkie, a liberal Democrat, and itching to run for Congress someday. In 1978 I went to the Democratic National Midterm Convention in Memphis and attended a panel workshop headlined by Senator Edward Kennedy. Although Kennedy gave a great speech, I found myself more intrigued by the panel's likeable, bushy-haired young moderator. I'd read a news story about him, so he was familiar to me beforehand. Only five years out of law school himself, he had rocketed to the top of his state's political ladder. I wanted to know how he'd done it.

Hours after Kennedy and most of the spectators left, I hung around to meet the young moderator. It was late when the forum ended; I introduced myself, explaining that I hoped someday to follow him into politics, and asked if he thought law school was a good foundation for this ambition. A law professor himself, he smiled at the question. Then he began a ten-minute monologue, telling me that a legal education opened endless possibilities, especially in the political world. Stressing that politics gave one the chance to do the most good for the most people, he described how he'd parlayed his law degree into winning statewide office. "Law school gave me the opportunity to run for Congress soon after graduation, and then I became state attorney general just two years later, and last month I was elected our state's youngest governor in history," he said with a sense of well-deserved pride.

As he talked about his background, I soaked up our similarities. We both were born into fatherless homes: His father died before he was born, while my father abandoned my unwed mother when he learned she was pregnant. Each of us was raised by our grandparents in our formative years. Later, we each went to live with mothers who married and divorced alcoholics. Both of us witnessed our mothers' lives of hardship: His mother struggled as a nursing student, while mine raised four kids working odd jobs and collecting welfare and food stamps. Finally, we both grew up wanting to go into politics: A president he met as a boy inspired him, while a vice president I met as a boy inspired me.

I listened as he urged me to go to law school, focus on the noble goal of public service, and keep him posted on my progress. I was so impressed; how could one not admire this charming, gracious young leader who had accomplished so much already, and who held so much more promise? He left me wanting to be just like him.

Through a strange twist of history, he and I were reunited twenty years later. Unhappily, though, when our paths again crossed it was as combatants, not colleagues. The young moderator who encouraged me to go to law school and enter politics on that long ago night in Memphis was the attorney general of Arkansas.

His name was Bill Clinton.

"JIMMY, IT'S TIME."

A colleague's voice snapped me back to the awaiting task. Asa Hutchinson had finished his powerful presentation; now it was my turn. Leaving the Marble Room, I returned to my seat in the Senate chamber as the senators, House managers, and the president's lawyers took their places. I fidgeted nervously with the binder containing my speech.

Just before trial resumed, fellow manager and House Judiciary Committee Chairman Henry Hyde sensed my unease. Patting my arm, his tone was fatherly: "Listen, Jim. What you'll do here today is history. I'm very proud of you. More than that, you will remember this speech for the rest of your life. Someday your children will watch it on television, and your grandchildren, and your great-grandchildren . . ."

As I nodded appreciation for the encouragement, he finished his sentence with a wink:

". . . *so don't screw it up!*"

I was still chuckling when the chief justice of the United States called the impeachment court back to order. Then he intoned solemnly, "The Chair recognizes Mr. Manager Rogan." Rising to address the Senate, I couldn't help but think again about Memphis, and of the long, unlikely road that brought me from welfare to Washington.

ROUGH EDGES

1

FILIUS NULLIUS²

Nobody called Grandpa deaf.

Jimmy Kleupfer was just "hard of hearing," and if he didn't like you, then his problem was all your fault. "Get the goddamn mush out of your mouth and stop mumbling at me!" Grandpa liked to bark at some intruder trying to make small talk with him. The unwanted visitor would raise his voice in a vain effort to help an increasingly irritated Grandpa understand. Of course, Grandpa *never* understood.

The origin of Grandpa's deafness was a matter of family dispute and legend. Some said he had suffered a blow during a prizefight, when as a young man he boxed under the scrappy name of Jimmy West. Others said it came from a cop's billy club during the violent San Francisco wharf strikes of the 1920s, or in a brawl with a bar full of Chinamen in some murky port-of-call. However it happened, deafness suited Grandpa because it intimidated those he wanted kept at bay. With him, it wasn't a disability—it was an art.

Not that Grandpa needed deafness to ward off annoyances: on the natural, he scared the hell out of most people. Grandpa was gruff, bald, tattooed, and forever scowling. A veteran longshoreman on the rugged

---

²Latin: an illegitimate or bastard child.

waterfront, Grandpa spent his entire life in San Francisco's Mission District, the city's oldest neighborhood. The Mission took its name from Mission Dolores, an adobe church built by Father Junipero Serra in 1776. Now, tightly packed flats, cocktail lounges, and Spanish movie theaters encircled Father Serra's ancient church. The Mission became home to a hodgepodge of low-income, blue-collar immigrants: Mexican, Irish, Italian, Chinese, and African-American. It was a tough place, with little room for fanciness or airs. Neighborhood kids settled disputes with their fists; tired women bore too many children, and tired men bore too many calluses.

Grandpa and the Mission were a good fit. The neighborhood was so much like him: colorful, hardscrabble, struggling, and no-nonsense. In Grandpa's day, longshoremen earned their paychecks by sheer brawn: Things like automation, gender diversity, and worker's compensation were nonexistent. A day of missed work meant a day your family didn't eat, so in over forty years on the piers Grandpa almost never missed a day of work.

My grandmother, Helen Glover, was born in a tent in San Francisco's Golden Gate Park. A few months earlier, the city's devastating 1906 earthquake and fire had destroyed their modest family home. Her father, John Glover, was a trolley car driver before his Twin Peaks route was shattered by the catastrophe. When police let survivors return to their homes to salvage, John found only rubble. Holding his four-year-old daughter Della's hand, he wept as he picked through the ruins. My great-aunt Della remembered letting go of him just once that day, when in the debris she spied a 1903 nickel burnt black by the fire. She slid into her apron pocket all that remained of their home. (More than sixty years later, Aunt Della pressed that nickel into my youthful hand; it sits on my desk today, still as black as the day Aunt Della spied it in the wreckage.)

John Glover returned to work after the maintenance crews repaired the trolley lines. His family remained in San Francisco where Grandma grew up, finished high school, then met and married her longshoreman. If Grandpa ever promised his young bride future wealth and comfort, the promise went unfulfilled. Grandma lived her entire adult life on a dockworker's salary.

Grandpa and Grandma's eldest child, my Uncle Jack, was in many ways very much like his father: a bald, unsmiling, husky man who commanded his listener's attention with an intimidating voice and perpetual frown. Uncle Jack left home in his teens for a twenty-five-year stint in the army, seeing action in World War II, Korea, and Vietnam. To the children, Uncle Jack was a mythical figure. His furloughs home were few, but when he did show up with duffel bags in hand, we were in for a season of enthrallment and fear. I could have made a mint if I'd charged admission to all my friends who wanted to come and see Uncle Jack limp across the room. According to Uncle Jack, an ankle-to-hip machine gun blast from a North Korean tree sniper had caused that limp—but it was no big deal, he said: The head of the soldier seated next to him in the jeep got shot off and it fell into his lap. Tales like that made Uncle Jack and his limp an almost supernatural phenomenon every kid wanted to see.

We stared unendingly at the top of Uncle Jack's head, looking for some trace of the steel plate surgically implanted there after an enemy grenade supposedly blew off part of his skull. When little Tommy Eversole dared to doubt the existence of the steel plate, I felt obliged to defend the family honor. While Uncle Jack napped in a chair after devouring a hearty lunch, I tiptoed quietly past him and got my oversized, horseshoe-shaped magnet. I approached the snoring hulk nervously, then ran the magnet across Uncle Jack's bumpy head, seeking the gentle "pull" that would prove Tommy wrong. When my initial cranial sweep came up empty, I began another pass using firmer pressure. Suddenly, Uncle Jack's eyes popped wide open. I froze in terror as he jumped up and shouted undecipherable gibberish while the neighbor kids scattered like roaches in the sunlight. My response, although lacking in dignity, was appropriate under the circumstances: I wet my pants as Uncle Jack chased me out the door.

"It sounded German," Tommy said later of Uncle Jack's unintelligible rant. He was probably right; Uncle Jack always yelled at us in German when we ticked him off. He claimed to have learned German while a Nazi prisoner of war, which made his German yelling all the more menacing. Besides, we didn't need a Berlitz course to know all of Uncle Jack's German meant the very same thing: "Get your ass moving."

Friends begged to stay for dinner when Uncle Jack was in town, because meals with him were a time of special enlightenment. Hot dogs? Uncle Jack knew what went into those things long before anyone ever heard of Ralph Nader. As he chowed through his food, he happily pointed out how each course resembled something you'd see while disemboweling your enemy. The spaghetti on your plate looked like the guts of some little Nip bastard Uncle Jack once bayoneted. Cream of Wheat resembled the brain matter that splattered his boots when he put a bullet in the head of some big Hun bastard. After dinner, as Grandma washed the dishes, Uncle Jack oiled and cleaned his arsenal of guns while spinning tales for us of the dead Kraut bastard, the dead Dago bastard, the dead Jap bastard, the dead Cong bastard, or the dead Gook bastard from whom he inherited the trophy. In time, I became a discerning observer of Uncle Jack's ethnic nuances: Sometimes he substituted the poor dead Dago bastard for an equally unfortunate, but just as dead, poor Eye-talian bastard. No matter how he bracketed the noun, for many years I thought the word "bastard" meant some guy Uncle Jack killed to get a wartime souvenir.

Growing up, we never knew how many of Uncle Jack's stories of bullet wounds, bomb wounds, knife wounds, shrapnel wounds, hand-to-hand combat wounds, and prisoner of war exploits were real. Who cared? True or false, nobody wove better tales of bravery. Besides, after my magnet mishap, I certainly wasn't going to challenge Uncle Jack's candor. Growing up, every boy I knew wished he had an Uncle Jack.

My grandparents also had two daughters. Their middle child was my Aunt Bev, who ran off in her late teens to marry a sailor who dumped her when she got pregnant. When her newborn daughter Lynn contracted polio, Aunt Bev showed up on her parents' doorstep and asked them to take her baby; Lynn remained with them until adulthood.

Grandpa worked double shifts to save money for doctors and specialists. One doctor gave Lynn a cursory examination, then told Grandpa, "The kid's crippled. She'll never walk and she may die, and there isn't a thing you can do about it." My furious grandfather gave the doctor a lesson in bedside manner: He grabbed the stunned doctor by his lab-coat lapels and slammed him into the wall. *"She'll walk,"* Grandpa growled at the trembling medic before releasing his grip and storming out the door with Lynn in his arms.

When Grandpa got home, he began the Sister Kenny polio treatment he'd read about in a magazine. Placing an unending stack of hot towels across Lynn's legs, he massaged her tiny limbs. Night after night—year after year—this after-dinner evening therapy never changed: massage and hot towels until bedtime. He did it when he was tired; he did it when he was sick. Nothing else mattered. Over time, Lynn's leg muscle tone developed slowly; her limbs looked straighter. Later, Lynn could walk with assistance, and eventually she was able to walk by herself. By the time Lynn went off to school, there was little visible evidence of the disease that almost consigned her to a lifetime of steel leg braces and disability.

Grandpa was that kind of a man. If he said you weren't going to be crippled, then by God, you weren't going to be crippled.

Shirley Alice was my grandparents' final child. It was hard not to favor Alice. With rings of blonde curls framing a sweet face, Alice had the gift of charm—and it was a bequest often called into duty with Grandma's older brother Eddie. Uncle Eddie was a big truck driver with an even bigger Irish heart. All week he worked hard and teetotaled, but the temperance ended on Friday nights when he took his paycheck to the local pub and ordered drinks for all. Transitory friends soon drained his earnings, and by night's end Uncle Eddie was broke. Grandma kept calling the bar in a panic, begging him to come home. He always promised to leave any minute, but forgot the promise with the next round of drinks. Nothing could budge Uncle Eddie and his money from the bar—until Grandma spotted his one big weakness. Tying pink ribbons in Alice's hair, she walked her little daughter to the bar; Grandma waited outside as Alice toddled in alone and made a beeline to the big Teamster. Stuffing Uncle Eddie's money into his coat pocket, she cooed, "Please come home and play with me, Uncle Eddie." Then she slid her small hand inside his ham-sized paw and led him out the door without a whimper of dissent.

Pretty and popular, with the makings of a professional dancer, Alice left home after graduation and rented a Mission District flat with two girlfriends. Taking a cocktail waitress job at the Cable Car Village in San Francisco, Alice liked the bartenders who worked with her—two boyhood pals named Johnny Burton and Jack Baroni. Johnny was tall and quick-witted, with an infectious Irish charm: A future law student, he was street smart as well as book smart.[3] Jack was all Italian and just as charming. He had wavy dark hair, a slender athletic build from his years as a Golden Gloves boxer, a big smile, and an easygoing manner. Jack worked days as an apprentice carpenter, hoping to break into the construction business.

Jack and Alice began seeing each other after work, but she kept their dating a secret at his insistence. The secret ended when Alice started feeling sick each morning. Afraid of what her family doctor might tell her parents, she visited a girlfriend's physician, who confirmed her fear: She was two months pregnant. Filled with anxiety, she called Jack and told him they had to talk. When he arrived at her flat later that night, Alice broke the news. It didn't take long for Jack to shatter her illusions about their future.

"Oh, shit," he muttered. "Well, what am I supposed to do about it?"

The party was over. Jack told her he didn't love her; in fact, he was engaged to another woman. He was sorry, but those were the breaks. He told Alice she'd need a back-alley abortion, but not to worry—he'd take care of the details. "I'll call you," he said as he walked out the door, leaving her alone and numb.

Alice was devastated, but she couldn't bear to let her parents know. At

---

[3] Almost forty years later, on the day I became a member of the California State Assembly, the first member of the legislature to welcome my mother and me to the chamber was former United States Congressman, and the current chairman of the California State Assembly Rules Committee, the Honorable John L. Burton of San Francisco. Mom smiled as she greeted her ex-bartender colleague with "Hello, you old bastard!" As they embraced and kissed, Mom told him, "Johnny, you look out for Jimmy up here, or I'll come back and knock the hell out of you." During my tenure, Democrat John Burton fought many legislative battles against Republican Jim Rogan, but for as long as I was there, "Uncle Johnny" looked out for me.

her roommates' urging, she agreed to go through with the abortion. A week later, Jack called to tell her that everything had been arranged. At the appointed time, Alice waited nervously in her flat for the dreaded visitor to arrive. Her heart jumped at the sound of his low, rapid knock on the front door. A roommate answered; a swarthy man hauling a black bag entered and began looking under beds, behind curtains, and inside closets. Watching him skulk through her flat like a robber casing a liquor store before a holdup, Alice shuddered to think of him touching her with whatever was in that bag. As he approached, a surge of remorse and terror gripped her. Alice bolted from her chair and out the door, ignoring his angry shouts to come back.

A few blocks away she found a telephone booth. Sobbing as she called her father, she told him the truth. "Stay where you are, honey," he said quietly, "I'm coming to get you." He drove to her location, picked her up, and took her back to the flat to collect her things.

Grandpa carried Alice's few boxes to her old room back home without taking off his hat. When Grandma suggested he forgot to remove it, Grandpa told her icily, "I didn't forget." After carrying in the last box, Grandpa headed out the front door. "I'll be back later," he said, ignoring his wife and daughter's tense questions about his destination.

Grandpa drove to the Cable Car Village. He'd never met Jack Baroni, but when Grandpa saw him behind the bar, no introductions were necessary. Each man knew the other instinctively. "Let's go," Grandpa said as he motioned with his head for Jack to follow him outside. Under a streetlight, Grandpa lit his cigarette and took a silent drag. Then he delivered an unemotional but straightforward message: "You got my daughter pregnant. You need to do the right thing."

"How do I know I'm the father?" Jack pleaded. "Maybe I was her first, but maybe there were others. I mean, let's face it. She works in a bar; she's a dancer. . . ."

Grandpa's eyes narrowed: "She says there's been one guy. She says it's you."

"*But how do I know?*" Jack continued. "Besides, I can't marry Alice. There's another girl I'm in love with. We're engaged. We're getting married."

Grandpa heard enough. This little punk wasn't worth the ass-kicking he deserved, let alone worth having as a son-in-law. Shaking his head with contempt, Grandpa tossed down his cigarette in the street, extinguished it with the steel toe of his work shoe, and then turned and walked away.

Jimmy Kleupfer and Jack Baroni never saw each other again.

Jack Baroni's abortion remedy almost wasn't necessary. A highly toxic infection hospitalized Alice for the last month of her pregnancy. Her doctor said she'd probably die if she carried the baby to term, but Alice refused the alternative. After the grim prognosis, Grandpa visited her bedside. "If anything happens to me, Dad, promise me you'll take care of my baby." He squeezed her hand and nodded, unable to speak.

The doctor's fears were unfounded. On August 21, 1957, Alice delivered a healthy boy with no damage beyond a manly looking black eye. The doctor asked his name for the records.

"James Edward Baroni," she replied, and the nurse entered that name on my birth certificate.

When my grandparents visited Mom and me at the hospital, Mom passed me to Grandpa. "Here, Dad," she said with a smile, "come meet little Jimmy. I named him after you."

For the first and only time in my mother's life, she saw her father cry.

2

FORTY-SEVEN STAIRS

EXPIRES ON BIRTHDAY **CALIFORNIA LICENSE**
1967

ISSUED IN ACCORDANCE WITH
THE CALIFORNIA VEHICLE CODE

CHIEF, DIVISION OF DRIVERS LICENSES

DRIVER Y 48517
James Gordon Kleupfer
2714 Bryant St.
San Francisco, Calif. (Over)

| SEX | COLOR HAIR | COLOR EYES | HEIGHT | WEIGHT | MARRIED |
| M | Brn | Brn | 5-11 | 180 | Yes |

| DATE OF BIRTH | AGE | PREVIOUS LICENSE |
| Mar 10 1898 | 64 | Y48517 |

MUST WEAR CORRECTIVE LENSES ☐   SEE OVER FOR ANY OTHER CONDITIONS ☐

OTHER ADDRESS

CLASS D. MAY DRIVE 2 AXLE VEHICLE. MAY TOW VEHICLE NOT OVER 6,000 LBS.
Office Daly City   Date 5/22/62

= MUST BE CARRIED WHEN OPERATING A MOTOR VEHICLE AND WHEN APPLYING FOR RENEWAL

Like most families living in the Mission District, ours were permanent renters who stayed for generations. My great-grandparents had lived in the Mission; my grandparents (and their children) lived for decades in a third-floor flat at 2718 Bryant Street. As newlyweds, they bounded up the forty-seven stairs leading to home, but with years of toil wearing them down, their spring up those steps ultimately became a trudge. My mother negotiated those stairs with ease her whole life, but when she carried me up them that first time, she was also carrying the burden of unwed, abandoned motherhood. By the time she reached the top, she was trudging, too.

There was nothing swanky at the top of those stairs. The furniture in my grandparents' flat was the kind used to furnish motels. Cloth and vinyl, not leather, covered the chairs. Grandma's washer and dryer were a clothesline out the alley window and a scrub board in the kitchen sink—the same sink that she used to bathe her kids, and then grandkids, every Saturday night. If the Bryant Street flat was cramped physically, for my mother it was cramped emotionally, too. When Mom went back to dating, Grandma was afraid she'd come home pregnant again. Tired of the nagging, Mom moved in with a friend and took a new waitress job at the Tower Lodge, leaving me with her parents while she got back on her feet.

A few months later Mom met Jack Rogan, a tall, rugged, handsome stationary engineer working for the local school district. After a whirl-wind romance, they married. Jack Rogan never adopted me, but from the day Mom married him she used his last name as my own. The name *Baroni* never was mentioned, and I knew nothing about the circumstances surrounding my birth. From my earliest memory, I was Jimmy Rogan, and Jack Rogan was Dad.

With a new husband and another baby on the way, Mom wanted me to come live with them. But that was a nonstarter for Grandpa, who pleaded not to lose his little namesake. As a compromise, Grandpa moved everyone to a two-story flat next door on Bryant Street. Grandpa, Grandma, my cousin Lynn, and I lived on the bottom floor; Dad, Mom, and my new sister Teri (born in 1958) lived on the top floor. More children came in succession: Pat (1959), Christie (1962; she lived only one month), and Johnny (1963). Although there was a floor between us, we all lived under one roof; with so many visits back and forth each day, we might as well have lived in the same room. Nothing seemed peculiar about the arrangement; besides, I was too young to know better. I just figured every first-born lived with his grandparents downstairs, while the parents and younger siblings lived upstairs.

More than thirty years of marriage had passed between Grandpa and Grandma by the time I came along. Their mutual love was real, but it remained mostly unspoken. Neither was the type to express it; in our family, the adults knew love existed between them without being told. Besides, there was no time for romantic folderol while raising a polio-afflicted granddaughter and her newborn cousin. If my grandparents withheld their displays of affection for each other, they overcompensated with the affection they showed for Lynn and me.

Years later Dad told me, "I never thought your grandfather was all that nice of a guy. He grumbled a lot, and the kids running around and screaming always seemed to annoy him. But when he looked at *you*, there was something there. I never saw it with anyone else." Whatever that "something" was, it was mutual.

My adoration of Grandpa dates to my earliest memory on earth—which is of Grandma trying to give me an enema. To Grandma's barbaric generation, a little enema now and then (like Thomas Jefferson's theory of revolution) was considered a good thing. There she stood, stirring some smelly mixture in a soup pot on her ironing board and fiddling with a long plastic tube. One end of the tube was in the pot, and Grandma kept trying to stick the other end into me. Bawling and wiggling for all I was worth, I was down to my last ounce of resistance when Grandpa appeared with a disgusted expression: "For Christ's sake, Helen!" he yelled at her, "Get that goddamn hose out of the poor kid's ass—and don't ever cook with that pot again!" In that moment, a lifelong reverence for Grandpa was born.

No boy ever had a finer example than Grandpa: He was tough, hard-working, loving, and right-doing. His conduct became my template for manly virtue; when he called us the "men of the house," the designation added inches to my stature. I took the label seriously. The fact that Grandma and Lynn didn't intend to be bossed around in Grandpa's absence by a child meant nothing to me. If Grandpa said we were the men of the house, then the womenfolk had better learn to suck it up.

One night Grandpa and I curled up in his chair to watch his favorite program, *Gillette Friday Night at the Fights*. As he explained the finer points of the brawl, an earthquake struck our flat like a wrecking ball. The dresser tipped over, kitchen dishes smashed to the ground, and plaster fell from the ceiling. Grandma, a survivor of San Francisco's *big one*, had seen one too many Hollywood reenactments of it, with streets cracking open and swallowing whole neighborhoods. "Oh, my God!" she screamed. "Everybody! Get under the door jamb or we'll all be killed!" Since Grandpa didn't move, neither did I. My panicky Grandma yanked me from the chair, grabbed Lynn, and dragged both of us under the doorway. Grandpa, unfazed, still watched TV. "So," he shouted over the sound of breaking glass, "do you think the whole house is gonna collapse, but leave the door jamb standing?"

As more pictures fell off the walls, Grandma was approaching hysteria—but her pleas only irritated Grandpa. "Goddamit, Helen, I can't hear the fight announcer!" As the ground still rolled, Grandpa reached for his glass of scotch, picked out a chunk of plaster, and sipped his drink without moving from the chair. The city might get buried in rubble, but as long as the TV worked, no earthquake was going to get between Grandpa and the eighth round.

Nothing thrilled me more than going with Grandpa to the docks. Staying as close to him as possible, I watched as he barked orders to his pug-ugly subordinates, who all resembled buccaneers. One longshoreman had a metal claw for a hand, just like Captain Hook; others had eye patches, missing teeth, facial scars, and stubs for fingers. They had tattoos, big knives on belts, sledgehammers for hands, and smelled of Ben-Gay and sweat. These dock pirates terrified and captivated me. They were the most menacing bunch I ever saw, and yet they were respectful, even deferential, to Grandpa—*my Grandpa!* As I followed him among his crew, I noticed that he parted from them with handshakes. This was odd: When Grandpa bade me goodbye or goodnight, it was with a kiss. That night, as Grandpa tucked me into bed, I asked him why. "Well," he explained, scratching the back of his neck, "men don't kiss each other. They shake hands." When my bedtime story ended, Grandpa bent over to kiss me goodnight. I recoiled and thrust out my hand with great seriousness. "Men of the house don't kiss," I told him. "Men of the house shake hands."

Grandpa and I did everything together. On weekends, I never went with Grandma on her errands, preferring to stay home and play with Grandpa. One of our favorite games was "Lincoln Logs"—*our* version of it, anyway. As Grandma got ready to leave, Grandpa and I went through the motions of making wooden cabins. The minute Grandma left, we dumped the can upside down. Amid the shower of logs tumbled out Grandpa's green felt casino pad, a small plastic roulette wheel, crap dice, a deck of cards, and a pile of poker chips. With Grandma gone, Grandpa taught me all the important life skills: whether a straight beats a flush, how to cut the deck with one hand, and various ways to exhort crap dice to bring home to daddy a new pair of shoes. When Grandma returned, we'd bury the evidence of our Vegas adventure beneath handfuls of Lincoln Logs, laughing at our shared secret.

To the world, and indeed to most of his own family, Grandpa was a growling bear. It wasn't a front: He really was that way. Still, that rough shell never fooled the grandchildren he raised. For all his grunts and scowls, Lynn and I knew that Grandpa was a soft touch. The one big exception was Lynn's social life, where Grandpa's sucker streak crashed and burned. When Lynn hit her teens in the early 1960s, she became a poster child for the permissive decade. Lynn was into rock and folk music, shaggy hair on boys, and the other hints of cultural pollution Grandpa saw festering around the Mission. He had no use for dirty beatniks hanging around coffee houses. Much to his chagrin, though, those were the only boys Lynn brought home. "The dirtier they are, the better you like 'em," he often griped as he vetoed yet another suitor at our doorstep.

One day we drove through the Haight-Ashbury, now teeming with the cartoonish characters Grandpa despised. "This used to be a nice neighborhood," Grandpa lamented. "Now it's filled with assholes." Lynn rebuked him: "They're called beatniks, Grandpa, because they hear a different beat and march to a different drummer. They're called hippies because they're hip to a better world, a world of peace and love. A world with no nations, no hunger, and no crime, where we'll all share everything . . ."

Grandpa ended Lynn's sermon by rolling down the station wagon window and, with a thunderous *hhhaaacch, pttooo*, launched a mouthful of phlegm onto Haight Street. "You can call these dirty bastards anything you want," he said as he rolled the window back up. "In my day, we just called 'em bums."

I remember one night when Lynn was getting ready for her date with some guy named Sam. Grandpa insisted Lynn's dates come inside and meet him before she was allowed to leave with them, so Lynn warned Sam in advance not to honk the horn for her. After dinner, as Lynn dressed for her date, Grandpa drove to the liquor store to get a pack of smokes. He returned fuming: "Some jackass damned near ran me down! His van came around the corner so fast it was on two wheels."

Just then, I looked out the window and saw a banged-up microbus pull in front of our house. "Hey, Grandpa, what color did you say that van was?" Grandpa walked to the window and looked outside. Suddenly his eyebrows arched. "That's the son of a bitch and his van right there!" he exclaimed. Not only had Lynn's date, Sam, arrived in a van—with no windows in the back, mind you—he'd almost run over Grandpa in the process.

This was going to be good.

When the doorbell rang, Lynn (who was always late for dates) yelled for me to let Sam in. I looked forward to opening that door more than I did opening Christmas presents. Sam didn't disappoint: His long and scruffy black hair had pieces of weeds in it, probably from rolling in the hay with someone else's granddaughter. He sported a Satanic-like goatee (strike two); multicolored, ragged clothes; a rope belt; and sandals that exposed his dirty feet. A drumstick (the musical kind, not a chicken leg) stuck out of his back pocket. Sealing his doom, Sam carried under his arm a pair of bongos. Before he said a word, I knew this guy was going to rocket Grandpa's blood pressure off the Lynn Date-O-Meter.

Sam's idea of making a good first impression was to look Grandpa up and down, and then ask, "Hey, old timer—is Lynn ready for our gig?" For a moment Grandpa just sat in his chair blankly, cigarette protruding from his mouth. Then he reached over and ground his cigarette stub into his favorite ashtray, a little ceramic baseball player trying to field a grounder between his legs. "Lynn's not going out with you," he said. "Not tonight or ever. Take a hike." When Sam protested, Grandpa explained the way things worked under his roof:

"I'm gonna count to ten. If you and your shithouse van aren't outta here by then, your ass'll race your bongos down the stairs."

Sam grew indignant. "Man, you can't talk to me—"

"One, two, three . . ."

"You can't tell me—"

"Four, five, six . . ."

"It's a free country, man. I got my rights."

"Seven, eight, nine . . ."

Grandpa jumped the gun at "nine," springing from his chair and advancing. Sam had the sudden good sense to flee, but his reflexes were too slow. Grandpa gave him a mighty heave, and the sound of Sam's sandals whapping against his heels followed him down the staircase. Grandpa went back to his reclining chair, lit another no-filter Lucky Strike, and returned to the TV.

A few minutes later, Lynn appeared looking for her date. "He left," Grandpa told her. "He said something about having to go learn his rights."

Lynn argued with our grandparents over things like dates, makeup, and bare-midriff tops, but the worst imposition on her life was having to baby-sit me. To Lynn, I was a smart-aleck little brat who lived to torment her for my own amusement. In reality, I viewed driving Lynn crazy as a patriotic duty.

In the 1960s, with rising Cold War tensions fueling the James Bond "spy" craze, boys stopped shooting space invaders with index-finger guns on the playground, and now targeted evil masterminds seeking world conquest. Since future spies needed to hone their espionage skills, I honed mine on Lynn, and reported her every misstep to HQ (Grandma). At first I used old-fashioned eavesdropping technology, like listening through a water glass pressed against a wall, picking up the extension phone, or watching her make out with boys through the front door peephole. But when Grandpa bought me the birthday present I wanted more than any other, I took espionage to the next level. It was the coolest toy ever made then or now—Topper Toys' *Secret Sam*.

To the untrained eye, Secret Sam was a black plastic toy attaché case, but inside was a one-man arsenal of freedom. It had a pistol with rifle stock and barrel extension that shot white plastic bullets; a periscope attached to the gun sights to spy on people while hiding. Best of all, the attaché case had a built-in hidden camera that took real black-and-white photographs. The possibilities now were endless.

The next time Lynn baby-sat, she sent me to bed at my usual time. While she was on the phone, I stuffed pillows under my blankets, sneaked into the living room with Secret Sam, and hid behind Grandpa's chair.

When Lynn thought I was asleep, she called Jerry the Jerk (Grandpa's name for him) and invited him over. Obviously, Grandpa didn't like Jerry, so my thrill threshold increased when I heard he was coming. Later, as Lynn and Jerry settled on the couch, my small periscope popped up from behind the chair. I made note of their behavior to Sam Cooke albums, pizza, and Cokes. As smooth-operator Jerry edged closer, my periscope extended higher. Soon they were in the clinches, making out on the couch. Amid the kissing and pawing, I positioned my hidden camera and clicked away. Then Jerry got a bit too frisky; Lynn pushed him back, but Jerry kept advancing. "Stop it, Jerry! I mean it!" Lynn demanded, but Jerry ignored her. As Lynn struggled, the dynamic changed: I went from being little fink to mighty defender. Lynn needed help! With Grandpa gone, I was the man of the house. This called for armed intervention.

I broke down the periscope and attached the rifle stock and barrel extension to Secret Sam. While loading plastic bullets into the magazine, Lynn told Jerry to leave right now. "Come on, baby, relax!" he said as he pulled her closer. Jumping up from my hiding place, I let out a rebel yell, startling Jerry so badly that he kicked the hi-fi and scratched his new Sam Cooke album.

Plink–plink–plink!

Three white plastic bullets bounced off Jerry's head. Lynn started to laugh, but Jerry was as furious as his testosterone. "Come back here, you little prick!" he shouted as he chased me down the hallway. I kept shooting him from over my shoulder as I ran away, which made him madder. Jerry cornered me in my room, but just as he moved in for the kill, we heard the sound of the front door slam shut. "What was that?" Jerry asked. I smiled, knowing the answer. "See ya, Jerry!" I called out as Grandpa grabbed him by the scruff of the neck.

A couple of days later Lynn came into my room. "Oh, Jimmy, I have bad news. Grandpa was letting me practice backing the car out of the garage. I don't know how it happened, but your Secret Sam was on the garage floor. I must have backed over it." Then, with a big smirk, she said, "I'm so *frightfully* sorry!"

• • •

Growing up with grandparents introduced me to the concept of death early, since people they knew kept dying. Although I hated funerals generally, I didn't mind too much when Grandma's Irish relatives died, because they held their funerals at Duggan's Serra Mortuary in Daly City. Old Bud Duggan made sure the next of kin's rented-limousine ride to the cemetery included a freshly basted turkey. While the adults hovered over the casket for one last look, we kids sneaked out the back door looking for the Lincoln smelling of giblets. If we got to that turkey ahead of the mourners, the hearse would reach the cemetery with two carcasses to bury.

After Cousin Paddy's funeral (Paddy was a neighbor; he was everyone's cousin by agreement, not ancestry), Grandpa begged off from attending any more of Grandma's Irish wakes. For the first few hours of Paddy's funeral, appropriate hushed decorum reigned. Then someone stood up to say a few kind words. The charming Irish story first brought chuckles, then laughter, and then guffaws. More testimonials followed, each more lively and outrageous than the last. When another mourner broke out a hip flask and proposed a toast, hip flasks and Dixie cups appeared out of nowhere. Soon Gaelic dance music blared from a loudspeaker. One drunk tucked a whiskey bottle and a Tanforan Park horse-racing form underneath Paddy's lifeless arm. Others added more "souvenirs," leaving Paddy lying in what looked more like a wastebasket than a coffin. Then a relative staggered forward, proclaiming that Paddy never wore such a silly grin. He reconfigured the corpse's facial expression, pushing and poking at his sewed-shut lips and cotton-stuffed cheeks. Still dissatisfied, he invited fellow mourners to try their hand at improving Paddy's look. By the time we left, a laughing woman was ratting Paddy's hair while others formed a conga line.

News of Mrs. Cleppick's death broke my young heart. She was a kindly, white-haired old lady in a wheelchair who baked fresh bread each day for the neighborhood kids. On the day of her funeral, Grandma dressed me for what I thought would be another ride to Duggan's. Instead, we walked to Mrs. Cleppick's house, which was packed with people. While the adults visited, I wandered around sampling food on trays. Suddenly, I stopped in my tracks: Seated in her rocking chair was old Mrs. Cleppick! Her head was bowed and her eyes were closed; a shawl draped her shoulders, and pince-nez glasses rested on her nose. I thought, "She's not dead! Grandma just thinks she's dead because she's asleep in her chair!" When I told a few relatives that Mrs. Cleppick was only sleeping, they brushed me off. Taking matters in my own hands, I called her name a few times. It amazed me how Mrs. Cleppick slept through this racket! One of the older kids watching the scene with devilish amusement said, "Come on, Jimmy, go rock her chair. That'll wake her up!" I began pushing the chair back and forth, first slightly, then with more vigor. Mrs. Cleppick moved suddenly, but not as I expected. She moved in one piece—onto the floor. Random chatter now turned to a collective gasp. There I stood, wide-eyed and open-mouthed, with Mrs. Cleppick frozen in a fetal position at my feet. Grandma yanked my hand so hard it almost severed from my arm. Apparently, it was time to go.

Over dinner that night, Grandpa didn't seem to mind that I dumped Mrs. Cleppick's corpse. He was too busy ridiculing Mr. Cleppick for having laid out his dead wife at home in her rocker. Grandpa shook his head in dismay: "They had to break all the old lady's bones to get her in the coffin after the wake, because she got stiff when rigor mortis set in. If you ask me, the stiffest bone in the joint was the one in Old Man Cleppick's head."

Grandpa's vast shadow obscured my view of Grandma. Since he played friend and "good cop," by default Grandma became nursemaid and disciplinarian. My new school pants always had ripped knees in a day or two. Grandpa didn't care about torn knees; he wanted to know if I scored a run sliding into home plate. Grandma was the wicked witch with the unglamorous job of nagging her grandson into appearing presentable, not shabby. Looking back, I understand how often I missed her handiwork in character building.

Flip through your family photo album and you'll see a picture of my grandmother. You can't miss her—she's the woman who appears much older than her age. Only 51 when I was born, Grandma looked old and worn out. She was a big woman with fleshy triceps that hung like ballast: Even her voice was big, often substituting shouting for speaking (from spending decades with a deaf husband). Just getting out of bed brought her unpleasantness: A lifelong diabetic, Grandma began her day jamming an insulin-filled hypodermic through the thick accumulations of scar tissue covering her thighs. Her few dresses were dowdy; she wore the same old pair of white nurse's shoes. When Grandpa gave her money to buy something for herself, Grandma diverted it to her priorities—new clothes and shoes for the grandkids. Like Grandpa, there was a forceful, straightforward manner about her. Unlike Grandpa, there was no mischievous streak underneath. In Grandma's world, there was no time for mischief. There were children to raise and work to be done. Hers was a universe without pampering: Things like personal trainers, *au pairs*, and weekend spas were as likely to land in her lap as a lightning strike.

Before I was old enough to attend school, I stayed home with Grandma all day. An insomniac, Grandma didn't sleep much at night, so by early afternoon she grew drowsy. After lunch, she took me to the movies at the New Mission Theater every day. Grandma said she couldn't nap at home, and she felt I'd be safer watching movies or playing inside a theater under the watchful eyes of the ushers. Each week our neighbor George (a New Mission usher) slipped Grandma handfuls of free passes. When Grandma napped at the New Mission, she insisted that it be in "her" seat on the corner aisle, rear right. If someone else sat there, George's job was to bounce the interloper to another row. While she slept, I spent my time watching movies and making friends with kids in the balcony while we tossed our popcorn down on the people below.

Although Grandpa never spanked me—he didn't believe in it—Grandma didn't play by those rules. Not only did Grandma spank me, she patented her own method for doing it. Grandma never used the word "spatula"; she called it a "pancake turner." I don't know why she called it that, because I never saw her turn a pancake with one, but she wore out plenty of them on me. When we left for an errand, she went through her checklist of handbag necessities to ensure they were all there: keys, wallet, lipstick, pancake turner. If I acted up, discipline didn't await privacy. Wherever we were, her response came with surgical swiftness: Down came my britches and out came the pancake turner. With a few fast whacks, my bottom was as red as my tear-streaked face. If the *Jeopardy* game-show answer is "the St. Francis Soda Shop, W.H. Kress Department Store, the Hibernia Bank, and the New Mission Theater during intermission," then the question must be "Name some places Grandma pancaked Little Jimmy." When she pancaked me in the confessional booth of St. Paul's, she undermined centuries of international law recognizing churches as places of sanctuary. Even Mussolini didn't go that far!

My salvation from the pancake turner came the day Grandma made the mistake of pancaking me in front of Grandpa, and he went ballistic: "What the hell do you think you're doing? Don't you ever hit Little Jimmy again! Do you understand me?" Grandma didn't know it at first, but when Grandpa took away her spatula, he handed me a bludgeon:

If Grandma spanks me, she gets in trouble!

Ruthlessly exploiting this discovery, when I suspected pancake turner therapy was near, "I'll tell Grandpa" became my favorite refrain. That worked for a while, but Grandma wasn't one to let a six-year-old boy use her as a doormat for very long. The question was *how* to enforce discipline (and maybe a little revenge) without leaving any fingerprints. When it came time to enroll me in first grade, Grandma struck. "I was just thinking," she suggested to Grandpa over dinner, "why don't we send Little Jimmy to St. Peter's?" Since St. Peter's schooled all their children and grandchildren, the suggestion seemed an innocent progression of family tradition. "By the way," Grandma mentioned casually, "Sister Mary Clarence still teaches first grade there. I called her and she said Little Jimmy could be in her class."

Sister Mary Clarence—an old battle-ax back when she taught Uncle Jack first grade in the 1930s—had a craggy face and thick glasses that made her a dead ringer for Harry Truman. She wore a traditional nun's habit with a flowing black robe and wimple, white collar, and crucifix.

The leather strap hanging from her belt wasn't a fashion accessory: That suited Grandma, who viewed corporal punishment as a tuition benefit.

When the morning bell rang, Sister eyeballed each student, searching for some grooming or uniform irregularity. If she found it, *whack!* A wooden ruler slammed into the waiting upturned palm. Stoicism was mandatory during punishment, and failure to abide by manly etiquette had its own consequences. Tears, flinching, and other effeminate demonstrations during ruler rehab paled next to the mother of all infractions— *smiling.* That was a big problem for Rollo, my chubby-faced, dumb, happy-go-lucky classmate cursed with both a forever-untucked shirt and the suicidal habit of laughing at inappropriate moments. A typical inspection morning went like this:

"Rollo, is that your shirttail I see untucked? Hold out your hand." *Whack!*

"Rollo, is that a smile I see? Hold out *both* hands." *Whack–whack!*

"Rollo, you're still grinning. Do you think I'm funny? Hold out both hands again." *Whack–whack!*

Poor Rollo was a perpetual double-whacker; Sister needed extra rulers from other classrooms just to accommodate Rollo's smirk. Classmates appreciated Rollo; by the time Sister whacked that silly grin off his face, she was too tired to hit the rest of us. When I accidentally kicked the classroom ball on the roof, I was so terrified of Sister's reaction that I did something inexcusable: I blamed the mishap on Rollo. My plan to finger the poor kid never stood a chance. Under Sister's cross-examination and my own tremendous sense of guilt, my alibi folded like a cheap suit. After confessing, Sister led me by the ear to the front of the hushed classroom. "Before I punish Jimmy for his horrible wrongdoing," she announced, "he will explain to us why he blamed poor Rollo for kicking the ball on the roof." She then turned over the program to me. After collecting my thoughts, I tried to salvage some noble Christian purpose from the wreckage: "Well, Sister tells us each day that it's a blessed thing that Jesus suffered by taking the punishment we deserve. Sister also told us we should be more like Jesus every day. So, I was just trying to help Rollo be more like Jesus."

Whack–whack–whack–whack. . . .

Sister Mary Clarence was the subject of my first recorded use of profanity. One day after school, Grandma asked what I thought of my teacher. Using a phrase I picked up on the playground, I replied, "Sister scares the shit out of me." Grandma's eyes bugged out in shock. Although she couldn't paddle me, she felt sure my using curse words against one of God's holy nuns guaranteed that Grandpa would lift his spanking embargo when he got home. Grandma licked her chops all afternoon, almost giddy anticipating Grandpa's arrival. That night, when he came home from work, she was so eager to squeal that she almost jumped out of her skin: "Do you know what your grandson said today? Would you like to know?" Grandma drew out the drama a bit longer before she dropped the S-bomb: "He said that Sister Mary Clarence scares the *s-h-i-t* out of him!"

Grandpa stared blankly at me for what seemed like an eternity. Filled with despair, I expected my best friend and hero to disown me. This was the worst feeling I had ever known.

"She scares the shit out of me, too," he replied. "What's for dinner?"

3

MAN OF THE HOUSE

In the summer of 1964, Grandpa decided to get the kids out of the crowded, crime-infested Mission District. Leaving the neighborhood he had called home all his life, we left the city for the suburbs: Mom and Dad chose the sunnier climate of Pacifica, and Grandma picked the neighboring city of Colma, which made easier her biweekly pilgrimage to family gravesites at Holy Cross Cemetery. Colma's plethora of cemeteries gave the city its claim to fame: It boasted more dead people than living. Despite these ghoulish boundaries, I loved our little rental house at 840 Lausanne Avenue. A neighborhood surrounded by graveyards meant quiet, safer streets—very different from the Mission—and safer neighborhoods meant Grandpa gave me greater outdoor playing freedom. Once I mastered riding my two-wheel bike, Colma became mine for the exploring. It made me feel older, more independent, more like Grandpa.

Shortly after starting second grade in Colma, I went to visit Mom's for the day in Pacifica. As my brother Pat and I rode skateboards down steep Redwood Way, Mom called from her window for me to hurry inside. Meeting me at the door, her expression told me something was wrong.

"Grandpa's had a heart attack," she said.

What did that mean? She said Grandpa got sick at work, and now doctors at the hospital needed to make him better. No, she said, I couldn't see him just yet. The hospital didn't permit children into something called the intensive care unit.

The next days blurred, but then the telephone rang and the call was for me:

"Grandpa!"

He sounded tired, but he assured me he'd be home soon. Grandpa explained that his heart stopped beating for a while; he regaled me with stories of riding in an ambulance, having nurses cut off all his clothes, and getting tubes stuck up his nose and down his throat. But the worst part came later, when doctors told him he couldn't eat hot dogs any more. "They're saying we'll have to come up with a new favorite food," he chuckled. "Well, we'll see about that!"

Although I still couldn't visit him, when he could get out of bed, Mom drove me each night to South San Francisco and parked on the street in front of Kaiser Hospital. At a prearranged time, Grandpa appeared in the corner window waving to me. All day I waited for that wave, and never tired of returning it. One night Mom walked me to the front door. "The hell with these rules," she said, "let's go." Hiding me inside her huge coat, I stood on her insteps as she walked past the nurse's station. When I reached Grandpa's room, I rushed to his bedside and hugged him for all I was worth. Then some nurse stepped in, her arms folded across her chest: "Excuse me, but no children are allowed in here. The boy will have to go."

"Goddamn it!" Grandpa barked in a voice sufficient to collapse the roof. "Can't you see it's my little grandson? How the hell do you expect me to get better if I can't see my grandson! Well, I sure don't give a damn about your rules. He's in here now—and he's staying in here!" Grandpa then produced a paper bag hidden under his blankets. Lowering his voice and giving the nurse a wink, he said, "Listen, honey, I'll make you a deal: Keep your mouth shut and I'll give you a present." With that, he reached into the bag, pulled out a contraband hot dog (snuck into the ICU by one of his wharf buddies), and tossed it to her.

The nurse caught the frankfurter, studied it for a moment, took a bite, and then left the room.

I stayed that night until Grandpa said it was time for me to go.

Grandpa's homecoming was my happiest day. Because his doctor told him to take a couple of months off work to rest, we spent more time together than ever. He walked me to school each morning, and then back home in the afternoon. We threw the football, the baseball, and a new toy called a "Frisbee"; we made model airplanes, used walkie-talkies at the cemetery, and played just about every board game invented. He even sang to me each night at bedtime. Since Grandpa knew three songs and no lullabies, his repertoire never changed: "School Days," "I'm Gonna Sit Right Down and Write Myself a Letter," and "My Bonnie Lies Over the Ocean."

Grandma cautioned him to take it easy, reminding that the doctor said that he shouldn't exert himself. For once Grandpa took orders, and he felt better every day. His color returned; he looked relaxed. Grandpa even swapped his trademark heavy Pendleton work shirts for cardigan sweaters. He was on the mend and he knew it. Then, in mid-December, he got the news he awaited: The doctor said he could return to work on Monday the 21st. "It's the best Christmas present anyone could give me!" he said, and I never saw him happier. He missed the docks, the ships, and his men.

On that last Saturday before he went back, Grandpa proclaimed it a day for the men of the house only, and we spent it together. We did everything I wanted: Grandpa even got down on his hands and knees and played G.I. Joe with me. That was a huge leap, since Grandpa balked at buying me a G.I. Joe. I had to convince him that Joe wasn't a doll—he was an "action figure." Dressed in battle fatigues, Joe's standard accessories (hand grenades, .45 caliber pistol, and an M-1 rifle) satisfied Grandpa that Joe wouldn't turn me into a sissy.

"Come on," he said when his knees ached, "help me wrap some Christmas presents." I needed no urging there, but to my disappointment, Grandpa wanted help wrapping clothes, not toys. He had already done my toys and put them under the tree. As we wrapped my new pair of slippers, I pleaded with him to let me open just one toy, but my earnestness only drew a chuckle: "You'll have to be patient a few more days," he teased.

Our "men of the house" day almost ended on a sour note. That night the family came for dinner; Grandpa played cribbage with Uncle Tom while "Mr. Magoo's Christmas Carol" played on TV for my benefit. Instead of watching cartoons, I preferred jabbing Grandpa with the sword Uncle Tom brought me. I must have poked Grandpa in the wrong spot, because he spun in his seat and gave me a swat on the behind. Everyone stared in disbelief: For the first time, Big Jimmy had spanked Little Jimmy. Inconsolable, I ran to my room and threw myself across the bed. The swat hurt my feelings more than my rump: It meant Grandpa didn't love me anymore. Things never would be the same between us.

A few minutes later Grandpa came in, sat on my bed, and dried my eyes. "Hey, c'mon," he said, sporting a rare smile. "That wasn't a spanking; it was just a 'love tap.' Love taps don't count, okay?" He assured me our "never been spanked by Grandpa" record remained unbroken. I still pouted; Grandpa pointed his two V-shaped fingers at me, buzzed them like dive bombers overhead, and then brought them down to tickle me until my whimpers turned to cackles.

Grandpa tucked me in and turned off the lights. "I'm leaving early tomorrow morning to have breakfast on the docks with some of my boys," he told me. "I need to catch up on a few things before I start back Monday, but when I get home, we'll spend another day together, okay? It'll just be us men of the house. And *maybe* I'll let you open one of those toys under the tree."

We were pals again. With the hallway light illuminating his silhouette, Grandpa extended his hand to me the same way he did since I announced the "no-kissing" rule. This time I made an exception: Pushing his hand aside, I wrapped my arms around his neck, pulled him toward me, and kissed him goodnight.

Nothing ever felt more like Christmas.

Too excited to sleep, Grandpa woke up the next morning a few minutes before the alarm rang at 5:30. He couldn't wait to get to his breakfast on the docks. While I snoozed in my bed a few feet away, he and Grandma whispered about family Christmas plans. Reaching over to turn off the alarm before it went off, he told Grandma, "No sense in waking up Little Jimmy." As he rolled over to get out of bed, Grandma heard him say something she hadn't heard in years:

"I love you, Helen."

Then a heavy thud sounded in the darkened room. Grandma called his name; when he didn't answer, she fumbled for the lamp. The commotion woke me just as the lights went on. I sat up amid the confused scene of Grandma screaming for my visiting cousin Debbie in the room next door. Grandpa lay face-up on the floor between our beds. His eyes were closed; blood trickled from a small cut on his forehead. I heard Debbie shouting our address to someone over the phone while Grandma cried, "He's dead . . . Oh, dear God, he's dead." Kneeling next to Grandpa, I saw a slight smile on his face—the same one I saw when he consoled me last night. Shaking him gently, I knew he'd get up for me. I whispered in his ear that he'd be all right. Grandma and Lynn needed us—we were the men of the house. His smile remained, but his eyes didn't open.

Soon firemen led me from the room; they carried Grandpa to an ambulance, and Grandma rode away with them.

A steady stream of red-eyed adults showed up at our house that morning. Nobody listened when I said Grandpa was all right because I saw him smiling. Then, a couple of hours later, Grandma came home. She walked past everyone else and came over to hug me.

"Jimmy, Grandpa died this morning. You're the man of the house now."

The man of the house was seven years old.

They buried Grandpa on Christmas Eve at Holy Cross Cemetery. I wasn't permitted to attend his wake or funeral—Uncle Jack said I should remember Grandpa as he was. Later that night, the family gathered at our house for Christmas dinner. The adults tried to put on a game face for the kids' sake. Uncle Jack suggested I open an early Christmas present, and then reached under the tree and handed me a box. I didn't want it. At his gentle insistence, I removed the wrapping paper. Inside, I saw the slippers

Grandpa and I wrapped on that last day. I put them down, went to my room, and closed the door.

Christmas didn't come to my house in 1964.[4]

Writing these words, forty Christmases now have passed without Grandpa. It's funny, but when I think of the man, his image is in black-and-white, not color. That's probably from replenishing memories of him over the decades with black-and-white photographs. Or maybe it's because Grandpa had black-and-white standards: If something was right, do it; if something was wrong, don't. A year before he died, Grandpa suffered serious injuries from a twenty-foot fall into the cargo bay of a ship. It was his employer's fault; they knew it and wanted to settle. Some lawyer promising a big payday showed up at our house offering to sue. Grandma thought it a great idea; we could use the money. Grandpa kicked him out. "That company put food on our table and clothes on our kids' backs during the Depression," he reminded Grandma.

Black and white.

My grandfather rose before dawn every day. He never called in sick. He worked hard, willed a crippled granddaughter to walk, and loved his family deeply. He never owned a house; he lived paycheck to paycheck, and he died with empty pockets. He also raised a little boy who one day went to Congress, rubbing elbows along the way with royalty, sports giants, war heroes, Hollywood superstars, and seven presidents of the

---

[4]Later, I learned that the optimistic prognosis for Grandpa's recovery was a ruse for his benefit. After the first heart attack, the doctor told Grandma, "He has blocked arteries. There's nothing we can do for him. He may die tomorrow, and he may die a year from tomorrow. Nobody can say. I suggest you not tell him; let him go back to work if that's what makes him happy. But understand he's on borrowed time." True to the doctor's advice, Grandma never told Grandpa or anyone else. Now, of course, this problem is treated with angioplasty or other routine medical procedures. Back in 1964, blocked arteries meant a death sentence.

United States. All of them fell short in comparison: The greatest man I ever saw cross the stage wasn't a politician or celebrity.

Someday, when we're reunited, I'll tell him so.

Grandma faced problems beyond a widow's grief. Soon to graduate from high school, Lynn wanted to move out and be on her own. Meanwhile, Mom told Grandma she wanted me back. I began to hear awful arguments between them. Grandma asked me, "If a judge or policeman ever wants to know, will you tell them you want to live with your mother or with me?" The question scared me. Finally, Mom asked me to move and be with her. I told her no: She and Dad had three other kids, and when Lynn left, Grandma would be alone. Grandpa wouldn't like that, so I was staying put.

We no longer could afford to stay in our little house in Colma. Aunt Bev took over the logistics, finding for us a small apartment on Como Street. A borrowed truck showed up; Aunt Bev said most of our stuff wouldn't fit in the new place, so we'd have to store it. On the truck I saw an open box with some of Grandpa's things: a Grace Lines pocket knife, a baseball signed by the 1932 Chicago White Sox, and his lucky "half-half dollar."[5] I put them all in my coat pocket, and I'm glad I did: When Aunt Bev failed to pay the storage bill, the company disposed of or dumped our belongings.

Como Street was lonely for Grandma and me. Instead of playing outside, I stayed indoors so she'd have company. The long walk to school became my only outdoor activity. A couple of local bullies looking for lunch money and amusement kept rolling me. Not wanting Grandma to worry, I kept the ongoing problem to myself. My shiner?

---

[5] As a boy, Grandpa saw a tramp sleeping on the railroad tracks get run over by a locomotive. The train cut the tramp in half, along with a half dollar coin in the tramp's pocket. Grandpa found the halved coin at the scene, and carried it the rest of his life for luck. Maybe that coin brought Grandpa luck for fifty years, but it sure didn't do much for the tramp on the tracks!

"The tetherball hit me in the eye at recess." The scraped knuckles? "I tripped over something."

Grandma's cousins urged her to return to the Mission District. In the summer of 1966, she agreed. We moved to a small flat at 1466 Church Street in the city. Now Grandma had visitors each day. Her older sister Della took me for weekends to 1839 Eighth Avenue, the house where she and Grandma grew up. Aunt Della was getting too old and infirm to maintain the family home; before she sold it, she wanted me to see where they once played as little girls. Stories of Grandma as a child softened my image of her. Grandma also helped with the softening: She seemed calmer; she yelled a lot less, and she hugged me a lot more. For the first time since Grandpa died, life slowly inched back.

Though our birthdays fell two days apart, Grandma and I always celebrated on my birthday, August 21. Since my ninth birthday in 1966 coincided with her sixtieth, she planned a special celebration. That morning Grandma told me how proud I made her. "You really have become the man of the house, Jimmy. I depend on you so much. When your Grandpa died, I wasn't sure what would happen to us. But you know what? I think we're gonna make it." Like her husband, Grandma almost never smiled, so when I saw one I believed her.

During our birthday party, Grandma didn't eat any of the food she had cooked. I overheard the adults pleading with Grandma about something, but she waved them away with a laugh. When I investigated, she told me, "Oh, all these fools want me to go to the doctor just because I have some pains in my stomach." Since she laughed (a new phenomenon) I thought nothing of it at first, but I grew concerned when she agreed to go. Just like Grandpa, she hated doctors, which meant she feared them. If she agreed to see one now, it wasn't a good sign.

The doctor performed tests; Grandma came home and said she needed an operation. "They told me I have some kind of blockage in my stomach. But if they operate on me, they can fix it and these pains will go away." Grandma's concern was about me, not herself: While she recovered, I needed to stay with Mom and Dad. "You'll have to start school in Pacifica," she told me. "But as soon as I heal up, you'll come home with me, and we'll start you at your new school at our new home. I promise it won't be very long."

After packing a suitcase, I went to live with Mom and Dad for the first time in my life.

I didn't know Mom and Dad's marriage was on the rocks until I moved in. During these early years, Dad battled alcoholism—an addiction bordering on a death wish.[6] Mom had her own addiction: An obsessive shopper, she bought everything imaginable for her kids to camouflage the home life fractures. She overextended the family finances on secretly obtained credit cards, and then hid the evidence from Dad, who learned of the sprees when creditors garnished his wages. This pushed him closer to the bottle, which pushed her closer to department stores. It was a destructive cycle.

I tuned out their loud and unending quarrels, remembering that this backdrop was temporary: When Grandma felt better, I'd go home again. Meanwhile, it was great being around my younger siblings. Although we grew up in separate homes, Pat, Teri, Johnny, and I remained close-knit. As the oldest, baby-sitting responsibilities fell to me while Mom and Dad worked. I didn't fail them on the big-ticket items (meaning I didn't kill the kids or sell them to gypsies), but since rules and parental authority were minimal at Mom's, it felt great to jettison responsibility and cut loose for a while. "Having fun" was something that died with Grandpa; now leading a brood of unsupervised kids, mischief became a tag-team activity.

The Rogan kids rained hell on the neighbors we disliked: We ran around at night covering their houses and lawns with rolls of moist toilet paper, soaping their car windows, chalking their garage doors, ringing their doorbells and fleeing, or playing the theme song from *Rat Patrol* on

---

[6]Dad suffered years of private hell before he walked into an AA meeting, found his sobriety, and kept it. Dad dedicated his later years to sharing his testimony with any alcoholic—from bank presidents to San Quentin convicts—needing to hear a big dose of truth.

my school loaner trumpet next to their bedroom window. When we tired of terrorizing the locals, we combed the telephone directory for Chinese surnames, having discovered that newly arrived immigrants were more likely to fall for our prank phone calls. We found plenty who believed we really were from the power company and needed to know if their refrigerator was still running (*"It is? Then go catch it, stupid!"*); we found lots of deli employees willing to tell us that yes, in fact, they did have pickled pigs' feet (*That's disgusting—go put on your shoes!*). But we never found an all-night tobacconist dumb enough to tell us he had Prince Albert in a can (*"No, we let him out an hour ago—now get to bed, you little bastard!"*). One night Teri discovered in the phone book some poor soul going through life bearing the name "Reddy Bonar." His late night harassing calls ended only when he disconnected his service.

"Safe and Sane" fireworks left in our hands were neither. Since Mom and Dad paid no attention to gardening, our yard was filled with waist-high weeds. One day we tried to make a Piccolo Pete fly, so we lit it upside down. It flew, arced in a loop, and then landed in the weeds. Soon the entire yard was an inferno. The fire department put it out before we burned down the house. A fire inspector searching the weeds picked up something, slid it in his pocket, and then walked over to us: "Were any of you kids playing with fireworks back here?" Oh no, we assured him, we'd never do that. "Then how did that fire get started?"

"Well, we were just sitting here on the patio. Suddenly the entire yard burst into flames. I think maybe someone threw a lit cigarette from an airplane flying over our house, and it must have landed in our back yard."

"Then how did this get into your yard?" The inspector reached into his pocket and held out the charred Piccolo Pete. We all looked at each other: "Uh . . . I think that's what the guy lit his cigarette with."

General mayhem aside, we always looked for ways to make an extra buck. When our stupid poodle Coco ate a bag of glitter, we discovered a digestive marvel. Soon we salted all of Coco's food with glitter, and then bet the neighbor kids that we had the "world's only glitter-shitting dog." Some doubter always put up a quarter to bet we didn't. Suspecting that we might try to pre-glitter Coco's stool specially for the occasion, the gambler insisted on following the dog around the yard until she had to go. If that took too long, we threw Coco some Ex Lax to help speed the exhibit. Eventually, Coco delivered the goods. "Hey, I'll be damned! Your dog really does shit glitter! Here's your two bits. Sorry I called you a liar." Sturdy as she was, the continuous concentration of glitter and Ex Lax took its toll on poor Coco. We found her one morning cold and stiff in the garage; nearby was her last glittery gift. Out of respect, admission to her final phenomenon was free.

While hiking through the hills near Terra Nova High School, we discovered the huge pipes leading to the underground sewers. Soon we were in the guided sewer tour business. With noses pinched to avoid the stench, we led our clients through waist-high waste, shining our flashlight on the rats, sludge, "brown trout," and other unspeakable discoveries. The pocket change flowed to us from boys eager to experience this poor man's version of Disneyland's Jungle Cruise ride.

We'd push a huge surplus truck tire up Redwood Way, and for a dime, we let kids curl inside the hole, and then we rolled them down the street. The tire ride was a dizzying thrill, but a constant complaint (in addition to our "no refund" policy if the tire crashed into a parked or moving car) was that the ride ended too quickly. We hit on a bright idea: *automated* rides—which involved substituting Mom's clothes dryer for the tire. Before inaugurating the new adventure, I selected Pat as the test pilot. I stuffed Pat into the dryer, set the dial on "fluff and fold," and flipped on the switch. Assuming Pat wanted a nice long ride, I ignored the "bump-BUMP, bump-BUMP, bump-BUMP" of Pat bouncing inside the dryer and went to the kitchen for a snack. After making my sandwich, I joined Mom in the living room. A few minutes later she said, "Jimmy, go get your sneakers out of the dryer! That bumping sound is driving me crazy—I can't hear the TV." Still eating my sandwich, I replied casually, "That's not sneakers. That's Pat." Fortunately, mouth-to-mouth resuscitation revived him just in time.

Our eagerness to make money, or let Mom save some, only went so far. We battled against the 25-cent haircuts at the Pacifica Beauty College, where teen students possessed all the styling finesse of a mudslide. No matter how much we squawked about the awful haircuts, Mom didn't care: It was too good a bargain to pass up. Once I asked the barber why they had a sign on the wall reading, "We reserve the right to refuse service to anyone." The student barber replied, "We don't cut the hair of dirty kids—we worry about lice getting in our combs." That gave me an idea. Before our next haircut, Pat and I collected dead flies from dusty windowsills, and bugs from our yard. Along with little Johnny, we slopped Dixie Peach Pomade on our hair, and then set off in Mom's car for the Beauty College. Riding in the back seat, Pat and I quietly embedded the insects in our scalps, and covered the collection with gooey strands of hair. At the beauty college, we tried not to laugh as the students pinned white towels around our necks. Suddenly, screams pierced the air: As the girls combed our hair, bugs (both alive and dead) dropped all over the white towels. "Oh, my God!" shrieked my barber. "They're infested! Get these filthy kids out of here!" My shocked mother jumped out of her chair: *"What did you call my children?"*

"You heard me—get them out of here! They're infested!"

With Mom and the supervisor now yelling at each other, my brothers and I shook out the evidence and stuffed it in our pockets. When Mom marched over to inspect our scalps, we wore innocent and hurt expressions. Mom stormed out the door with her kids in tow, shouting lawsuit threats over her shoulder along the way. Whimpering deliciously, Pat asked through his fake sniffles, "Mommy, how come those mean ladies don't like us?"

Grandma had her surgery; the next day Aunt Della brought me to the hospital. Tubes hung from Grandma's nostrils and arms. She greeted me with a weak but lasting hug: "Don't worry about me, I'll be fine. Tell me all about your new school." As days followed there were more visits, but I felt uneasy. Grandma grew weepy when I visited; no date was set for her to come home. Adults dropped their voices when discussing her condition in front of me. Then one day I overheard a whispered word foreign to my vocabulary: *cancer.* When I asked Mom what that word meant, she gave a nondescript answer. Then the visits and telephone calls stopped. "Grandma's in a coma," Mom told me. What did that mean? "It means she's sleeping; she's sick today. But don't worry. Don't worry."

Alone one night with Grandma in her hospital room, Mom listened to her comatose mother's labored breathing under an oxygen tent. Mom left to have a cigarette; when she returned a few minutes later, Grandma was gone. Mom broke the news to me the next morning, saying Grandma's exploratory surgery a few weeks earlier revealed a ravaging stomach cancer. The doctors closed her up. They could do nothing.

"Honey, you'll be living with Dad and me from now on."

The day after Grandma died, Mom took me to Church Street to get my things and to select an outfit for Grandma's burial. There wasn't much from which to choose. A couple of old house dresses hung in her closet; under her bed lay those old white nurse's shoes Grandma always wore. My grandmother died owning two shabby dresses and one old pair of shoes, while I had neatly pressed, new clothes hanging in my closet.

Two days after Grandma's burial, a car struck my younger brother Pat. He spent months in a full body cast and had to learn to walk anew. His near-fatal accident cranked up anxieties around an already tense home. Between Dad's drinking and Mom's spending, their fights became more ugly and profane. Both preferred to stay away from each other, which meant neither came home much during waking hours. Fun time again was over: I got a battlefield promotion to surrogate parent. "You're the oldest," Mom said. "You're the most responsible, so I count on you." There were far fewer high jinks now: At age nine I cooked, cleaned, gave baths, settled arguments, helped with homework, fixed skateboards, enforced discipline, got them up for school in the morning, and put them to bed at night. Sometimes Mom or Dad came home after dinner; sometimes it was long after we went to bed.

With each battle royal between Mom and Dad, coupled with my grandparents' back-to-back deaths, I grew more dejected and withdrawn. Staying focused in school became a problem; I got into fistfights with any kid looking for trouble. At home, I ate meals alone in my room to avoid the quarrels. I played less outside and took care of more chores inside. Mom depended on me because I was the oldest. When only the kids were home, I needed to be the man of the house.

One day in Mom's garage I saw an old family photo album atop a pile of things to be thrown out. I saved the photos, and then looked to see if anything else needed salvaging. Among the castoffs lay a legal-looking document from St. Luke's Hospital. A piece of trash covered the surname, but I could see the first two names on it were mine: *James Edward*. I couldn't believe Mom threw out *my* birth certificate. When I picked it up I saw the full name: *James Edward Baroni*.

"Who's that?" I wondered. "Is this some cousin or something?" Examining it further, I saw that the birth date and place were the same as mine, and it listed Mom as the mother; but the father's name wasn't Jack Rogan; it was somebody named John Baroni.

I don't know how long I stared at that piece of paper trying to sort this out. Random memories came back. *Jimmy's not a real Rogan,* some of Dad's relatives whispered to my young brothers and sister. *You're not my son,* Dad had yelled at me one night while on a bender. *You're not my son*—What did that mean? When I asked Mom, she shrugged it off, saying that people who drink say stupid things.

That night, when I confronted Mom with the certificate, her face lost color. "Oh, shit," she mumbled. She sat me down, hastily lit a cigarette with trembling hands, and began a halting explanation as her eyes darted around the room: "Dad—Jack Rogan—isn't your real father. I met a man named Jack Baroni. He's your real father. You never knew him because after we were married, but before you were born, he was killed in the Korean War. Then I met Jack and we got married."

I was an avid history reader, and by now I knew a little biology, too. "Mom, the Korean War ended in 1953. I was born in 1957. So how was my father killed in the Korean War?" Mom backpedaled on the Korea story, but told me no more. She was hiding something.

Relatives later confirmed what happened: While working as a cocktail waitress, Mom became pregnant by John Baroni, who then left her. They never met him or his family and knew no more about it. After he disappeared, Mom married Jack Rogan, and everyone embraced the story that he was my father even though he never adopted me.

Those sketchy details didn't satisfy me. Who was John Baroni? Is he hurt or sick, I wondered? Has he looked for me? Is he dead? Do I have a whole family I don't know about—brothers, sisters, some lonely grandmother in a nursing home? I wanted the truth, and it became clear I'd have to get it for myself.

I spent long weekends at the public library looking up the name "John Baroni" in every telephone book in the San Francisco Bay Area, and then in California. I called every "John Baroni'" and "J. Baroni" listed. After getting Mr. Baroni on the line, I asked if he ever worked as a bartender at the Cable Car Village in San Francisco. The answer was always no. When I ran out of John's and J's, I called all the Baroni listings. I never found the bartender or anyone who knew him. Over the years I continued searching, checking genealogical, church, and government records. I wrote to Social Security and each branch of the military. Nothing ever came of it. The search for answers regarding my biological father ended, and I accepted the inevitable: John Baroni was dead.

This discovery added to my deepening grief. I loved my family but I hated our situation. I didn't feel like I belonged here; I wanted to be back with Grandpa and Grandma. It made me wonder if that meant I wanted to die, too.

4

ONE LESS GEOLOGIST

"Take care of Little Jimmy for me."

Grandma whispered this appeal to her older sister before slipping into her final coma. Aunt Della squeezed Grandma's hand to acknowledge the promise; after Grandma died, she made good on her pledge, dropping by or calling to check on me almost daily.

Aunt Della bore a striking resemblance to Grandma, but the similarity ended with physical appearance. Unlike my solemn Grandma, Aunt Della had an infectious and mischievous sense of humor. Her sunny disposition not only tolerated childish shenanigans, she instigated them. Once when I made eye contact with her during Thanksgiving dinner, she looked around to make sure nobody else was watching. Then she crossed her eyes, popped forward her dentures, and clacked her false teeth at me. I laughed so hard that I spewed my milk across the turkey. While everyone yelled at me for ruining the bird, Aunt Della smiled, feigning deep concern over "the poor dear's little spell."

Even Aunt Della's unfailing sense of humor faded as she noticed her once cheery great-nephew growing gloomy and introverted. "Hey, why don't you come over and spend the night?" she began asking. "We'll do whatever you want!" She and her late-in-life boyfriend Ralf Olson teamed to snap me out of the doldrums. Visits to her new Westlake apartment at 25

Poncetta Drive involved nonstop activity: wall tennis at Park Merced, swimming at Fleishhacker Pool, viewing the seals at the Cliff House, hiking to the Broderick and Terry dueling site,[7] or munching bowls of Jiffy Pop while watching old movies on TV. Aunt Della loved any old movie that didn't star actor Victor Mature. Decades earlier, when she worked as a hotel telephone operator, she called to tell Mr. Mature that his car and driver awaited. The drunken actor repaid the courtesy by slurring, "Hey lady, go take a shit in your hat!" Aunt Della boycotted Victor Mature movies ever since.

My random overnighters to Aunt Della's soon extended to weekend stays; later, they stretched to a week or more at a time, and I couldn't get enough of them. Seeing a great emotional need for stability in my life, she and Uncle Ralf poured all their attentions into steering me back on track. Life with them wasn't life with my grandparents, but nothing ever came closer.

Happy and upbeat while at Aunt Della's, I grew sullen and melancholy back home. I wanted to live full-time with her. Had that happened, I might have ended up a geologist, which is what Aunt Della wanted me to become. Instead, a chance occurrence launched me on another trajectory, and that fuse was lit not at Aunt Della's, but at Mom's.

I wish there was a more romanticized way to say this: I was elected to the United States Congress in 1996 because our garbage man overslept one morning in 1966.

Mom's inability to pass by any sales "bargain" left her not only mired in debt, but with a home décor possessing all the chic of a garage sale.

---

[7]Because I loved history, Uncle Ralf said he knew a special place to visit. We hiked down a dirt trail near Lake Merced through eucalyptus and pine trees until we came to a forgotten clearing. There two stone markers showed where U.S. Supreme Court Justice David Terry killed U.S. Senator David Broderick in a duel on September 13, 1859. It was an eerie, quiet place, and we often visited the site of the deadly encounter. Decades later I took my nephew to show him the site. The eucalyptus trees and the dusty trail were gone; tennis courts and condominiums now encircle the little stone markers.

Clutter and unmatched furnishings filled each room. A neighbor once joked about Mom's hallway table decoration: Stacked on the table, from bottom to top, was a food warmer, a brass spittoon, and a large plaster replica of King Tut's head. Mom bought the pieces dirt-cheap somewhere; I never noticed the bizarre combination until it was pointed out. In our house, totem poles of junk like this were everywhere.

Mom bought her groceries at the Mayfair Market in Daly City. When I was in the fourth grade, Mayfair offered a promotional giveaway of small statues of the presidents of the United States and a Styrofoam stand shaped like the U.S. Capitol steps upon which to display them. She brought home statues each time she shopped; I lined them up and rolled rubber balls at them. My lack of gratitude or historical reverence didn't matter to Mom, who brought them home compulsively.

When Mom opened the display stand packaging, she removed its plastic wrapper and tossed it atop the still-uncollected trash. Later, the star-studded border of the wrapper caught my eye; when I picked up the bag to examine it, out fell a booklet Mom had overlooked: "The American Presidents Album." Without much thought I stuffed it into my notebook and headed off to school. During a lull in class, I pulled it out and flipped through it. Knowing nothing about presidents beyond Washington's cherry tree and Lincoln's top hat, these photos and brief profiles now teased my interest. Who were these men, and what were they like? How did they get their chance at greatness? I read and reread the pamphlet. Still intrigued, I went to the school library and checked out a book on presidents. I went back for another book, and another, and yet another. After reading all the books on presidents in our school library, I found another library.

Because of our circumstances, the stories of presidents coming from humble backgrounds fascinated me. Yes, the rich often filled their ranks, but those ranks also included plow drivers, tailors, Indian fighters, store clerks, realtors, preachers, reporters, miners, flatboat pilots, railroad time-keepers, surveyors, bookkeepers, insurance salesmen, rail-splitters, haber-dashers, and cattle herders. One future president was an indentured servant; another was a bankrupt; still another hanged criminals. Some came from mud-floored, claptrap shanties on desolate prairies; many had little or no formal education. For every son of privilege to occupy the White House, there were sons of mule traders, drunks, gamblers, grocers, and dirt farmers who got there, too. These stories planted the seeds of an important subliminal truth: People inherit money, but they can't inherit greatness. That comes from hard work, honor, and perseverance. Rich people may get a head start in the race, but marathons aren't won in the sprint.

One question puzzled me: What set these thirty-five men apart from everyone else? Then I stumbled on a magazine article that answered my question—and killed forever Aunt Della's dreams of a geology career for me. The story was of a young pharmacist's first visit to Washington during the Depression. Seeing the Capitol and the monuments in all their glory brought him a newfound passion. In his hotel room that night, he rushed off an excited letter to his fiancée back home. After admonishing her not to laugh, he wrote that if he applied himself, maybe someday he could return as a congressman. She didn't laugh; they married, and she watched her husband climb the political ladder to mayor, U.S. Senator, vice president of the United States, and candidate for president. Along the way, ex-druggist Hubert Humphrey helped shape almost every landmark law of his era, including expanding Social Security protection for old people, and drafting the Medicare and Civil Rights Acts of the 1950s and 1960s.

Civil rights? I remembered that phrase: Grandpa once said something about it being why we could now have neighbors like my across-the-street friend Greg and his little sister. Before the laws changed, Grandpa said Negro families like Greg's maybe couldn't live on our block. Instead, people like Greg's family were treated badly, and sometimes beaten or killed, just because they were black. That story rattled me deeply; I was sure glad the laws changed for Greg and his family. Social Security and Medicare? That's what Aunt Della told me kept her going. Since her massive heart attack and stroke, she couldn't work anymore. Aunt Della said she lived off her $103-a-month Social Security check, and if it wasn't for that and Medicare, she couldn't buy the digitalis heart medicine that kept her alive.

This magazine story showed me the nexus that brought all of these future leaders to Washington—the Indian fighter, the hangman, the coal miner, the servant boy, and now the pharmacist. For some it was sheer worthiness; for others it was dogged determination; for a few, it was dumb luck.

But for all of them, it was politics.

If politics gave a Walgreen's druggist from Minnesota the chance to help millions of families like Greg's and mine, then why didn't everyone want to be in politics? Why would I want to do anything else? Just like Hubert Humphrey in that letter to his future wife, if I applied myself and set my sights high, someday I could be a congressman and write laws to help people like Aunt Della and my grandparents. To write better laws, I figured being a lawyer would help.

There was my equation: *The law + politics = helping people.* Once I connected those dots, my compass was set. I wanted to be a congressman when I grew up, and none of Aunt Della's thrilling tales of geology ever enticed me away.

No one awaited the start of 1968 more eagerly than I: After two years of studying history, politics, and presidents, now I'd get to see my first presidential election. We spent weeks studying the campaign in Miss Firpo's fifth grade class. On the Democratic side my new hero Hubert Humphrey was running, as were Senators Robert F. Kennedy and Eugene McCarthy. The Republican nomination looked like Richard Nixon's to lose, but who cared? If Humphrey was a Democrat, then so was I.

Living in California brought added excitement to the race: Our state's June 4 primary might well decide the Democratic contest. Humphrey wasn't on the ballot, but for Kennedy and McCarthy, California was make or break. Miss Firpo urged us to visit their campaign headquarters and bring back posters and stickers to decorate the classroom. I rooted for McCarthy only because Cheryl Briones, the freckle-faced girl on whom I had a secret crush, was for him. We were in the minority; most of the kids were going "All the Way with RFK" and decorating the classroom with Kennedy posters. On Election Day, we bet our best baseball cards on the winner. Mike Dittman pinned to my coat a blue Kennedy badge; I stuffed it into my pocket before Cheryl saw it. That night, tragedy struck: After delivering his victory speech, Kennedy was assassinated. I awoke the next morning to the news, which we watched on a neighborhood novelty—a small color television. The networks replayed color footage of the fallen candidate, his head resting in a spreading pool of maroon blood. I felt sick to my stomach.

In class that day, yesterday's rivalry gave way to shock and overwhelming sadness. Miss Firpo tried to explain the horror to her children in a room still decorated with a dozen Kennedy posters. His picture on the banners, frozen with a half-smile, bore the haunting aura of death. Later that day, something sharp in my jacket pocket pricked my thumb: the Kennedy campaign badge Mike gave me. Destined originally for the junk drawer, now I treated it as a historic relic. I laid the badge inside a small box lined with cotton. I didn't know it at the time, but I just started a lifelong hobby that added to my unquenchable interest of history and politics. Collecting campaign artifacts somehow brought to life all those stories I read about the lives of politicians.

If this political enthusiasm disappointed Aunt Della's hope that I would come to my senses and learn about geology, she never let it show. A few weeks later, on a trip to Reno, Aunt Della and Uncle Ralf let me hang out in the "Humphrey for President" headquarters while they played the nickel slots at Harrah's. Inside, I found a chaotic room swarming with volunteers answering telephones, stuffing envelopes, and marking precinct maps. When I tugged on someone's sleeve and asked what everyone was doing, her answer thrilled me: "What are we doing? We're electing a president!" I stood for hours watching with fascination; before leaving, I doubled my collection by getting an "HHH Humphrey" badge and matchbook.

Later, I wandered into a coin store with the pocketful of dimes Aunt Della gave me for lunch. As the owner entertained friends with jokes in the corner, I scoured his display cases for stray campaign buttons. "Hey kid," he called, "you collect coins?" No, I told him, I was just looking. Then I saw it: Amid a row of silk ribbons thumbtacked to the wall, one ribbon proclaimed boldly, "Sons of Old Soldiers—Harrison and Morton Club of Indianapolis." From my studies I knew its origin: It was an 1888 parade ribbon supporting Benjamin Harrison and Levi P. Morton for president and vice president. I wanted to buy it, but the owner said the ribbons were for decoration, not sale. "Everything's for sale," I said, mimicking a line I once heard in a movie. I dumped out my dimes and, after counting them, shoved the pile toward him: "Mister, I'm prepared to offer you four dollars and ten cents for that ribbon. Take it or leave it." After enjoying a big laugh at my determination, he took it.

All the way home from Reno I held that ribbon with a sense of awe. In my imagination, I saw men from a bygone era wearing tall hats and starched collars, with walking sticks and handlebar mustaches, parading through town singing Harrison songs and wearing my ribbon. To me, finding and collecting such artifacts was like unearthing dinosaur bones or fossils, linking our political and historic past to the present. Maybe that's why Aunt Della didn't mind my hobby: In a way, it made me something of a geologist after all.

Aunt Della put aside a few dollars each month to help me add to my library of books or collection of campaign items. I earned money working after school each day as a stock boy at King Norman's Kingdom of Toys, where the owner paid me $1.00 an hour under the table. Every couple of weeks Aunt Della drove me to the Cow Palace Flea Market, and while she waited in the car, I searched for old campaign treasures. Soon I was adding memorabilia from candidates long remembered and long forgotten: Teddy Roosevelt and Alton B. Parker, Franklin D. Roosevelt and Alf Landon, Woodrow Wilson and Wendell Willkie. Before long, I needed more cotton and a bigger box.

Uncle Ralf suggested I write the president and ask for his autograph, saying it would make a nice addition to my collection. I never thought a president would write me back, but to humor Uncle Ralf I wrote President Johnson and asked for a signed picture. A few months went by with no reply. Each day Aunt Della sent me to get her mail, and I would ask our old mailman Cliff if I had a letter from the president today. "Nope, not today!" he'd laugh, presuming I was joking. Then one day he pulled from his mailbag a big envelope, did a double take, and then handed it to me with a twinkle in his eye. The return address left me speechless: *The White House.* I was too nervous to open it, so Aunt Della did it for me. Inside was a letter from the president's secretary, along with a color photograph signed, "With best wishes, Lyndon B. Johnson."

Sadly, the dear man who encouraged me to write the letter didn't live to see the reply. A doctor diagnosed Uncle Ralf with an ulcer; he entered the hospital for surgery to remove it. Just as it happened with Grandma a couple of years earlier, the doctors found inoperable stomach cancer. Uncle Ralf never came home from the hospital.

With Uncle Ralf's death, Aunt Della's entire focus now shifted to me. Despite her nagging feeling that all politicians were crooks and that I'd still be better off digging for rocks, she gave up that expectation to support my political interests. She got me a 1950 Underwood typewriter so I could write more letters to politicians (and make the ones I wrote legible), and loaded me up with envelopes and postage stamps. Soon the postman delivered mail from Presidents Harry Truman, Dwight Eisenhower, and Richard Nixon; Congressman Gerald Ford; Governor Ronald Reagan; Ambassador George Bush; Chief Justice Earl Warren; and countless senators, governors, cabinet members, and former presidential and vice presidential candidates.

Aunt Della redeemed all of her S&H Green Stamp books for two metal bookcases to organize my growing collection. To help combat my shyness and fear of public speaking, she bought me a small phonograph. "If you're going into politics," she said with a smile, "you'd better learn how to give a speech. Otherwise, well, there's always geology!" She handed me a record album, *A Memorial Tribute: The Speeches of President John F. Kennedy*, and told me to go listen to him. Every couple of months she bought me a new spoken word album so I could learn speechmaking: *Great Moments with Mr. Lincoln, Franklin D. Roosevelt in His Own Words, Eisenhower Memorial Tribute*, and *Historic Speeches of the American Presidents* were but a few. I wore out record needles doing more than just listening: I tried mimicking the orators' cadence, inflection, and style until I could recite from memory Lincoln's Gettysburg Address, Kennedy's Inaugural Address, General MacArthur's "Old Soldiers Never Die" speech, FDR's declaration of war against Japan, and many others. At a church bazaar, I knocked over all the lead milk bottles with one throw of the baseball. The barker told me to pick any prize; skipping the catcher's mitt, I chose the album *Everett Dirksen's America*, featuring the Illinois senator speaking words to great patriotic songs. As I walked away with my prize, I heard the bazaar carnie say, "Hmmm—weird kid."

I spent so much time at Aunt Della's that I enrolled in middle school near her. At the end of my first day at Ben Franklin Junior High, I saw a tall kid with a notebook bearing a Hubert Humphrey sticker. From that moment, Dan Swanson and I became best friends, spending our free time together volunteering on campaigns, studying government, and collecting political autographs and campaign buttons. In Mr. Lasley's advanced government class, which was like being in a yearlong model U.S. Senate, I met two more classmates—Roger Mahan and Clint Bolick—who completed our quartet of political junkies, memorabilia collectors, and friends.

Mr. Lasley took my youthful determination to serve in Congress someday and turned it into a passion. He taught us the legislative process, parliamentary law, and the rules of debate. Under his guidance we introduced bills and amendments, debated their merits, formed coalitions, and used procedural tricks to advance or block legislation. He even taught us to attack opponents diplomatically: "Mr. President, I rise to congratulate my distinguished colleague for his remarks. Were I learned in the art of obfuscation, I might comprehend his meandering bloviations. . . ." All my energies went into that class: I couldn't wait for it to start each day, and I hated when the dismissal bell rang. Our little political mafia spent nights and weekends brainstorming on strategies and tactics. Since we took it so seriously (and the rest of our classmates didn't), we took over the Senate: I became president pro tem, Dan became majority leader, and Roger led his own one-man Conservative Party.[8]

---

[8]Many years later, after my election to the California State Assembly, I used my old class notes from Mr. Lasley's class to refresh my memory on parliamentary law and tactics, and they still served me well! Later, when I was in Congress, I called Mr. Lasley's wife and told her to have my former teacher (now battling brain cancer) watch C-SPAN at a prearranged time. To his astonishment, I gave a floor speech in Congress paying tribute to him and his advanced government class, sharing how much it inspired Dan, Roger, Clint, and me in our later pursuits. Mrs. Lasley told me her husband wept through the whole speech.

When we weren't focused on advanced government strategies, Dan, Roger, and I spent our leisure time at the Daly City Public Library looking up more addresses of retired political leaders in the "Who's Who" reference books so we could write for autographs and advice. If one of us got a good reply, the others wrote to replicate the luck. When we found an article reporting that President Johnson used a secretary to sign his autograph requests, we all felt defrauded by the counterfeit treasures sent us. The race was on to be the first to convince Johnson to send a genuine autograph. Repeated sincere polite requests were rebuffed; even shameless lying failed ("Dear President Johnson, My sister was playing in a house when the boiler room blew up. As the firemen dragged her burned and scalded body from the rubble, she screamed out in agony, '*Genuine Johnson autograph!*' If you will send my sister a real autograph, and not a phony one, it will help her get better. PS: Please inscribe it to Jim Rogan, so I can keep it in case she doesn't pull through . . ."). It wasn't until I asked Mrs. Johnson to intercede with her husband that I got the real McCoy.

Getting Harry Truman's address from the library came in handy for one school project, although not without causing some indigestion along the way. When my English teacher, Mr. Puhr, assigned us to write a seven-page biography of a president, I picked Harry Truman. Instead of spending the allotted three months on the project, I finished it in three days, so I mailed my only copy to Truman and asked him to look it over. It never dawned on me that it wouldn't be returned in time. Months passed; when the paper came due, I was empty-handed. Mr. Puhr rejected my explanation, called me a liar in front of the class, and gave me an "F" grade. "Besides," he sputtered, "Truman's been dead for almost twenty years! I should know: I watched his funeral on television."

As time went by, I forgot about the incident. Then one afternoon Aunt Della handed me a large envelope postmarked from Independence, Missouri. Inside I found my report returned, along with an autographed picture and a note written on Truman's personal letterhead: "Dear Jim: I was very pleased to have your letter and manuscript. I am sorry I cannot help you with it, as I have a rule against working on another author's paper. It is clear, however, that you did your homework well. With best wishes for success in your life. Sincerely yours, Harry S Truman."

The next day in class, I walked up to Mr. Puhr's desk and showed him my proof. His face reddened as he read the letter and report; he said sternly, "Take your seat." After humiliating me earlier, he refused to acknowledge his mistake. I fumed for the rest of class, so when the recess bell rang, I jumped from my desk and blocked the classroom door. Holding aloft my treasures, I called to my classmates, "Hey, if anybody wants to see the letter and autographed picture I got yesterday from the *late* President Harry Truman, I'll show it to you on the playground!"

When Mr. Puhr again refused to accept my paper, I went to the principal and argued my case. She overruled Mr. Puhr and ordered him to receive it. Later, Mr. Puhr handed back my paper in front of the entire class, telling me that he marked me down for repeated punctuation errors in that I failed to put a period after Truman's middle initial. I said that the omission was intentional, because the "S" didn't get a period— it *was* his middle name. Mr. Puhr grabbed Volume T of the Encyclopedia Britannica, turned to Truman's entry, and cackled aloud: "The encyclopedia lists him as "Harry *S-with-a-period* Truman! What do you say to that?"

"The encyclopedia's wrong."

"So! The encyclopedia is wrong and Mr. Rogan is right! My, aren't we lucky to have such a brilliant student in our midst!" Classmates laughed as Mr. Puhr mocked me for the rest of the period, and for days afterward he called on me to "confirm" things like Columbus discovered America and George Washington was our first president. Growing tired of the abuse, I took matters into my own hands: "Dear President Truman, You won't believe this teacher of mine. . . ." I laid out the story for Truman and asked him to settle the issue.

The school year ended without any reply, and again I forgot about it. As summer vacation ended, another letter from Missouri arrived: "Dear Jim, The "S" in my middle name stands for the first letter of the first name of each of my grandfathers. In order to be strictly impartial in naming me for one or the other, I was given the letter "S" as a middle name. It can be used with or without a period. I was glad to autograph your engraved picture of the White House and it is being returned to you herewith. I appreciate your very kind comments and send you best wishes. Sincerely yours, Harry S Truman." Now, for the first time, I noticed Truman's engraved letterhead: sure enough, it bore the name "Harry S Truman" with no period after the middle initial.

On the first day of the new school year, I showed up early looking for Mr. Puhr. He looked baffled when I entered his classroom, as if I had made another mistake. I walked to his desk and showed him the second Truman letter. He still refused to regrade my report, but changed his mind when I threatened to have the principal intervene again. As I walked away, Mr. Puhr called to me sharply: "Rogan," he said, "I'm very glad you won't be in my class this year."

Writing letters to politicians was a great way for us to expand our collections; later, Dan, Roger, and I discovered a better way. When I heard that my hero Hubert Humphrey would appear the next morning with Senator Edward Kennedy on Jim Dunbar's TV news show, we concocted a plan to cut school and try to meet them in person. Well before dawn, we rode a trolley car from Daly City into downtown San Francisco, then we walked for blocks down dark streets, passing hobos sleeping in doorways and winos drinking from bottles wrapped in paper bags. It was a spooky journey for three kids, but we arrived at KGO Studio in one piece, and a kindly doorman told us where to wait for Humphrey and Kennedy's arrival.

Kennedy got there first, climbing out of his car and walking toward the entrance. We were so nervous that we almost let him pass by without meeting him. He was very gracious as he signed autographs and posed for a group photo before going in for his interview. A few minutes later, Humphrey strolled over and shook our hands, signed autographs, and posed for pictures. Gregarious and charming, he wanted to know our names, where we lived, and where we went to school. When he heard we loved politics, he beamed with enthusiasm, sharing his joy of public service and encouraging us to keep up our studies. I was so tongue-tied that I couldn't do much better than mumble back my thanks.

What a thrill! Here was Hubert Humphrey in the flesh—the guy whose letter I read in that magazine article years earlier, who almost became president and might still become president—now encouraging *me* to get into politics! The experience left me breathless; I don't think I would have sold that autograph for a million dollars. Back at school, Mr. Lasley was so impressed with our chutzpah in meeting Humphrey and Kennedy that he ran interference for us on our truancy problem.

Over the next few years, Dan, Roger and I became regular fixtures outside KGO Studio. Whenever newsman Jim Dunbar interviewed any national political figure passing through San Francisco, we waited outside to get autographs, take pictures, and solicit their advice on getting into politics. We met almost every governor, senator, congressman, and presidential candidate making their way through town in the early to mid-1970s; we became so familiar that Jim Dunbar let us inside the studio to watch his interviews from the control booth. Decades later, during the Clinton impeachment trial, my press secretary Jeff Solsby fended off scores of press interview requests that came each day for me. Despite my backbreaking schedule, Jeff knew to put through every interview request from Jim Dunbar, who thirty years later still broadcast the news at KGO.

Each visit to KGO was memorable, and making these personal connections with national leaders taught me an important lesson beyond autograph collecting: No matter how famous or powerful, there was nothing mystical about these people. In fact, once I got beyond the "celebrity factor," very few struck me as extraordinary. From these encounters, I got many autographs, but I also got something far more important: the confidence that someday I could do this.

5

FRANK, ROCKY, AND
THE APARTMENTS

One day, as the end of junior high school approached, I took the bus after class to Aunt Della's. When I arrived, I realized I had forgotten my key. Aunt Della wasn't there to let me in; she had planned a day of lunch and shopping with Lynn. I heard her TV from the hallway, but she often left it on to ward off burglars. Annoyed by my own forgetfulness, I did my homework in the lobby while waiting for her to return. Minutes turned to hours, and it grew dark outside. Lynn wasn't home when I called her house, so now I worried they might have been in an accident.

My mother picked me up; together we drove to the manager's office, where a receptionist gave me a spare key to Apartment 110 with nothing more than my assurance that I lived there. We drove back to Aunt Della's, and while Mom parked, I went inside. I found Aunt Della at her small dinette, with her face buried in her arms atop the table as if napping. An extinguished cigarette lay on the table nearby; it had fallen from the ashtray and burned a small hole in the table. I called her name, but she didn't move. Rushing over, I tried to lift her; the skin on her face and arms was bluish-black. I stepped backward, tripping over the books that I'd dropped on the floor when I entered the apartment. Aunt Della slumped back onto the table.

At the funeral a few days later, Lynn told me she and Aunt Della had gone shopping and to lunch as planned. Lynn dropped off Aunt Della at home, and then borrowed her car for a few hours. After turning over the car keys to Lynn, Aunt Della picked up her mail, entered Apartment 110, turned on her television, lit one of her Bel-Air cigarettes, and, sometime before I came home from school, suffered a massive heart attack.

Mom took me back to Apartment 110 one last time to collect my things. Aunt Della's unfinished cigarette still rested on the table; the hamburger she thawed for our dinner sat rotting on the kitchen counter, leaving a stench in the small quarters. On the day she died, a letter from U.S. Senator Ed Muskie came in the mail for me; during Aunt Della's final minutes, she positioned it on my memorabilia bookcase so I'd see it when I got home from school. There it remained, untouched.

For two generations of nieces and nephews, Aunt Della's home offered a haven of affection and nurturing. Only a silent, haunting tableau now remained. When I walked out of Apartment 110 for the last time, I didn't look back.

Again I lived full-time at Mom and Dad's, but that didn't last long. Their quarrels continued; one night she rounded up the kids, stuffed us in her car, tossed hastily packed suitcases in the trunk, and drove away. She didn't know where to go, but with $150 in her purse, it wouldn't be far. She wended her way across the San Francisco Bay Bridge and headed north, stopping after about thirty miles in Pinole. Pulling in front of the first apartment building she saw, she told us to wait while she talked to the manager. A few minutes later, after writing a check she hoped wouldn't bounce for the rent and security deposit (it did), she signed a lease for a unit in the Pinole Crest Garden Apartments.

Mom told Dad where we were, but rejected his plea to come home. Dad tried to reconcile, but in the end, he agreed reluctantly to her demand. The marriage died without any bitter contest; she sought no legal settlement, since Dad sent money each month voluntarily. She denied him visitation rights, refusing to bring us back until the dust cleared. Dad accepted her terms; the next time I saw him, I was five years older.

With more than a decade of marriage behind her, Mom found herself single with four kids and little money. Applying for welfare and food stamps, she joined all the other single welfare mothers in the apartments collecting government relief.

On the day we moved in, the manager, Mrs. Fall, led us to our second floor unit. To get there I had to step around two hoodlums seated in the stairwell. As I approached, they snickered at me, letting me know I didn't fit in. Didn't fit in? With unfashionably short hair, and clothes bought by an old woman whose style dated to the raccoon-coat era, that was no revelation. With the wardrobe I carried from Aunt Della's closet to Pinole, the only fashion accessory I lacked was a sign around my neck reading "Please Pick on Me."

If my clothes looked purchased at a retirement-home rummage sale, then these guys on the stairs were outfitted at Thugs-R-Us. The older guy had a bizarre Caucasian combination of black nappy hair and pale blue eyes; he dressed like James Dean redux, with a pack of Marlboro's rolled inside his tee shirt sleeve, dirty Levi's, thick black leather belt, and battered motorcycle boots. His husky pal had straight jet-black hair, a Latin-looking complexion, and a long black leather jacket. Other than that, he looked like the other guy's clone: Both had cigarettes dangling from their lips in menacing fashion (I later learned the "dangling cigarette" look was *haute couture* at the apartments).

As I carried a box up the stairs, I tried to move by these twin obstructions; they made no effort to get out of my way. "Excuse me," I said politely. The nappy-haired guy sneered: "Excuse you? Why, did you fart?" They both laughed at Nappy's insult coup. I squeezed by; as I did, the same guy added, "Don't bump me." When finally I got past them and entered the apartment, I said a silent prayer that these two jerks were transients passing through. Then Mrs. Fall asked me, "Did you meet Frank and Rocky outside on the stairs? Frank's your next-door neighbor. You'll be seeing a lot of him!" I asked which one was Frank. "Frank's the older one," she said, "the one with the nappy hair." Her answer almost made me an atheist.

The next day Mom asked me to go to 7-Eleven and pick up some milk. I grimaced at the idea, not wanting to run into those two goons from the stairway. Sure enough, there they were—loitering under a carport with their gang of apartment friends.[9] They laughed and played loud rock music on a transistor radio; a sickly sweet smell wafted from the hand-rolled joint they passed around. I ignored them and kept walking, but heard their whispers and titters as I passed. "Hey dude," Frank yelled out, "who dressed yah'?" He and his buddies chortled as I continued on my way. "What a dork!" Frank yelled, turning to accept the approval of his gang.

My clothes might have been dated, but a longshoreman raised me—and my first grammar lessons came straight from the waterfront. Grandpa also taught me to stand up to a bully and get a few licks in; walking away only guarantees he'll bully you forever. This frizzy-haired neighbor acted like someone Grandpa had in mind, and I had my fill of him by now.

"Hey, Frank," I called.

Frank looked puzzled that I knew his name; when everyone looked my way, I jabbed a finger in his direction and finished my sentence: *Fuck you.*

At first the pack stood silent, then hoots and catcalls erupted: "Go on, Frank, kick his ass!" As I geared up for the fight, I sensed Frank's hesitation. He didn't appear afraid (it was more the other way around), but he also didn't look anxious to get into a scrap. Still, with the gang taunting him, he needed to save face. Frank sauntered over and struck a bravura pose; his eyes squinted and his still-dangling cigarette drooped from his mouth: "Come on, punk, take your best shot," he snarled. I told Frank no—he started the trouble, so if he wanted a fight he'd have to start that, too. Our back-and-forth argument over who needed to throw the first punch annoyed our spectators, who now took out their frustration by turning on Frank, calling him too chicken to take a swing at me. Mutually sensing the need to get some action going (and avoid a more hostile crowd), we took turns shoving each other, punctuating the ballet with the same refrain: "You hit me first"; "No, you hit me first." Long after the irritable crowd grew bored and left, Frank and I remained under the carport pushing each other. Fatigue set in, which made our intermittent shoves

---

[9]I use the word "gang" in the traditional sense, meaning a group of friends, rather than the criminal vernacular suggesting an organized criminal enterprise (although in the apartments the lines sometimes blurred).

more of a formality than an expression of hostility. Meanwhile, we chatted about a variety of subjects: girls, Joe DiMaggio, where we lived before moving to the apartments, siblings, what we did in our spare time.

About two hours later, Frank began wincing each time I pushed. "Hey," he said, "my shoulder's getting sore from you shoving me in the same spot. Can you push me on the other side for a while?" That underscored the silliness of our pushing match. We laughed, shook hands, and agreed that if anyone asked, we'd each say the fistfight began right after the crowd left, and continued until the cops arrived to break it up.

Later that night, I heard a loud knock on my door. There stood Frank and his Latin-looking buddy Rocky. "My mother told me to come over," Frank said sheepishly. "She says I need to make friends with a guy who's smart. She says I might learn something." Then, pointing to the big Latin, he added, "This is Rocky. His mother told him to come over, too." Rocky said they didn't come only because of that: They decided that a guy who doesn't take any shit was okay with them.

As we got acquainted, they showed great interest in my political memorabilia collection. Frank pointed to my boxes of books: "Have you read all those?" he asked. When I said I had, he nodded in awe, then turned to Rocky and said, "Someday I'm gonna work for this dude, so I'm gettin' in on his good side right now!" Rocky nodded his agreement, and a three-way lifelong friendship was born.

Frank Debrose looked much older than fourteen. A year older than me, and light-years ahead in street smarts, his biker wardrobe and expletive-laced vocabulary spoken in a Marlon Brando/*Godfather* timbre added to his street punk mystique. Frank probably knew how to fight, although we never saw him in one because would-be troublemakers chose targets that looked far less menacing (like the campaign button collector wearing yellow socks). Still, under his sinister look was a guy who'd give a friend the shirt off his back. Frank had an old-world sense of honor when it came to family, and to be Frank's friend meant one joined his family.

As for Frank's "Latin" companion, I'm probably more Latin than Curtis Piehu "Rocky" Iaukea IV. The hefty son of an even heftier Hawaiian wrestler, nobody believed Rocky was only twelve. He stood six feet tall and weighed 220 pounds. His dark piercing eyes gave him the deportment of a hired killer. Rocky got expelled from sixth grade for beating up an entire group of his classmates; when the principal stepped in to break up the fight, Rocky beat him up, too. Bartenders served alcohol to Rocky without asking for identification. Unlike Frank, Rocky had a nurturing home life. His single mother, Phyllis, doted over her only child, but she took no guff from him, either. When Rocky went too far with his mom, Phyllis chased him through the apartments with a broom handle, whacking him on the head or threatening to shove it in an uncomfortable place.

We were three of the most unlikely companions imaginable. I was shy and serious; they were loud and obnoxious, but we spent all of our free time together. At their urging I shed the Aunt Della–styled wardrobe for threads more suitable to the apartments: Boots replaced black leather loafers, faded Levis replaced wool slacks, and dirty tees replaced dress shirts. Visits to the barber became fewer; soon I looked as shaggy as any Pinole native. Frank and Rocky did more than help change my outward appearance: They coaxed and teased me out of my shell. Because they put their imprimatur of approval on me, the gang of teenagers hanging out each day in the apartments accepted me.

When I moved to Pinole I was pretty naïve about girls, but between Frank's sordid tales and nature taking hold, the basics became clear. As time went by, and with a bevy of pretty young ladies living in the apartments, female inspiration never lacked for our group of testosterone-raging teenage boys.

The first night I hung out with the gang, they started a game of spin the bottle. On the first boys' spin, the bottle landed on me. Sensing I was new to the contest, Rita Rodriguez whispered some guidance: "Now remember, when you go out back to kiss the girl, you're supposed to 'French kiss' her." Until then I assumed all nationalities kissed alike—the same way actors did in old movies: pucker up, push lips together, hold for appropriate amount of time, and release. When Rita described the French adaptation, it sounded like the boy and girl were supposed to chew on each other. Rita assured me that using teeth would be a grave social blunder; she urged me to trust her description and not improvise. It didn't sound very sanitary, but I wanted to make a good first impression.

My worries about contracting germs evaporated when the next bottle spin landed on the luscious Darlene, my shapely raven-haired neighbor. The boys were envious; Frank termed it "beginner's luck." Everyone whooped as Darlene took me by the hand to lead me to my French lesson. Then the hooting stopped suddenly: Darlene's nutty brother Anthony, nicknamed "Perp," showed up. My luck ran out as fast as it arrived. Darlene had to be adopted, because nobody that pretty could be the sister of a troll like Perp. A huge guy with ratty black hair jetting from his scalp in all directions, Perp had the look and temperament of a caged baboon. Everyone feared Perp. He sold drugs and carried both a straight-edged razor and a switchblade. For amusement, Perp drove around looking for police cars; when he spied one he pulled alongside so the officer could see him drinking from an open liquor bottle. Perp then hurled the bottle out the window, smashed it into the squad car, and sped away laughing with enraged cops in pursuit.

Perp spewed profanity at Darlene for making out with boys, and then turned his ire on me. I played dumb, saying I just moved here and didn't know Darlene was his sister. Besides, Frank and Rocky brought me to the game, and I told Perp they'd vouch for me. Friendship aside, as I turned to get some backup, I saw Frank and Rocky trying to slip out the back door. Perp yanked them back. "So," he exclaimed, "you three dickheads wanna play with Darlene, eh? Well, let's take 'the Ride of Death' and talk about it!" Perp shoved the three of us into the rear of his old black jalopy, and then he got behind the wheel and started the engine. Frank was apoplectic: Perp had taken him on "the ride of death" once before, and Frank didn't want to reprise the experience. Perp cranked up the acid rock on his favorite underground FM station, and then sped off down the street. The rear of Perp's car had no floorboards, so we wedged ourselves between the front and back seats to avoid being dragged or run over. Perp ran over a curb and drove on the sidewalk, knocking down garbage cans and sending trash flying. He tore across a vacant lot behind the apartments, sailed off the sidewalk and back into the street, ran every stop sign, bounced off a mailbox, and then careened down Pinole Valley Road on the wrong side of the street. Drivers in oncoming traffic waved their arms and honked their horns, swerving to avoid head-on collisions; Perp never once swerved. Trying to remain calm, I volunteered some basic rules of the road, suggesting we not drive down the wrong side of the street. "Asshole," Perp replied, "if I drove on the right side of the street, then it wouldn't be called the Ride of Death, would it?"

Perp's satanic laugh drowned out our backseat pleas. As the car caromed off more unfixed objects, Frank made the sign of the cross while Rocky chanted to something called Kahuna. After a couple dozen more examples of random property damage, Perp threw us out where the ride began, and the gang cheered our survival. After Perp left, Frank told them that the ride ended only when Frank threatened to kick Perp's ass if he didn't pull over.

A few weeks later Darlene joined the gang looking for a favor: "My date for tonight's Sadie Hawkins school dance is sick and can't make it. Would one of you guys like to be my date?" All the boys looked at each other; there were no takers.

Frank and Rocky's genetic code made them immune to embarrassment. I learned that painful lesson the day Rocky and I grocery shopped for our mothers at the nearby market. We got in line to pay, with me in front. After the clerk rang up my groceries, I pulled out Mom's neon-colored USDA food stamp coupons. I hated using the demeaning tickets, which flagged for everyone that we were on welfare. Then horror struck: In the next line over I saw Colleen Hazzard, a girl in my sociology class on whom I had a big crush. She saw me and flashed a dazzling smile as I hid the food stamps behind my back. I managed to pay without Colleen seeing them; however, I had change coming, and the store did not give back cash to food stamp users. Instead, welfare customers got back change in scrip, and my cashier was out. Before I could stop her, the cashier picked up the microphone and announced, "ATTENTION, MANAGER: CUSTOMER NEEDS FOOD STAMP CHANGE ON AISLE THREE." The manager brought the scrip; my head hung in shame as the clerk counted it for me. Then the old woman behind Colleen turned to my heartthrob and snipped, "I certainly hope those boys on welfare really are poor. There are so many cheats out there, you know!" Like me, Rocky heard the old woman's comment to Colleen. Unlike me, Rocky could have cared care less.

"Ah, shit," Rocky bellowed after the clerk rang his few items. "Did I leave my food stamps at home?" Then, after turning all of his pockets inside-out with dramatic flair, Rocky produced his food stamp booklet. Waving them over his head, he called to me as I tried to flee from his performance. "Hey, Jimmy, everything's okay! Look! I found my food stamps! Thank God! For a minute I thought I'd have to spend my beer money on food!" The face of the woman next to Colleen contorted in disgust as Rocky continued his soliloquy designed for all to hear: "You know, I love America! When my eleven cousins and me came here, we were afraid we'd have to go out and get jobs. But once we saw we could get all the welfare and food stamps we wanted, we wrote to the rest of our family and told them to come over, too! This sure is a good deal here."

Turning to the woman next to Colleen, Rocky continued: "See this beautiful leather jacket, lady [pointing to the faux leather coat his grandfather sent as a birthday present]? You know who paid for this? You did! See that white Cadillac in the parking lot [pointing to a stranger's car outside]? You bought me that, too! Yeah, this is a great country. Hey, clerk, by the way, can I buy a pack of smokes with these food stamps? What? I can't? What a rip-off. How the hell else am I supposed to get cigarettes—pay for them out of my own pocket? This sucks. . . ." When we got outside, I would have killed Rocky if he wasn't so damned big. Rocky shrugged off my complaint that he shamed me in front of Colleen: "Trust me on this," he said. "I'm tellin' you—chicks dig food stamps—it turns them on!" That was the stupidest thing I'd ever heard. I was so angry that I walked home alone.

The next day the dreaded moment of seeing Colleen in class arrived. I wanted to crawl under the desk as she walked by me. "Oh, hi, Rogue!" she cooed. "Hey, you and Rocky are a riot. You guys must have done that comedy routine before."

"By the way," Colleen added with a smile, "I'll be in the cafeteria at lunchtime. Want to join me?"

Frank found food stamps useful, but he didn't waste them on food.

He preferred them for barter when negotiating prices with Oakland streetwalkers. Frank was the undisputed Lothario of the apartments—by his own admission. Each day he regaled us with tales of his unending sexual triumphs, and the same stories grew more outlandish with each retelling. The yarns ended with the object of his conquests shouting eternal gratitude for Frank's boundless capabilities, his hitherto unknown techniques, his European instincts, and of course his superhuman proportions. In Frank's own mind, he was a one-man Kama Sutra.

When Frank's stories revved at full-throttle, one could see he actually believed what he said. This enthusiasm made him grow furious when we laughed and mocked these fantasy escapades. The more we laughed, the madder Frank grew for doubting his "word of honor." Rocky especially loved puncturing his preposterous tales and exaggerated pride. Frank's festering indignation merely served to increase Rocky's needling. Frank usually stormed off in a huff, foreswearing any further friendship with Rocky (who still teased Frank as he stalked away). They were empty threats: The next day Frank couldn't wait to rejoin us and share the news of his latest triumph. We always welcomed Frank back to the fold because, whether he meant to or not, Frank entertained us. In fairness, for all his boasting and outlandish claims, he had more action with women than the rest of us combined. We never understood how beautiful women found attraction in a chubby sluggard who lacked formal education, refused to get out of bed for job interviews, and went through life constantly mispronouncing words. "I can't explain it," a girlfriend of his once told me. "Frankie's like a teddy bear. He needs to be hugged and loved."

When we were teenagers, the bewitching Yvette lived in the apartments. Pretty, older, and with a slinky appeal that filled us with raw carnality, Yvette later married, moved away, and dropped out of sight. A few years later, I worked nights as a pizza cook when Yvette called me unexpectedly, saying she was divorced and lonely. Yvette invited me over when my shift ended. I hung up the telephone, rubbed my eyes until they were red, then ran to my boss and told him I had to leave early for a family emergency ("Terrible news, boss. Grandma Rogan just died."). I rushed home, jumped in the shower, combed my hair, and doused on cologne when Frank (now staying with me) investigated the commotion. I boasted of Yvette's call. Frank surprised me by showing disgust instead of envy. "You're showing a side that I've never seen before, and it's a side I don't like," he said. "We've known Yvette for ten years. Sure, we all fantasized about her, but the minute her life crumbles, you want to take advantage of it. I wouldn't do this if I were you, and if you do, I'll lose all respect for you."

Frank's words humbled me, and I felt so ashamed that I called Yvette and canceled the date. Frank put his arm around my shoulder. "I'm proud of you, Jimmy," he said. "I knew I raised you right. Don't you feel better?" In truth, I did. We shook hands; I said goodnight and went to bed. Sleep came easily with a clear conscience.

The next morning Frank was gone, along with my car keys and the directions to Yvette's house. Three days later he returned wearing Yvette's baseball cap and a big grin: "I said I wouldn't go to Yvette's if I were *you*. I didn't say anything about *me*."

Frank, Rocky, and I talked often about our future goals. My aspirations never varied: college, probably law school, and someday Congress. Rocky wanted to be a professional wrestler, following in his father's footsteps. When I first met Frank, he wanted to be a professional criminal. Luckily, he proved incredibly inept at his chosen trade. First, he tried pimping for Tammy, the apartments' resident hooker, but he became his own best customer. Next he tried selling pot, but he gave away his minimal inventory to friends on credit who then disappeared when payment came due. He even botched simple petty theft: Once I rode with Frank and a couple friends in Perp's car. Perp stopped at a red traffic light and pulled alongside a large delivery truck stockpiled on both open sides with soft drink cases. Perp's rare show of respect for the Vehicle Code meant he saw a chance for a quick ill-gotten buck. He ordered Frank to lean out the window and grab some soda cases; Perp wanted to sell them to the shady manager of a nearby convenience store. Frank did what Perp said: He grabbed two cases of soda and heaved them into the car as Perp sped away. Of all the soft-drink brands in the world to steal, Frank grabbed two cases of diet strawberry soda—the one soft drink nobody buys.

Wanting to get a toehold into the big time, Frank started hanging out with a crop of two-bit punks from nearby Richmond. Frank's initiation required him to commit a strong-arm robbery. Frank and the crooks drove around Richmond until they saw a well-dressed older man walking down the street two blocks away. The wheelman pulled the car to the curb, kept the engine running, and gave Frank his instructions: "You jump out of the car and get a running start. When you catch up to the old man, grab him and make him give you his wallet and jewelry. Then we'll pull up and you jump in the car."

Frank suppressed his troubled conscience, got out of the car, and started running. Fortunately, Frank was a heavy smoker and out of shape (the only weights he lifted were supersized cheeseburgers to his mouth). The would-be bandit fatigued quickly; by the time he reached the old man two blocks away, Frank gasped for air. The old man, fearing Frank was having a heart attack, helped him to a nearby bench. The car with Frank's former associates raced by: "Dude, you're pathetic!" one yelled at Frank as they drove off and abandoned him in Richmond. Adding insult to injury, the old man gave Frank a ride home in exchange for gas money: Frank's last $3.

Frank grew out of his romanticized notions about the criminal life. His decision was inevitable: Criminals cheat and hurt people. Despite all his tough talk, Frank could do neither. For someone in trouble or need, Frank was the softest touch I knew. That's not to say his professional goals matured rapidly: Even as a young adult, he once said his ambition in life was to own a topless bar. I shook my head in disgust. "A topless bar is the extent of your life's ambition?" I asked.

"Well, not just any topless bar," Frank replied defensively. "I want a *classy* topless bar. Something upscale, you know?"

"Oh, an *upscale* one. I get it—your girls maybe talk about the Magna Carta or Socrates while they grind for your customers, right?"

Frank tried rehabilitating his dream without success; I said his goal proved the gutter drew him like metal to a magnet. Lighting another cigarette, a slight grin crossed his face: "Well, maybe I'm drawn to the gutter now and then, but as long as you and Rocky are around to look out for me, I'll never end up there for good."

. . .

Whenever Frank got kicked out of his home, he ended up on our doorstep, which meant he lived with me quite a bit during our teens. Despite Mom's slender financial means, she always made room for stray dogs, cats, neighborhood kids like Frank, and even strangers in desperate straits. I remember when one of Mom's coworkers was brutally murdered. At the funeral Mom tried to console Nancy, the dead man's now-homeless girlfriend. Mom invited Nancy to stay with us until she found a job. Marginally attractive, Nancy had curly red hair, owlish round eyeglasses, and a very full figure. Nancy spent days scouring want ads in some newspaper she specially ordered; one day she asked me to keep her company on the drive to San Francisco for a job interview. On the way into town, I asked Nancy what kind of work she did; she answered that she worked in customer relations.

We found the building, parked her car, and then walked up a few flights of stairs. Nancy told me to wait in the hallway while she went inside for her interview. Nancy knocked on the door, whispered something to a man, and then went inside. Later, an elderly businessman with a flushed face walked out. The door locked behind him as he bent over to tie his shoes. "Hey, mister," I asked, "what kind of a business is in there?"

"Well, kid, I guess you could call it a 'relief office.' "

Nancy got the job. Each day she commuted across the Bay, and then returned to our Pinole apartment at night while Mom encouraged her to stay until she got on her feet. Soon we learned that Nancy's job description didn't include "getting on her feet." One morning little Johnny rummaged innocently through Nancy's open suitcase. He came walking down the hallway carrying a leather bullwhip, steel handcuffs, and a magazine featuring full-color pictures of nude lesbians in bondage scenes. When Mom saw the paraphernalia, she sprang from her chair and wrenched it from his hands. After Nancy returned that night, Mom summoned her into the bedroom. Mom's angry voice carried through the walls; a few minutes later, Nancy headed out the door, bags in hand, and said goodbye.

"Hey, Jimmy, come visit me sometime in the city," Nancy purred as she left, "*when you're just a little bit older.*"

6

NO RULES

Most high school kids have photo albums filled with snap-
shots of family vacations. Mine looked like *Who's Who in American Politics*: President Nixon and future presidents Ford, Carter, Reagan, and
Bush were in there. Other prominent politicians of the era like Spiro Ag-
new, Nelson Rockefeller, George McGovern, Barry Goldwater, Walter
Mondale, Bob Dole, Henry Kissinger, Sam Ervin, George Wallace (recov-
ering from an assassination attempt), John Connally (wounded during
the assassination of President John F. Kennedy), and Alf Landon (1936
GOP presidential nominee defeated by Franklin D. Roosevelt) were there,
too. From many of these encounters I brought home great treasures for
my memorabilia collection.

Former Vice President Hubert Humphrey's personal story was an
early motivation for my political interest, but he also remained a favorite
of mine for the unending kindness he showed to young people. I retain a
great memento dating from the time I met him in May 1972, only days after the near-fatal shooting of presidential candidate George Wallace.
Running for president at the time, Humphrey had just finished an interview at KPIX in San Francisco when he came out and saw my brother Pat
and me waiting outside the studio. He walked over to greet us, and then
agreed to handwrite for my collection a favorite campaign quotation. His

Secret Service detail pleaded frantically for him to get inside his bullet-proof car, but Humphrey waved them away. Strolling over to a nearby mailbox, he used it as his writing desk, using slow and careful pen strokes to complete the task. Meanwhile, his fidgety bodyguards watched rooftops, passing cars, and the spectators now gathering. Humphrey handed back to me a sheet of U.S. Senate stationery with this inscription: "If I am permitted to be president, I intend to be president. I've noticed most presidents are like that. They don't take orders from vice presidents or anyone else. Hubert Humphrey as vice president is a member of a team. Hubert Humphrey as president is captain of a team. There's a lot of difference—Hubert H. Humphrey."

That summer I attended the 1972 Republican National Convention in Miami. I tagged along with the Young Voters for the President (YVP) delegation. They limited their membership to diehard Richard Nixon fans aged 18 to 30. I was fourteen and a Democrat, but who cared? Political conventions are to aficionados what Valhalla is to dead Vikings. I just wanted to go to a convention, and I especially wanted to go to one on the other side of the country for a week with no chaperone! The plane flight to Miami gave me a glimpse of what goes on behind the scenes at these things. As soon as our charter plane took off from California, young Republicans roamed the aisles partying. One opened the galley and passed out all the liquor. Rock music blared over the intercom; people danced on their seats. The airborne jubilee continued throughout the night, growing louder and merrier as we jetted across the country. My traveling companions shattered my stereotyped image of young Republicans: These folks were young, hip, fun, and (within minutes of takeoff) drunk.

Once in Miami, at the end of the convention eve rally I spied a neat piece of memorabilia that I wanted for my collection. Shimmying up a pole near the speaker's platform, I reached over and snatched the convention seal off the lectern. Had I been caught, they'd probably have shipped me back to California on the next plane. There must have been backups, because I saw another on the podium the next night. Anyway, I carried that seal under my arm during the week and got it autographed by all the dignitaries I met. Among the signatures adorning this treasured memento hanging in my office today are those of President Richard Nixon, Congressman Gerald R. Ford, Governor Ronald Reagan, and United Nations Ambassador George Bush. I got the autographs of the three future presidents at the same unlikely place. Each morning organizers brought the YVPs to our holding center, a large tent pitched on the athletic field of Nautilus Middle School. Although it was hot and muggy under that tent, nothing dampened the enthusiasm of the YVPs. While we spent the day painting rally signs or helping with convention logistics, a parade of dignitaries arrived to say thanks. Jerry Ford arrived in an old station wagon; he leaned heavily on his cane (following knee surgery to correct an old college football injury) and walked unrecognized among the YVPs. Not many people bothered to come and hear Ford's pep talk, but he got a hearty response from those who did when he urged the group to go home and help him achieve his greatest ambition in life: to become Speaker of the House. George Bush came to Nautilus twice: once while en route to play in a celebrity tennis match, and another time to address our group. Like Ford, nobody else recognized Bush when his car first pulled onto the field and he walked to the tent to thank the volunteers.

Anonymity was not an issue when the town car carrying Reagan pulled up. YVPs rushed from all corners and crammed underneath the tent to hear him, and a great cheer rang out at his introduction. Although the sticky weather never eased up, Reagan looked crisp and fresh throughout, with his hair and necktie neatly in place. Unlike the other speakers, one had to fight for a spot underneath the tent to hear Reagan, who stayed half an hour discussing the Nixon campaign and the future of the Republican Party. He took a couple of questions at the end of his impromptu talk; when someone pleaded for him to run for president in 1976, an enthusiastic whoop erupted. The YVPs chanted for five minutes, "Reagan '76! Reagan '76!" Reagan's only response was to cock his head and flash a coy grin, a pose destined to become familiar to the next generation of voters.

In October 1972, my brother Pat and I snuck into a Democratic fundraiser at the Fairmont Hotel in San Francisco, attended by the national Democratic congressional leadership. Near the end of the evening, I saw House Majority Leader Hale Boggs, who was expected to become the next Speaker of the House. While Boggs chatted with two colleagues, I waited to introduce myself. A diminutive woman tapped me on the shoulder and asked if I'd like to meet Congressman Boggs. I told her yes, but I didn't want to interrupt. "Oh, I promise he won't mind if we interrupt," she said as she grabbed my arm and led me over. At first I tried to beg off, thinking the woman was crazy, until she said, "By the way, I'm Lindy Boggs—Hale's wife. What's your name?" Mrs. Boggs broke up the powwow and introduced Pat and me, telling her husband I wanted to run for Congress some day. Then she took my camera and clicked a group photograph.

The story doesn't end there: A week later, an airplane crash in Alaska claimed Hale Boggs's life, along with Congressman Nick Begich. Their plane disappeared in the wilderness snow and to this day has never been found. A few months after his death, Lindy Boggs won a special election to succeed her late husband. I mailed her the photograph she took that night at the Fairmont; she replied with a gracious letter, remembering our discussion about my wanting to run for Congress someday. Since I was now fifteen, she said I'd be constitutionally eligible to join her in ten years, and ended her note by saying she'd wait there for me. I didn't make it in ten years, but I did in twenty-five, so I tracked down Lindy's address after my 1996 election (she had retired a few years earlier). Sending a copy of the letter she wrote long ago, I penned a note on my new congressional letterhead: "I am so disappointed—you didn't wait for me!" A few weeks later, we had a lovely reunion over lunch. When she later served as U.S. Ambassador to the Vatican, I visited her in Rome and told that story during my toast to her exceptional service to America.

When I made my first appearance as a congressman on the ABC News *This Week* Sunday morning show with Cokie Roberts and Sam Donaldson, my interview segment was broadcast from Los Angeles via satellite. Just before airtime, I heard Cokie through my earpiece thanking me for coming on the program (she was in the Washington studio). While we waited for the show to start, I mentioned my story about her parents, Hale and Lindy Boggs. Suddenly my earpiece went dead. Within minutes, we were on the air, and Cokie interviewed me without missing a beat. A few weeks later over lunch, Cokie told me why I lost audio: She had become teary-eyed at the mention of her father, and needed to go compose herself before airtime. The last time she ever saw him alive was the night I met him. After all those years, the searing pain of losing her dad never diminished.

In 1973, my friend Eldon Jernigan and I crashed the luncheon speech of Governor Ronald Reagan at the Boundary Oaks Restaurant in Walnut Creek. Before leaving, Reagan gave me his handwritten stack of 4-by-6 speech note cards for my collection, signing the last page at my request. Each card bore his written notes on one side while the other side had notes typed in large font. Reagan explained that the typed side was his reading copy of an earlier speech. Not one to waste paper, Reagan said he used the back of those typed speech cards for today's address. "I sat in my hotel room last night and wrote out today's speech in longhand on the back of the other speech," Reagan said. "So you see, you're really getting two speeches for the price of one."

There is an interesting footnote to this episode. In eight years, with Reagan in the White House and me in law school, I didn't have enough for tuition and faced being kicked out. I sold the Reagan speech note cards for tuition money, but I was heartbroken to lose this special historical gift earlier given to me by the man who was now our new president. All was not lost: Twenty years after that, while in Congress, I flipped through an auction catalog of political memorabilia and saw for sale the speech note cards I had sold—and I got them back! Martin Anderson, a former aide to Reagan who has researched and written multiple books from Reagan's handwritten archives, told me that these notes are the only known complete set of Reagan's famous 4-by-6 handwritten speech cards outside the possession of the Reagan Library, and the *only* known set autographed by Reagan in existence. Apparently, nobody thought to ask Reagan to sign his speech cards before I came along, and nobody bothered to ask after.

Getting from Pinole to San Francisco (where I went for most of these political events) was difficult. I got up early and walked two miles down unlit streets to catch the 4 A.M. bus for the two-hour ride downtown. The trek was long and cumbersome, but it beat the alternative: A few times, when I didn't have bus fare, I hitchhiked. When I first started making the trips, Pinole police pulled me over routinely. The sight of someone scurrying through the shadows at 4 A.M. made them think I was a runaway or prowler. Once they came to know me, they'd pull over and ask who I was going to see.

I skipped school to attend these political functions, and none of my absences were excused. Justifying my conduct was easy, at least in my own mind: My classmates studied and read about national leaders who now called me by my first name. When choosing between watching filmstrips in science class or seeing a presidential candidate speak, politics always won out. At first, I worried about getting in trouble for cutting classes, but Frank taught me how to game the system. During the first week of school, everyone received some bland notice requiring a guardian's signature. Frank told me to sign it for my mother: "The school uses this form to get a record of what your old lady's signature looks like," he said. "If *you* sign it, you can write your own excuses from now until graduation." I did as Frank suggested; soon typed notes "signed" by Alice Rogan flooded the attendance office, listing all of the doctors' appointments and funerals that needed my attention. Once, Frank and I were standing in the crowded hallway between classes when I mentioned that Humphrey planned a three-day campaign swing through Northern California; I wanted to go see him, but I couldn't get away with a three-day disappearance. "I'll show you how to get three days off," Frank promised. He peered around the lockers until he saw a teacher approaching. Then he pulled out his Marlboros, lit two cigarettes, tossed one to me, and kicked over a trashcan. When the teacher investigated the ruckus, she "caught" us smoking and hauled us to the assistant principal, Mr. Mackey.

"Boys, I want the truth," Mr. Mackey said. "Were you smoking?"

Frank jutted out his jaw and struck a Washingtonian "I cannot tell a lie" pose: "Mr. Mackey, I'm not gonna BS you. We did it, we knew we shouldn't do it, we thought we could get away with it, and you caught us fair and square."

"I'll have to suspend you boys for three days for smoking," Mr.

Mackey said. "But off the record, I admire your honesty and your willingness to take your punishment like men. But remember, you can't come back until your mothers sign the suspension notification I'm sending home with you." Frank and I looked at each other, thinking we were too clever for words.

Had I limited my absences to political treks, it might not have mattered much, but then I started missing classes for another reason. For the first time, school bored me, especially when measured against my new-found amusement of loafing through the day with my chronically truant buddies. At school's end, I'd return to the apartments and be regaled with glamorized tales of the gang's off-campus day. It might have been a romantic rendezvous with pretty girls, a manly brawl with Richmond or Martinez punks encroaching on our turf, or surviving another maniacal Perp ride. Whatever the adventure, they were having fun cutting school and I wasn't having any fun attending. After years of feeling buried in responsibilities, I liked the liberating feeling of carefree goofing off. Since I didn't know anyone who went to college, nobody explained to me the nexus between high school grades and college acceptance rates. For all my self-perceived smarts, I didn't have enough common sense to figure that one out on my own. Universities were for smart people, so I figured when I was ready to get serious I'd just show up, take some sort of IQ test, and get in. Operating under this foolish delusion, truancy had all the earmarks of a pain-free vacation.

With Frank in the same grade (Rocky went to a different school), we became a malingering daily duo. Each class we cut put us farther behind; the more behind we fell, the less inclined we were to try catching up. Getting caught? No concern there: The punishment for cutting was *suspension*! Like Brer Rabbit, we begged to be thrown into that briar patch. On days when Frank and I made guest appearances at school, we dared teachers to sanction us. In foreign language class, I wouldn't translate our German homework phrases "My name is Karl Heinz" and "I can't find my rubber overshoes." The reason? I told the teacher my name wasn't Karl Heinz, and I didn't own rubber overshoes. My final test grade: F. In physical education class, Frank and I showed up in street clothes rather than required gym attire. When asked why we weren't suited up for basketball, we told the coach we were poor and couldn't afford gym clothes. Recognizing us for a couple of goldbrickers, the coach said the school had extra uniforms for such cases. Frank and I grew indignant at the suggestion, telling him we didn't take charity. Our final grade: F.

My English teacher, young Ms. Price, had a subtle rebellious streak of her own. She once said the way to end all discrimination and wars would be to make everyone walk around naked, because people behave differently when they can't hide behind their clothes. That idea was sure provocative: For the rest of the year, it provoked every male student's imagination of how the fair Ms. Price might look sauntering through her nudie Utopia. Anyway, she assigned a book report on Ray Bradbury's novel, *The Illustrated Man*. I never read the book; instead, I wrote my report on why I found science fiction a waste of time, and that I read only political books because it pertained to my career goal. I expected an F, but Ms. Price called my hand. She found my "I'm not reading your assigned book" approach gutsy, and she gave me a "B" for spunk. Of course, I told her I couldn't accept the B as a matter of principle. My ultimate grade: F.

The exception to this pattern of academic hostility was debate class: I never wanted to miss it. Unlike other subjects with no relevance to Congress, I viewed debate as the *sine qua non* of political preparation. Despite a knee-knocking fear of public speaking, I volunteered for every topic offered and approached each assignment in earnest. On the eve of the 1972 presidential election, I debated in favor of Democrat George McGovern's candidacy. My classmate-opponent went first; he trembled through his five-minute softball outline of President Nixon's record. When my turn came, I pulled out the thirteen-page typed manuscript I had prepared and began shredding into Nixon as my startled opponent's mouth gaped open. At five minutes' end, I hadn't even warmed up; I hammered away despite the teacher's repeated admonition that time had expired. The class liked my moxie: They chanted my last name in unison as the instructor unsuccessfully continued her demand that I cease. My soliloquy ended only when three football players (at the flustered teacher's direction) physically picked up my desk with me still seated in it, deposited both desk and debater in the hallway, returned to the classroom, and locked me out.

The combination of my distraction with politics and hanging out with buddies caused my grade-point average to collapse. By the end of tenth grade, straight Fs decorated my report card (except for my D in German because Frau Doktor Milek liked me). At least I had Frank beat: His had all Fs. So what?

So nothing—if one doesn't mind an approaching train wreck.

When I moved to Pinole, my idea of substance abuse was eating too many Hershey bars in one sitting. Smoke marijuana? Forget it. I figured smoking dope was suicidal. After seeing that 1930s movie *Reefer Madness*, I knew what became of potheads: The girls turned into gang-raped sluts and the boys became lunatics finishing out their days in padded cells. As for alcohol and cigarettes, those graphic school films of corroded livers and lungs taken from autopsied winos and cigarette fiends made me never want to join their club at the morgue.

Still, peer pressure to *really* be a part of the gang dulled those burnished memories eventually. Fortunately, my body resisted when my scruples flagged. At my friends' repeated urging I tried cigarettes, but I could never suppress the gag reflex when inhaling. Somebody always had a bottle of cheap wine around for guzzling, but this wasn't for me either. I couldn't disassociate the grape's bouquet from the toxic stench of Thunderbird or Ripple that commingled in the vomit puddle Frank or Rocky just heaved near my shoe.

Smoking and drinking aside, the gang's early "high" of choice was marijuana, and pot was in plentiful supply. All the gang smoked pot, yet none of the boys turned into maniacs, and (with the exception of Tammy) the slut factor among our girls appeared minimal. The only consistent symptom my dope-smoking cronies showed was laughing a lot and acting silly. My favorite cousin smoked pot: She told me all it did was relax her. Even one of my teachers, a hip woman who encouraged her students to call her by her first name, tacitly admitted to our class that she and her husband toked up. How dangerous could this stuff really be?

Besides Perp, who bragged about how little "dope" there was in the dope he peddled, another regular pot supplier from the apartments' gang was Wobbly Jay, a fat, smelly, heavily perspiring guy with a neurological disorder that made his head wobble from side to side. Ten-dollar bills burned holes in the gangs' pockets for a "dime bag" from Wobbly Jay. The exchange method never varied: Wobbly Jay took the cash, looked around to make sure the cops weren't watching, dug his clammy hands into his underwear, fished around near his groin, and then produced a damp plastic bag filled with marijuana. I didn't get it: Putting aside pot's danger, how could anyone smoke something that had fermented all day in Wobbly Jay's crotch?

Month after month, the gang urged me to try it; month after month, I declined. In time, curiosity replaced fear. One day someone passed me a lit joint. After they assured me (and then reassured me) it didn't come from Wobbly Jay, I took a hit. The room didn't spin and the psychotic effect never materialized; the only thing I felt was the backslapping approval of the gang. "Congratulations," someone said to me. "Now you're *really* one of us." That was something I wanted to be, and lowering my standards of right and wrong seemed like a good bargain at the time.

Looking back, who knows what we really smoked back in those days? If guys like Perp supplied the pot, adulteration was a virtual guarantee. Whether our high was more psychological than pharmacological didn't matter. We still acted out the part: After a few tokes, we staggered and laughed about how loaded we were.

The first time Frank saw me with a joint in my mouth, his response surprised me. He offered no congratulations; instead, he looked irritated. He yanked the smoke from my mouth and said, "I expect more of you." Just as my feeling of disappointing a best friend sank in, Frank turned and walked away, smoking the same joint he just confiscated from me.

Each of my pot-smoking experiences had me taking a drag or two— just enough to maintain my social standing. I didn't like smoking pot any more than cigarettes (inhaling smoke of any kind made me feel sick). Although I could stumble around as convincingly as the next guy, I don't remember ever feeling under the influence of anything. Besides, nobody shared marijuana for long with someone who wasn't buying it and reciprocating. I'd never waste my money on drugs or booze: Every extra dollar of mine went for bus fare to San Francisco, a new book, or campaign buttons, posters, or historic autographs for my collection.

Besides smoking dope and drinking, getting into fights was another gang diversion. Losing a decent fight was considered honorable, but cowering from one meant excommunication. When insulted or challenged, our unwritten bylaws required either an apology or a scuffle. Under these rules, I had my share of fights; I lost most of them. I wouldn't hit smaller guys (benevolence was permitted as an exception to the mandatory fight rule), but I foolishly refused to back down from bigger guys. I never fought unless provoked, and my friendship with Eldon Jernigan provoked more fights than I care to remember.

Eldon (a Pinole Valley High classmate) and his family lived in the apartment above me. Raised by a single mother and three older sisters, Eldon's effeminate voice and mannerisms dogged him in an era when those traits weren't socially acceptable. Obviously, Eldon wasn't part of our gang; in fact, we teased him mercilessly. Since two of Eldon's sisters were named Yvonne and Yvette, we nicknamed him "*Yveldon*." When he returned fire with his girlie voice, we laughed and increased the teasing.

Since Eldon was so meticulous, and we were such slobs, Mom started paying him to clean our house. Each time Eldon came over to dust, Frank, Rocky, and I made a sport of mocking him. Eldon took it, and dished it back in spades, which of course we secretly admired. As we came to know him better, we discovered to our surprise a bright, witty, and outrageously entertaining guy. It was an even greater surprise that we started liking him. In time, Eldon stopped being the butt of our crude jokes. Maybe the plenary gang didn't care much for Eldon, but its Frank–Rocky–Jim subcommittee adopted him as a friend.

Eldon's only known heterosexual experience was with Big Joanie, an obese, wealthy, older woman. Eldon was Big Joanie's gigolo: She forked over money, clothes, and newly leased cars in exchange for Eldon's company. Eldon always invited us to ride in his latest acquisition. If we suggested driving to Disneyland or San Diego while on our way to the grocery store, Eldon thought nothing of changing course on a moment's notice and driving all night to go there. On these long drives, Eldon regaled us with the details of his homosexual relationships and, at the other end of the spectrum, Big Joanie's requirements for Eldon earning his car keys. The visual images created by Eldon's graphic accounts made us shiver with disgust. Still, like Cub Scouts listening to spooky tales around the campfire, we had a macabre fascination in wanting to hear how his gruesome story ended. Eldon's loud laugh as he grossed us out made the story twice as funny.

Hanging out with Eldon created a bit of a problem: Because he was so dramatically gay (and didn't care who knew it), local troublemakers assumed anyone with Eldon must be gay, too. If one of them insulted us while out somewhere with Eldon, the prescribed ritual required Frank, Rocky, and me to jump out of the car, adopt an aggressive stance, and ask, "Who you callin' a fag?" After the big mouth sized up Frank and Rocky, an apology always came to them. Since I never perfected the psycho killer look of my two friends, I ended up in the fistfight to preserve "our" manly honor.

One day we were with Eldon when a local punk we called Fleabag and a couple of his friends saw Eldon and yelled out some "fag" slur. When Frank, Rocky, and I confronted them, Fleabag followed the script and apologized to Frank and Rocky. Then, without warning, he spun around and threw a sucker punch I never saw coming. After shaking off the stunning blow to my head, I dove into him returning fire. We traded punches; after I landed a hard one to his jaw, Fleabag backed up and reached into his pocket. He whipped out a switchblade, clicked it open, and lunged at me. Thankfully, Rocky kicked the knife from his hand and grabbed it away. Now without his weapon, we laid into each other until he backtracked. That "apology" only cost me two black eyes, a split lip, cuts and scratches, and a near-stabbing. Maintaining the apartments' manhood code was an expensive proposition.

When I later complained to Frank about Fleabag's cowardice in hitting me without warning and then pulling a knife on me, Frank brushed off my grievance. "On the streets," he told me, "there ain't no rules."

My pot-smoking exploits ended the day a friend gave me a "super charge." The gang smoked their pot either in hand-rolled cigarettes, a bong pipe, or from a super-charge pipe. A cardboard toilet paper roll served as the super-charge pipe by slicing a small hole into the side, pushing tinfoil into the opening, and punching pinholes into the tinfoil to create a makeshift screen. With the marijuana placed and lit atop the screen, the friend sealed his mouth over the lit pot, covered with his hand one of the two open ends of the roll, and then blew hard. My job was to put my nose into the opposite end of the roll and inhale the smoke as he blew. I inhaled deeply through my nose when the smoke concentration rushed toward me, but he blew so hard that the tinfoil screen failed, sending burning marijuana embers straight up my nostrils. I rushed to the sink, turned on the faucet, hung my head upside down, and ran cold water up my nose. I almost drowned trying to put out the fire. When we told everyone about my super-charge experience, the laughter and teasing I expected didn't happen. Instead, some of the more brain-fried users thought I had stumbled onto a new method of getting high: *snorting* lit marijuana. Their experiments never went beyond the first try. As for me, just as the associational smell of cheap wine and vomit made me a virtual teetotaler, mentally I connected forevermore the aroma of marijuana with the stench of burning nose hair.

Film historians may be right that *Reefer Madness* is one of the worst films ever made, but my time in the apartments taught me that its ultimate message was true: Casual marijuana use was dangerous. My offhand assumptions about marijuana being safe faded when I realized that everybody I knew who used it soon wanted to try something harder. The neighborhood lexicon now brimmed with nicknames for new things to try: *bennies, dexies, speed, crank, coke, reds, tabs, uppers, downers, smack, angel dust, acid, hash.* Some in our gang paid big money to lick small pieces of perforated paper treated with LSD; others started carrying hype kits with a thick rubber band to tie around their arm, a spoon and flame to liquefy heroin, and a shared dirty injection needle. As usual, plenty of dope dealers hung around to supply the demand for a more potent menu.

I drew the line at smoking pot; I wanted nothing to do with the rest of this poison. I knew too many drug peddlers laughing about how they cut their dope with things like rat poison to make their supply go farther, and I knew people who OD'd while experimenting with stronger drugs. One neighborhood kid went to prison for killing a guy during a drug-induced high; another committed suicide; still another so abused drugs that his heart gave out during routine surgery. Once I went to a school dance with Rose, a black-haired Italian beauty. In time Rose lost her looks, and then her life, undergoing dialysis for kidneys ravaged by years of drug abuse. Maybe smoking marijuana didn't turn people into lunatics right away, but it was always the first step in the downfall of too many acquaintances.

Perp still lived next door and still sold drugs, but even he showed signs of slowing down from his lifetime of bad habits. When his petite, bespectacled girlfriend Rae Jane became pregnant, Perp did right by her. As a new husband and father, Perp acted differently. The rides of death ended; now Perp checked his blind spot and used turn indicators and seat belts while driving. The sight of him pushing a baby stroller, with his head held high and a stogie in his mouth, became a familiar one around the apartments. He looked so out of character. Then one night, two loud explosions from Perp's apartment rocked the evening stillness. Anxious neighbors found Perp's crumpled body inside the bathtub; the aftermath of a shotgun blast directed at Perp's chest left his bathroom walls splattered with blood. They found Rae Jane's corpse in the bedroom; nearby lay their baby in the bassinet, crying but unhurt. The word circulated quickly on the street: Perp and his habit of cheating people in drug deals had collided finally with the wrong guy.

Drug use brought no mind expansion to our apartments' gang: It brought only lost opportunity, misery, and death. The old Latin maxim applied to me: *Qui tacit consentio* ("He who is silent gives consent"). My fear of taking a stand against drugs because it might cost me friends backfired; I still lost friends, only now I lost them to the jail or the graveyard.

If only I had come to my senses about school as quickly as I did about drugs. One day when Frank and I got caught cutting algebra class, we were sent to the boy's dean, whose perfunctory manner seemed odd. He never looked at me or stopped munching on his sandwich while signing an official-looking form. Then he said, "Rogan, I'm suspending you for three days for cutting class. Do you know what that means? It means you've joined the Twenty Club. That's the club reserved for guys with twenty days of suspension. When a student joins that club, it also means something else: You're expelled."

Expelled? I felt too stunned to speak: Nobody warned me that I was teetering on this edge. In one devastating moment, I saw my life's ambitions slipping away forever; I tried unsuccessfully to suppress a sudden trembling. Regaining my composure, I asked for just one chance and offered to accept any conditions placed on me. Swearing I'd reform overnight, I now begged, *"Please, please, don't expel me."*

"Sorry," he said, "no more chances. You're gone. And since your pal Frank now has eighteen suspensions, he won't be far behind. But if you're sincere about proving yourself, maybe after a year at a continuation school we'll welcome you back with open arms. You start there tomorrow. Send us a postcard."

The continuation school: That's where they warehoused out-of-control troublemaking teenage boys, and hid pregnant teenage girls from sight. No amount of pleading changed the dean's mind. Why should it? Frank and I defied authority with impunity; we preferred hanging out with guys more interested in taking drugs than lecture notes. All I wanted to do was impress my apartments' friends. Well, at least I didn't fail there. They'd all be impressed by my expulsion.

It only cost me my future.

As hard as this news hit me, a more devastating revelation eclipsed it.

Handing me some forms before dismissing me, the dean said, "Give these papers to the principal tomorrow at Gompers." Gompers Continuation High School in North Richmond was one of the worst schools in one of the worst school districts in America. That's where they hauled every predatory punk unfit for public school. Its reputation around the apartments was that white guys went to Gompers only if they wanted to get knifed.

The only neighborhood guy I knew at Gompers was John "Crazy" Cutlip. Legendary stories of Crazy Cutlip's fights with gang members at Gompers circulated throughout the apartments. Cutlip always had some new tale of a fist or knife fight he had at Gompers. Nobody wanted to tangle with Crazy Cutlip unless they were crazy, too. Now I'd be going to a school filled with Crazy Cutlips. The dean might as well have ordered me to report to San Quentin. After I threw away my future to have friends, I don't think I ever felt so alone.

The next morning my deeply disappointed mother drove me to Richmond. Not wanting Mom to worry, I kept my safety concerns to myself. When I saw the front entrance of Gompers lined with thugs, I told her to drive around back. Nobody was around a rear door, so I jumped from the car and sprinted into the building. In my first few minutes I heard things like, "We're gonna cut you after school, white boy" and "You're dead, honky." Ignoring the taunts, I kept walking, looking for the principal's office. Relieved to find it, a school administrator met with me. A severe man with unfriendly eyes, he dished out a terse overview of the rules like a prison warden lecturing a new inmate. He said school had two sessions: morning session and afternoon session. I'd get morning session, which meant school started for me at 9 A.M. and ended at 11:15. Jabbing his finger in my chest, he said, "You be in your desk for homeroom at nine *every day* or I'll come looking for you. Homeroom's only ten minutes, so you can handle that. But you'd better be there for homeroom, and don't give me no goddamn excuses why you didn't make it. After that, hey, you're a man. If you want to stay here at school, stay. If you've got things you need to do, then go. That's all up to you. But you better be in your homeroom class at nine, or you deal with me. After homeroom, do as you please. But don't you miss your homeroom class, or you and I have got a big problem."

Baffled by his emphasis on homeroom's ten minutes and his disregard for where I spent the rest of my day, I asked why. His face moved so close to mine that I could smell the tobacco on his breath as he barked that they took attendance in homeroom, "and attendance is where we get money from the state." If I missed homeroom, then I would cost the school state funding. "Once you're in the attendance book, we get our money whether you stay or go. So don't miss homeroom, or I'll come looking for you. After that, do what you want."

After hearing his cynical confession, he told me of another Gompers "benefit" in having him as a school supervisor: "Now, a lot of the brothers here like to mix it up. You and one of the brothers might have a beef you need to settle like men. When a fight happens, someone comes running for me to break it up. That's my job, but I'll take the long way to make sure you guys have plenty of time to get your licks in before I interfere."

I told him to forget the courtesy if I'm in a fight: I wanted it ended immediately. "Don't worry," he smiled. "I'll make sure it ends, after you and the brother get your licks in."

In my first class, the teacher handed me a large sheet of paper and a pencil, and then gave me my one-hour assignment: Go draw. "Go draw what?" I asked.

"Whatever. Just draw." For the entire class, while the teacher read silently an unrelated book, everyone drew until the bell rang. At our next class, the teacher passed out another sheet of paper and a pencil: "Draw."

At least the educational failure in that "art" class was passive. In my first history class, I settled into a desk at the rear of a room occupied by almost all black students. The black teacher's lecture consisted of inflammatory claims that all Afro-Americans have been held down by greedy and evil white oppressors for three hundred years. White men sold black babies, raped black women, beat and brutalized black men, and maintained economic slavery over the black community today. The more the teacher ranted, the more nodding heads with angry eyes turned to look at me. When the bell rang, I wanted to be the first one out the door, running at full throttle several blocks to catch the bus back to Pinole.

Each day the scenario repeated itself: Mom dropped me off at the back of the school; I endured threats walking to and from class, and at the session's last bell I ran like hell to get away before anyone else was out of their desk. One morning Mom dropped me off in the usual place. Crazy Cutlip called to me from the opposite direction. He was behind me as I opened the door and encountered about six black male students blocking our entrance. "This is our door, white boys," a towering figure growled at me. "You mothers want to come in this door? Then you pay each of us a quarter." I tried squeezing past them while joking to lessen the tension: "Hey, I don't even like coming here for free, so don't expect me to pay to be here!" Their humorless spokesman shoved me hard as he shouted obscenities and grew more menacing. My mind raced: Crazy Cutlip was about to earn his nickname and start wading into these guys just as he said he always did. I remembered Uncle Ralf once said that if a group ever jumped me, I should try taking down the biggest one. Expecting action to break out in the next heartbeat or two, I drew a bead on the biggest extortionist, tightened my fist, and plowed it into his head as hard as I could. Shouting "Come on, John, let's take 'em down!" I turned to swing at the two guys behind me. That's when I saw Crazy Cutlip, already half a block away, fleeing at Olympian speed while my grinning tormentors closed their circle around me. The next thing I knew, I was on the ground protecting my head from punches and kicks landing all over me. Strangely, I wasn't focused on the fight; all I could think about was how stupid I was to believe the self-created legend of the formerly crazy (but now exceedingly sane and scampering) John Cutlip.

"They should call me 'Crazy Rogan,'" I remember thinking as blows rained down on me. "Crazy for believing Cutlip's bullshit."

I left Gompers that day and never returned. It turned out the school administrator never came looking for me for missing homeroom class; neither did anyone else.

7

SECOND CHANCE

STUDENT BODY ID CARD
Gompers Continuation High School
Richmond, California

Student's Name: Jim Rogan

Grade: 10   **1973**

I felt no long-term relief in leaving Gompers for good. Looking in the mirror and seeing a newly minted high school dropout gripped me with despair. Without completing high school, there would be no college, no law school, and certainly no politics. The idea of serving in Congress one day, given my present circumstances, was laughable. I had to get back and chase that diploma, but how? My old high school wouldn't take me back unless I spent a year at Gompers, and that wasn't going to happen.

After walking away from Gompers, I wandered the streets for hours trying to clear my head. Thinking came hard: My body ached from the six-guys-against-me street fight earlier; one of my eyes was nearly swollen shut. That paled next to the discomfort of knowing that I'd self-inflicted all my troubles. It was just about the worst day of my life.

I headed to Frank's apartment to break the news. My ribs hurt so badly that I could barely raise my arm to knock on the door. There was no answer; I cursed him for being gone when I really needed to talk to him. Walking around the apartments, I heard Frank's familiar "smoker's cough" coming from inside a carport storage shed. I cracked open the door and peered inside; when my eyes adjusted to the dark, I saw Frank's silhouette huddled over a gloomy candle. He looked startled and then embarrassed. A rubber surgical strap looped over Frank's bare bicep; he tried pulling it tighter by tugging on the other end of the strap with his teeth. Next to the candle rested a metal spoon holding a dark tar-like substance; a hypodermic needle lay nearby. Frank shrugged in silent acknowledgment of my discovery. "I wish you hadn't come," he said. "But now that you're here, do me a favor and help me tie off my arm."

I stared at this wretched scene. As bleak as things were for me, Frank had just trumped me in the hopelessness department. On the day I became a high school dropout, Frank was about to graduate—to heroin junkie. Seeing a best friend in a storage shed with a dirty syringe was the last straw. "Sure, Frank," I replied. "I'll help you tie off your arm. Get up so I can do it." Frank stood and handed the rubber strap to me. I wrapped it around his arm, and then yanked it so tight that it pinched his flesh. He yelped in pain and reached to loosen the strap; I grabbed the front of his shirt, jerked him toward me, and then cold-cocked him with a punch that dropped him like a sack of coal. The candle and drug paraphernalia scattered over the dirty storeroom floor as he toppled over. I stripped off my jacket and straddled him with both of my fists clenched. "Get up, you son of a bitch," I shouted. "You want to kill yourself? You want to die today? Okay, Frank, you can die today. Only you're gonna be a murder victim, not a suicide."

"I can't believe what you just did," he sputtered finally, still sprawled on the floor and rubbing his chin. "Are you crazy?"

"*I said get up*," I snarled as I kicked him.

"You're crazy—I'm not getting up until you calm down."

My advantage had nothing to do with size or strength: Frank never raised an angry hand to a friend, no matter how provoked. I didn't play by the same rules. Knowing this, Frank elected to remain on the ground. After spewing a mouthful of profanities at my horizontal friend, I told him, "Things are going to change around here for me, Frank," I said, "and they're changing for you, too—or I'll beat the living shit out of you."

Biting his lower lip, Frank said there was no arguing with a crazy man. Then he reached over and picked up his syringe, sighed, and then pressed the needle against the floor until it snapped. I helped him up, and then we went to his apartment where he flushed the heroin down the toilet.

"What a waste," he muttered.

That's how I felt about my life.

My plan to right the canoe wasn't complicated: Get a job and get back in (another) school. Night classes would let me do both, but getting a job proved problematic. Answering "no" to the "high school diploma?" employment application question usually meant automatic disqualification. Nobody asked or cared about how many presidents I had met; dropping out signaled that I couldn't follow through with the most fundamental of tasks. "Why should I trust my business to a screw-up who can't even finish high school?" one prospective employer asked.

The only jobs I found were menial and tedious; often, they involved working for less than the minimum wage, being paid "under the table," and getting no benefits. Over the next few years I worked a variety of full- and part-time jobs, including bussing tables, assembling bicycles for Christmas shoppers, dumping trash, crushing cardboard boxes, filling produce shelves in a market, fast food cook, cleaning toilets, washing dishes, janitorial work, and brush and soap salesman. When a local auto supply shop hired me for ten cents above minimum wage, I was delighted. Wanting to make a good impression, I asked Eldon (now working in a retail store)for some advice. He told me to show up the first day in a shirt and tie, and ask the manager questions about payroll and inventory. "That'll show your boss that you're focused on the business side of things. It will impress him and make him want to move you up the ladder." I did as Eldon suggested. On my first day I wore my only dress shirt and tie. Sitting with the manager while I filled out a tax withholding form, I asked about the payroll and inventory.

"What do you care?" he replied. After looking me up and down, he added, "Uh, you might be a little overdressed today. Your job's not here in the store doing sales. It's there." With his head, he motioned out the window to the warehouse, where a large delivery truck had just pulled up and dumped three hundred steel-belted radial truck tires. He said my job was to carry each tire to the top of the warehouse's metal gantry and stack them in the racks. Time dragged as I lugged the heavy tires up the rickety stairs one at a time. After six hours of nonstop work I finished the job in time for another truckload of tires to arrive. When I got home that night I was too tired to eat; my shirt, tie, and pants were ruined by crisscrossing tire tread patterns. I looked like I'd napped on the Grand Prix racetrack. The next day I asked the manager how long I had to stack tires before I worked my way into the store sales crew. "Sorry," he said. "Salesmen have to work with money at the cash register, and store policy forbids high school dropouts from doing that."

When I earned enough to buy a new shirt and tie, I answered an ad for a new job: door-to-door vacuum cleaner salesman. A gangly guy with a long neck who resembled Ichabod Crane interviewed me for the job. Everyone called him "Turkey Arnie" because when he spoke his head jutted forward from his neck and shoulders with each syllable, just like a turkey pecking at corn feed on the ground. It was a distracting habit: After talking with him for a few minutes, my head wanted to jet forward like his just to keep up the rhythm.

Turkey Arnie was a piece of work: He wore Day-Glo polyester coats with an elastic belt and rhinestone studs on the back in the shape of a large turkey. No matter how goofy his outward appearance, at least he didn't care if I had a high school diploma: "I only care if you can sell vacuum cleaners!" When I assured him I fit the bill (even though I knew more about cold fusion than vacuums) he hired me to work for straight commission. Here was a job that forced me to suppress my instincts toward shyness: Bashfulness had no place when trying to foist $600 vacuum cleaners down the throats of people who neither needed nor wanted the contraptions, especially when the average Hoover upright sold for about thirty bucks.

The work morning started with our ten-man sales team gathering at a small office storefront for coffee. Fritz, the portly sales manager, started the program by calling forward salesmen to share war stories from their latest sales deal, or (if it was a slow week) tales of the lonely housewife the salesman bedded while her husband went to work to earn vacuum cleaner money. When the gabfest ended, Fritz passed out homemade mimeographed songbooks. Waving his stubby fingers like batons, he led the vacuum cleaner choir. He expected salesmen to belt out each jingle with full-throated gusto, believing it psyched them up for the day's selling effort. The tunes were well-known ditties with lyrics adapted to denigrate the intelligence of our customers. One example was "Mary Had a Dirty House," sung to the tune of "Mary Had a Little Lamb":

Mary had a dirty house, dirty house, dirty house;
Mary had a dirty house because she was a pig.
Her carpets all were full of dust, full of grime, full of crap;
Her carpets all were full of filth 'cause she's a lazy broad.
But now her house is spic-and-span, spic-and-span, spic-and-span;
And now her house is spic-and-span 'cause I sold my machine.
And if she gets buyer's remorse, such remorse, sad remorse;
And if she gets buyer's remorse
Well ain't that just too bad!

When Fritz felt we were ready to sell machines, he piled everyone into a Volkswagen van and drove us into some of the worst ghetto areas of East Oakland. He randomly picked a neighborhood, synchronized his watch with ours, and then dropped us on different street corners with our expensive vacuum cleaners, a bulky box of attachments, and a 48-ounce bottle of Coca-Cola. The van sped away, not to return for two hours. The salesmen's incentive of self-preservation required getting into someone's house immediately for a two-hour demonstration before some marauding gang beat and robbed us of our $600 vacuum cleaner. After knocking on the first available door, the rapid patter went something like this:

Good morning, ma'am. My name's Jim Rogan. My company is marketing a brand new revolutionary home-cleaning service that is sweeping America, so to speak! We don't advertise on TV or radio; our owner believes that the best advertising is word of mouth from friends and neighbors. Your home has been selected for a free cleaning from top to bottom, and I'm here to present your reward. All I want from you is two things: First, you let me do all your housecleaning—you just sit back and relax. Second, if you know anybody who could use a machine like this, you'll tell them to call me. By the way, here's your free 48-ounce bottle of Coke. It's with my compliments for your kindness in listening to me. Now, why don't you pour yourself a tall, cool glass while I clean your home!

The complimentary bottle of Coke and my willingness to clean the house for nothing proved an appealing offer. Of course, once in the door, we never intended to leave without a sale. The pitch was designed to get the unwitting customer to keep agreeing with an avalanche of my loaded questions:

"Isn't it remarkable how this machine cleaned your rug?"
"If you had a machine like this, you'd certainly use it, right?"
"Don't your children deserve to sleep on a clean bed and pillow?"
"Ma'am, you don't want your baby playing on a carpet after your husband's shoes tracked in germs from the floor of some gas station urinal, do you?"

After getting them to say "yes" for two hours, I rushed through a 30-second financing explanation and then shoved a contract and pen under the customer's nose. The closing line was, "Well, now that you've told me how much you love the machine and how much you'd use it, my only question is, what color would you like your new machine to be?" Timing was everything: If Fritz and I kept to perfect schedules, he'd knock on the customer's door right about now and come in to "check" on me. He knew where to find his crew: At the start of the pitch, we left a colored placard in the front window to flag our location.

"Hey, Jimmy," Fritz declared as he entered the home, "I just called the front office. Remember that contest for a free vacation for you and your wife? It ends in twenty minutes! And guess what? You're only one sale away from being the winner! If you can get just one more machine sold today, you can take your wife on that vacation she's always dreamed about!" Turning to the customer, he mixed empathy for my nonexistent wife with the customer's desire not to live in this illusory filth. To sweeten the deal when necessary, he bartered away part or all of my $60 commission. One way or another, we almost never left the house without ink drying on a purchase contract.

Bringing Frank into the business, I sent him out to find us a sales lead; he came back with an address in nearby Berkeley. With Frank in tow, I lugged my vacuum cleaner up two flights of stairs in what looked like an apartment building. Frank knocked on the door; an older woman wearing a silk robe and makeup caked on her deeply worn face led us into a parlor looking like a Dodge City saloon. It had tattered red wallpaper, and heavy, musty red velvet drapes covered the walls, along with cheap oil paintings of cherubic nudes. A dozen or so scantily clad women in varying shapes, sizes, and colors sprawled on the couches and loveseats. Under the harsh midday light they looked more tired than pretty, but when we entered they smiled and bade us a friendly hello. "Ladies, this is Jim and Frank," the older woman said. Not surprisingly, a couple of them nodded to Frank like they knew him. Turning toward me, our hostess bowed regally as she proclaimed, "You are welcome to our place of business!" It didn't take a high school grad to figure out their place of business was a local whorehouse.

With no customers or television in the room to distract me, and a parlor full of bored working women looking to be entertained, I gave them the full pitch. The carpets and drapes were so caked with dust that it made my work easy. Also, I called up a trick Turkey Arnie taught me to use for special occasions. Since the human body sheds dead skin that is invisible to the naked eye, it collects and settles into bedding. Without asking permission, I picked up the machine and ordered everyone to follow me. Pushing open the first door in the hallway, I found a sparsely decorated room with a brass bed. With all the ladies in tow and watching with keen interest, I pulled back the blanket and sheets and threw them on the floor. Then I jammed a thin black buffing cloth between the vacuum hose and the attachment head, turning the cloth into a makeshift filter. As I vacuumed the mattress and pillow, a layer of flaky dead skin resembling white ash formed on the cloth. I removed the filter and handled it as gingerly as if it contained nitroglycerin. Holding it away from me at arm's length (and wearing a look of disgust), I explained how the ladies were laying in these flesh germs shed by their unsanitary clients each time they climbed between the sheets. Then, to ram home the revulsion factor, I flicked on a cigarette lighter and ran it underneath the filter. The stench of burning skin engulfed the room as I thrust the now putrid smelling cloth filter under the ladies' noses. "Sniff this! Can you believe this is what you've been sleeping in? Uh, well, maybe you're not *sleeping* in it, but. . . ."

They got the point.

When I put the contract and a pen on the table and asked what color they wanted their machine to be, the hostess said without hesitation "Red, if you have it." The ladies started pulling money out of their brassieres, and counted out $600 in cash. As a reward to Frank for the referral, I gave him half of my commission. The next day he was broke; when I asked what he did with the money, he grinned and said, "Well, let's just say I went back to make sure your vacuum cleaner still worked!"

One day Fritz dropped me off in East Oakland. Just as the van pulled away, a band of thugs came around the corner and started eyeing my machine. Expecting trouble, I ran up the first available flight of stairs. I was surprised to find no front door: Instead, a large cardboard refrigerator-packing box was wedged into the doorframe. Finding a family so poor that they didn't even have a front door would make me go elsewhere normally, but under the circumstances I couldn't afford to be picky. I rapped on the box; a few moments later it slid to the side and an elderly couple greeted me. I gave them my speech about cleaning their house and presented them with the bottle of Coke. "That's so nice of you," the old man said as he handed the bottle to his wife. "Sure, come on in and show us what you've got." Assuming the family couldn't afford a machine, I figured I'd just kill time cleaning carpets until the van returned. I was startled when I entered the home and found all hardwood floors! There wasn't a carpet fragment anywhere. With those punks still lingering outside, and my only bottle of Coke gone, there was nothing to do except stall for time and hope the couple had no plans the rest of the morning.

I ran out the clock improvising cleaning techniques. I took a fluorescent lamp and rubbed its edge along their worn couch, then held it up to show all the dust particles they breathed every time someone plopped on the sofa. Then I put on the hose attachment and "vacuumed" the air, getting rid of all their "indoor air pollution." I vacuumed their drapes, walls, floors, and ceilings with the machine. Near the end of my presentation I threw in this afterthought: "And if you ever get carpets, let me show you what else this thing can do!" By the time I finished, the couple feared their grandchildren were exposed to countless health hazards in their home.

When Fritz showed up, I bundled my equipment and whispered to him to nix the standard sales close. I just wanted to thank my hosts and leave. He wouldn't have any part of that suggestion. He overpowered the naïve old couple with a hard-sell sales pitch. Because they liked me, they really wanted me to win that contest prize for selling a machine that day. "Well, I'd sure like to see Mr. Jim get it," the old man said. "And I'd like to buy one of these machines for my missus. But the only money we got is my Social Security money." No problem, Fritz assured them, we'd tailor an installment contract just for them. My boss's smile camouflaged his unspoken thought: Let us take big chunks of your Social Security for three years, you stupid old people, so you can own the world's most expensive rug cleaner, even though you don't own a rug.

My conscience kept me from going along with this raw deal. The next day I called the old woman and said the machine was meant for carpets; any other benefits were incidental. I told her she'd do as well with a $5 dust mop. At my urging, she called Fritz and exercised her 72-hour cancellation right. Not surprisingly, when I reported for work Fritz fired me, swearing he'd fix me for screwing him out of that sale.

When I applied for my next job, I naïvely listed the vacuum cleaner experience; Fritz refused to answer repeated requests to verify my employment. When my new boss reached him finally, Fritz wondered aloud if I was that guy who left the company under a cloud of "*suspicion*, but no proof" of theft. When my new manager reported his statement back to me, I took my entire savings ($150) and hired an attorney, who told Fritz to retract the comment or face a lawsuit. When confronted by a lawyer, Fritz denied saying it.

A few days later my telephone rang. Fritz chortled into the receiver, "So, I hear you're broke as well as unemployed now!" He laughed loudly, and then slammed down the phone in my ear.

I had no time or inclination to hang out at the apartments any more. Not that it mattered much: Most of the old gang was gone. Rocky had moved to Hawaii to live with his father and learn the wrestling trade; Ken Cable had joined the Army, and his cute sisters Marie and Rose (on whom every guy had an abiding crush) moved to Martinez. Soon the Rogans also left for a new neighborhood. Only Frank remained, until he was kicked out of his house—again. With no place to stay, he showed up on our doorstep and asked to spend a couple of nights.

A year later he still was there.

Although Mom viewed Frank as another son, his unending presence and slovenly habits grated on her nerves. Many times she wanted to toss him out, but I always intervened. Still, Mom grew increasingly impatient with her lazy adoptee: "You've simply got to do something about Frank before he drives me crazy," she complained. As much as I loved Frank, he drove me crazy, too. We both messed up our lives in Pinole; I wanted mine back on track, but Frank preferred to watch my self-improvement efforts and then live vicariously off them. I worked all day and then went to high school night classes. Frank kept to a different schedule: He watched TV all night and then slept until late afternoon. When he did awaken, he ate like a predatory animal, smoked pot, secretly reconnected with his druggie friends in Pinole, or tried seducing Rhonda (my sister's pretty runaway girlfriend, also encamped at our place).

I worried about Frank's lack of ambition as much as his potential regression. When I got him a job interview with a well-paying janitorial service, he went to the interview and was rude and sarcastic to the hiring committee. He returned home without the job and then boasted about his obnoxious conduct. The reason? He didn't like the tone of my voice when I told him to get his fat ass out of bed for the job interview. "You pissed me off," he told me, "so I tanked the interview. Let that be a lesson to you." It was a lesson to me—and it also was the straw that broke the camel's back.

A guy in my night school class worked with a local U.S. Navy recruiting office. After listening to some of my Frank stories during coffee breaks, he said the Navy would make a man out of Frank: "He sounds like a good guy deep down, but he's never had any structure or purpose. The Navy could turn him around." With the Vietnam War over for almost two years, the Navy was more selective about their recruits; he said he'd have to pull a few strings to get Frank in. I said we'd see flying pigs at the recruiting office before we'd see Frank there, especially without me in tow. "Well," he asked, cocking an eyebrow, "what if Frank thought *you* were enlisting, too?" I nodded with complicity, and we hatched an irresistible plot. Frank had a childlike faith in me, and I never exploited it except for his own good. This, I decided, was one of those times.

Later that week, I returned home from school and told Frank I'd just cut a deal to enlist us in the Navy on the "buddy system." Not surprisingly, Frank didn't warm to the idea. For days I worked him over, telling him how the "new Navy" would treat us. The recruiter was a friend from night school, I assured him, and we'd get special treatment. He'd mark our files to indicate we were the sons of an admiral and a senator; they'd waive boot camp for us, and take us to special training school for VIP recruits. Our first tour was six months guaranteed in Hawaii, with an island renewal right. In case we didn't like the Navy, we had an opt-out clause that freed us with an honorable discharge as long as we gave thirty days' notice. As the days went by, the greater our "benefits" package grew: I now promised Frank that I had negotiated for us off-base meal privileges, food vouchers for restaurants of our choice, eight-hour workdays, our own personal jeep, officer's bars, and the like. One night I told Frank it was decision time: If he signed up now, they guaranteed we wouldn't be separated. "Goddamn it, Frank," I thundered, "I've already enlisted for four years, took my physical, and I've been sworn in. They're holding up my assignment waiting for you so we can ship out together. They're not going to wait forever for you to get off your ass and make the move."

In the end, Frank had no choice. If I left, he knew his meal ticket and shelter ended. When at last he agreed to enlist with me, I introduced him to my classmate and let the recruiter take it from there. In short order Frank took his physical, "passed" his high school equivalency test (proctored by my classmate), and took the oath as a new recruit. There was just one hitch: Thinking he'd get the last laugh on me, Frank returned from his oath ceremony and told me he changed his enlistment to *two* years instead of the four to which he thought I obligated myself. "Hey, just because you're a sucker doesn't mean I'm a sucker, too! I'm only goin' in for two years," Frank laughed. "So let that be another lesson to you!"

"Frank," I told him calmly, "this'll be a lesson neither one of us ever will forget."

Frank spent his final night as a civilian at his Uncle Horse's, where he loaded up on hookers and liquor. Early the next morning a small military van drove around the neighborhood picking up new recruits scheduled to report for induction. Frank and I already agreed that he'd get picked up at Uncle Horse's; I said I didn't want anyone around when I bid an emotional farewell to my mother. I told him my house was the last scheduled pickup, and to save me a seat next to him on the bus.

The next morning Frank staggered aboard the recruiting bus with one hell of a hangover. Taking a seat in the rear, he closed his eyes and paid no attention to those boarding at the remaining pickup sites—until the bus drove onto the freeway and headed for Oakland Airport. Thinking he must have slept through my boarding, Frank walked the length of the bus looking for me. Then he marched up to the officer in charge of the detail and said they missed picking up Jim Rogan. "There's no Rogan on my list of pickups," the officer barked. "Get back in your seat." The bus dropped off the recruits at the airport and herded them onto an airplane to ship off for basic training.

Months went by. Then one afternoon the telephone rang. When I answered, I heard the crackling voice of an overseas operator trying to talk over static. "I have a collect call from Guantanamo Bay, Cuba," she said. "Will you accept charges?" At first there was a pause, and then a familiar voice on the other end growled the world's longest delivery of a two-syllable word:

"A-a-a-a-a-a-a-a-a-ass-ho-o-o-o-o-o-o-o-ole. . . ."

At a dance one night Mom met Jose, an easygoing, middle-aged Filipino working as a supervisor for the BART commuter trains. They dated for a while and then married. Theirs was never a "head over heels" love; they were more like good friends deciding to give marriage a try. It didn't last; their decision to split up came as casually as the one to marry: no fuss, nobody hurt, and ending as it began—friends. Still, Mom benefited from their brief marriage by saying goodbye to the welfare culture of Pinole. We moved to Livermore, a small city in a rural valley near Oakland. In the mid-1970s housing tracts were just beginning to pop up among the Livermore orchards and farmlands. Lawrence Livermore Lab, where they designed and tested nuclear bombs, was the valley's major employer. The big joke among residents was that if the Soviets ever attacked America, nobody in Livermore would know, since the first atomic strike would be against us.

A wrinkle developed after Mom's marriage: During her time on welfare, she took side jobs as a toy store cashier to make ends meet. The welfare check didn't provide enough for her large brood. Knowing the government would slash her benefits if she took a job, Mom didn't report it. Shortly after marrying Jose and moving to Livermore, an investigator showed up to question her about this old case. When she told the truth, the police booked her for welfare fraud.

Mom rejected her defense attorney's advice to plead "not guilty" and get a bargaining chip with the DA. Since the charges were true, she wanted to fess up and put the issue behind her. She pled guilty, and the judge told her to return in a few weeks for sentencing. Mom's lawyer reassured her the standard sentence in first-time cases like this was probation and restitution, with no jail time. When she returned to court for her sentencing, Mom watched a parade of welfare-cheating women take their turn before the judge. The litany never changed: The women wept, apologized, and in response to the judge's question, promised never to do it again. Each received the standard minimum sentence. When Mom's turn came, she skipped the tears but otherwise followed suit: She said she did it, she was sorry, and she wanted to pay back the money with interest. However, when the judge asked if she would do it again, Mom veered from the script. Wanting to be candid, she told the court, "Well, judge, in all honesty, if I needed to do it to keep my family together, then I guess I would."

Wrong answer: Like the other women, Mom received probation and was ordered to pay restitution; unlike the others, the judge sent her to jail. Mom spent about four months in custody, dividing her jail time between Martinez County Jail and a work furlough halfway house in Oakland. Meanwhile, Jose and I held down the fort.

Doris Derby, Mom's high school friend, told me not to worry about her being in jail: "Your mother's *always* been a tough broad." Up to now Mom never appeared fazed by difficult circumstances, but jail could depress even the most buoyant spirit. I didn't know what to expect when I saw her there the first time. I entered the visitor's area, which looked like a large recreation room. Mom wasn't hard to pick out of the crowd: She was the only white inmate there. Wearing a standard-issue jail jumpsuit, she chatted merrily with her jailers and fellow inmates while crocheting a rug. Her eyes lit up when she saw me, and after exchanging hugs she introduced me to her new companions. There was Mary, who had torched her motor home for the insurance money. Next to her was doper Debbie, for whom Mom later got a job at King Norman's Toy Store at Eastmont Mall. Mom also introduced me to Annie, who taught Mom how to crochet: "Annie stabbed her boyfriend—or did you shoot him, Annie? I can't remember." A wispy woman with a shy grin, Annie rolled her eyes as if embarrassed by the fuss. With doe-like innocence, she peeked up and cooed, "I sticked him."

"Oh, well," Mom shrugged, "it doesn't matter. He was a no-good son of a bitch anyway." Then Mom introduced me to a giggly jailer from whom she bummed a smoke. "We've heard so much about you!" the mountainous female guard said. "And we just love your Mom!" I felt like I'd stumbled into a family reunion.

The county later sent Mom eventually to a work furlough program that allowed her to leave jail for her day job; she spent only nights in custody for the remainder of her sentence. For most middle-aged women, jail would be an inducement into clinical depression. For Mom, it wasn't much more than an inconvenience. Her friend Doris was right: Mom was a tough broad.

By early 1975, I got some unhappy news from a school counselor: It would take me about three years to earn my diploma attending night classes. Now almost eighteen, I didn't want to be in my twenties and still working my way through high school. Suddenly, Frank's situation didn't look so bad: If a Navy recruiter massaged it so Frank got his high school equivalency to enlist, then why not me? Once Frank got out, he'd have the GI Bill to pay for college and graduate school. I weighed my options: have my education paid for, serve my country, see the world, and have some excitement; or work in hash houses while slugging through night school for three years. It didn't take a genius to see I'd be better off enlisting. Unfortunately, the guy who helped Frank now was gone, and the passage of time changed the recruitment dynamic. When I visited Livermore's various recruiting centers to sign up, I heard the same message: With the Vietnam War long over, the military was downsizing. "Nothing personal," an Air Force recruiter told me, "but we're not bringing in guys like you; we're kicking them out early."

I was disheartened, but not for long. After more digging, I learned that in California, anyone eighteen or over could enroll in a community college *without* a high school diploma. The bar was set at eighteen to make sure high school students didn't quit prematurely and head straight to college. With my eighteenth birthday around the corner, it made no sense for me to spend years in night classes trying to finish high school when, in the same amount of time, I could be close to earning a bachelor's degree. I dropped the night school route, studied for the high school equivalency exam as a backup plan, but otherwise waited for my birthday to apply to community college directly.

On a spring day in June 1975, I had some unfinished business back in Pinole. Wandering through the apartments, I didn't see anyone I knew. Late that afternoon I stood under Ken Cable's old apartment, where our gang had hung out so many times, and watched over the fence as Pinole Valley High's Class of 1975 left their graduation ceremony. Clad in their caps and gowns and waving diplomas, my joyful former classmates headed for their graduation parties—parties I might now be attending had I not failed so miserably.

Watching them gave me an overwhelming feeling of melancholia, just as I knew it would. In fact, that's why I went to Pinole that day: to inject myself with a potent reminder of the high cost of failure. My resolve to reverse course was fixed; now I hoped I had the skills to match the determination.

8

TRANSITIONS

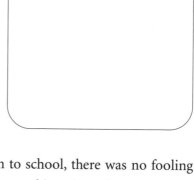

CHABOT COLLEGE
REGISTRATION CARD

559-25-4460 | | AUTUMN 1975

STUDENT I.D. NUMBER   COUNSELOR   VALID FOR QUARTER SHOWN

ROGAN JAMES EDWARD
STUDENT'S NAME

PRE-REG PRIORITY   199
NOT TRANSFERABLE

SHOW ON DEMAND TO REPRESENTATIVES
OF THE COLLEGE

AFFIX
A.S.C.C.
MEMBERSHIP
LABEL
HERE

STUDENT'S SIGNATURE

When it came to my return to school, there was no fooling around. Life had given gave me quite a spanking since the apartments, and it took me three years in menial jobs to get back my footing. In the fall of 1975, the doors first opened at Livermore's new Chabot Community College, later renamed Las Positas. I saw something symbolic in getting a brand new start in a brand new school. When Chabot opened, there wasn't much there: only eight classrooms, sixteen instructors, and wooden stakes with red flags marking the 147 acres upon which the campus administration hoped to expand. On August 21, my eighteenth birthday, I skipped the parties and spent all day in enrollment lines at Chabot. By day's end, I had my reward when I slid into my wallet a student body ID card. That piece of paper represented more than another form of identification; it meant I had another chance.

I discovered that college, unlike high school, is sink or swim: no truant officer enforced attendance. The choice belonged to the student: Show up and work hard, or don't and fail. I left nothing to chance. Although three years had passed since I'd dropped out of Gompers, my interim education taught me if I didn't do well now, I'd spend the rest of my life working alongside the Turkey Arnies of the world. What more motivation did a guy need to hunker down and hit the books?

The week before classes started, I fulfilled a lifelong dream. Saving enough money for the cheapest plane ticket and hotel ($15 a night at the Harrington), I took my first trip to Washington, D.C. I sent letters to each instructor telling them I'd miss the first few days of class because of the trip; later I learned they appreciated the notification—they assumed I was an overly conscientious student. Little did they know I'd done it to avoid any more "suspensions" for missing classes to run off to political events!

The nation's capital was a different city in 1975 than it is today: Metal detectors didn't screen visitors, barricades didn't encircle the plaza, and tourists explored the halls of the Capitol at will. I wrote ahead to many political leaders and asked if I could meet them while in town for advice on entering politics; in an era before terrorist alerts and anthrax threats, most wrote back and invited me to drop by for a chat.

The magic that Hubert Humphrey once encountered upon arriving as a young man and seeing his first glimpse of the Capitol dome lived on: When I caught my first view of it during a cab ride across the Potomac River from National Airport, the alabaster dome painted against the gray sky left me speechless.

One of the men I wanted to meet was Tom Clark, a retired U.S. Supreme Court Justice who also served as Attorney General under President Truman. Clark one-upped my request to meet: He sent back a handwritten note saying he'd pick me up at the Harrington that first morning and bring me to the Supreme Court for our talk! We met in the lobby shortly after I checked in; he was tall, white-haired, and distinguished, wearing one of his trademark polka-dot bow ties. Clark drove me around town showing me the monuments before we pulled into the justices' private driveway at the Court. It was thrilling to hear him tell old war stories from his years working with FDR and Truman, and then discuss his seventeen years on the Warren Court and the key decisions in which he participated. During our visit, Clark confirmed for me what by now I already knew: Law school was the ticket to politics. What better preparation for being a lawgiver than to study the law? His secretary echoed the sentiment: "I worked for my first boss for forty years, and that's the path he took," she told me. "Law school led him to politics. He became a prosecutor, ran for office, and then ended up here. You're a Californian, so you've probably heard of him—his name was Earl Warren."

I was amazed at how accessible so many leaders made themselves to a young nobody. Senator Edmund Muskie, the 1968 Democratic vice presidential nominee (and future Secretary of State), left a meeting with Vice President Rockefeller to spend a few minutes in his private office encouraging my pursuits. Senator John Glenn, the first American to orbit the Earth, showed me a scale model of his Friendship VII space capsule as he patiently explained its 1962 voyage. "This model is built to one-tenth scale, so it gives you an idea just how small the original was," Glenn noted. When I marveled that he could fit inside something so tiny, Glenn laughed and pointed to his balding head: "I think I lost a few hairs climbing out!" Judge John Sirica, *Time*'s 1974 Man of the Year who presided over the Watergate trials, invited me to his chambers at the U.S. District Court. He showed a special interest in my background and desire to attend law school. Sirica knew something about the school of hard knocks: He paid his way through school alternating between being a trash collector and having heavyweight boxing champ Jack Dempsey pound on him as a sparring partner. Sirica signed a photograph of us shaking hands, "To Jim Rogan, a fine young man who I believe is destined to be a great lawyer some day." When the time came a few years later, Sirica wrote me a law school recommendation.

I learned from these meetings that when one falls in politics, it's a long drop. The last time I'd seen Senator George McGovern, he was the 1972 Democratic presidential nominee, surrounded by an army of Secret Service agents as thousands of eager fans pressed forward to touch him. Now, having lost forty-nine states to Richard Nixon, I saw him walking the Capitol grounds alone and unrecognized. During our meeting in his office, he reassured me that public service was a noble pursuit, and if I felt led to participate, he said I should do all I could to get a good education and prepare myself. When I asked about his crushing defeat to Nixon, McGovern picked up from his desk a Gallup Poll taken after Watergate came to light, showing he would have defeated Nixon had all the facts been known. "This poll vindicated me," McGovern said with intensity. Dropping his voice, he repeated quietly the thought: "It vindicated me."

Sadness hung in the air during my meeting with Arkansas Congressman Wilbur D. Mills. Mills was a legislative titan, with four decades in Congress, including sixteen years as the powerful chairman of the House Ways and Means Committee. The *Los Angeles Times* once noted that "There were no tax, trade or government entitlement measures of the 1960s and 1970s that did not bear his mark; measures such as tax cuts and Medicare were enacted only when he was ready." That power evaporated in late 1974 when Mills was in a car crash following a drunken escapade with a nightclub stripper. Although reelected to his nineteenth and final term after the scandal broke, Congress stripped Mills of his chairmanship. He remained in Congress for another year, but to his colleagues he was a political dead man walking. Mills had covered his office walls from floor to ceiling with framed political cartoons touting his former power. One depicted a cowering President Nixon groveling before Mills, captioned, "I need a favor, Godfather." Another showed a huge Texas-style cowboy hat atop the Capitol dome with President Johnson's initials ("LBJ") on it; atop Johnson's hat was an even larger hat labeled "Wilbur Mills." Now these old cartoons seemed oddly out of place.

Mills invited me into his office; as I sat down, he continued signing a thick stack of letters without reading them. I shouldn't have asked why he signed letters he hadn't read, but I did. He brushed off the question with a shrug, saying, "My secretary reads them for me. I don't have time anymore." We spent little time discussing my ambitions; Mills talked mostly about his love for the House of Representatives and how he never wanted to leave: "The folks back home wanted me to run for the Senate as early as 1944, and I would have been unopposed. I decided to stay in the House and make this my home." Mills's eyes suddenly misted as his voice trailed off. "Yes, I decided to make this my home." A profound look of sadness covered his weathered face as he cast his eyes downward.

My unforgettable meeting with another giant convinced me that some of these guys needed to pack up and go home. The president pro tem of the Senate, Mississippi's James O. Eastland, was a gruff, cigar-chomping politician who served as chairman of the Senate Judiciary Committee longer than anyone in the twentieth century. When I got to

Eastland's office, his secretary pulled me aside and asked me a bizarre question: Did I *really* want to meet Eastland? She suggested she could arrange better things for me to do, like special Washington tours. When I declined her alternative, she heaved a deep sigh and then escorted me into a private office. She announced in a loud voice to an apparently empty room that I was here. I didn't see anybody until she led me by the arm to a high-backed Queen Anne chair facing the window. There, slumped down and looking half dead, was Senator Eastland. "Let's just do a quick picture," his secretary suggested, and called to a husky male aide, who lifted Eastland and led the shuffling legislator to his desk. The aide put my hand inside Eastland's clammy palm and snapped a picture. When I asked Eastland to sign an autograph for me, his staff exchanged worried glances. Eastland swayed his hunched shoulders as he slid into his desk chair and took a pen, writing his name with a weak and shaky script. We didn't discuss politics, career options, or anything else: During my visit, Eastland never uttered a word. When his pen finished scratching out the signature, his secretary tugged at my arm and told me to say goodbye. Before I left the outer office, she put her hand on my shoulder and whispered, "You know, the Senator's presence in the Senate is very important to the people of our state—*very important*. You understand what I mean, don't you?" I understood: She wanted me to keep my mouth shut about how the boss looked. I glanced down and saw a stack of pamphlets on a table in his reception area depicting Eastland. The hearty, smiling man pictured on the brochure bore no resemblance to the crumpled man slumped in the chair who currently stood third in the constitutional line of presidential succession.

Other meetings struck me as underwhelming. Senate Majority Leader Mike Mansfield offered to see me, but when I showed up, he proved cranky and irritable, and complained of being in a hurry. He had no time to talk; the picture taken of us shows two unsmiling subjects. Senator Frank Church, chairman of the Senate Foreign Relations Committee, lost track of time and forgot our meeting. His secretary apologized for the mix-up when I came to his office. She said her boss didn't want me to leave empty-handed: "He personally signed a photograph for you just before he left, and made me promise to present it when you got here." She excused herself to get it and stepped into an alcove from which I soon heard the whir of a machine. She returned moments later and handed me a photograph bearing a still wet, autopen-signed Frank Church photograph.

Those incidents were the exceptions. For the most part, the trip was the thrill of a lifetime. By the time I returned home, I felt like I had accessed most of the federal government personally. On that trip, I managed to meet Vice President Nelson Rockefeller and Senator Walter Mondale (future vice president); Senators Edward M. Kennedy, Strom Thurmond, and Ernest F. Hollings (with whom I later served in Congress); Senator Birch Bayh (who became my law partner thirty years later), and Senator Bob Dole (who twenty years later campaigned for me). I saw Senators John Sparkman (Adlai Stevenson's 1952 running mate), Barry Goldwater (1964 Republican presidential nominee), Tom Eagleton (George McGovern's running mate), Lloyd Bentsen (Mike Dukakis's running mate and future Secretary of the Treasury), John Tower (later rejected for Secretary of Defense for drinking and womanizing), Gary Hart (whose presidential campaign fizzled in a sex scandal), Jake Garn (who later became an astronaut), Harrison Williams (who later became a federal prisoner), Dale Bumpers (against whom I later battled in the U.S. Senate during the Clinton impeachment trial), Secretary of State Henry Kissinger, and many others.

Needless to say, my appointment with the great Hubert Humphrey promised to be the highlight. However, he missed our scheduled appointment in his office because of Senate votes. Instead, his intern escorted me to the Senate Members-Only Dining Room. I felt uneasy about interrupting Humphrey's lunch, especially after my grouchy Mike Mansfield episode, but when he came out and pumped my hand, he set me at ease. "Oh, nonsense to lunch, Jim," he gushed, "I'm glad to see you." Rather than take a picture with me and send me on my way, Humphrey overflowed with questions about my trip, treating me as an old friend instead of a nuisance. When I said my Washington experience had made me want to come back someday as a congressman, he exclaimed, "That's wonderful! I know exactly how you feel." Then he closed his eyes and rubbed his temples as if conjuring up a distant memory, and recounted the story of his first visit, remembering how he wrote to his fiancée to share his own dream of coming back as a congressman. How well I knew that story—it was one of my early motivations to politics, and I told him so.

"Well, Jim," he said with a parting smile, "when you get here as a congressman, bring honor to the place. That's the obligation of all who serve here."

When we moved to Livermore, I wanted to buy a used car. One of Pat's friends told me his older brother was selling his 1968 Pontiac LeMans for $250. Since this was in my price range, I went over to check it out. The gunmetal gray junker, nicknamed the La Bamba, was a mess: Chunks of the black vinyl hardtop blew off when driving at freeway speed; a Boy Scout belt held the rear fender on; a coat hanger subbed for the radio antenna, the glove compartment was duct-taped shut, and glass packs made the engine rev to painfully high decibels. Despite all this, the car met two of my basic needs: The engine started when the key was turned, and it lurched forward when the accelerator was pressed. I bought the car.

More important than the car purchase was the friendship I struck up with the La Bamba's seller, Bob Wyatt. It turned out we were the same age, classmates at Chabot, and shared a love of history, government, and politics. In no time, we became inseparable friends. Bob helped me land a job with him as a cook at Livermore's Straw Hat Pizza. We went to school during the day and worked nights making pizzas for about $2.75 an hour. It wasn't much money, but it paid for schoolbooks and supplies, gas money for the La Bamba, and dates. Bob was the "oven man," meaning he stood at the 525-degree ovens with a shovel on a long handle, spinning and moving the baking pizzas to keep them from burning. I worked both the cash register and the oven alongside Bob. You could tell the oven men from the rest of the crew: We were the guys with vertical scars striping across our right forearms (the result of accidentally brushing one's flesh against the red-hot oven door while spinning pies). College-aged women made up more than half our crew; when we burned our arms on the oven door, they usually fussed and babied us. A couple of times I tattooed my arm on purpose just so Debbie or Sylvianne could nurse my injury with their own version of health care in the dimly lit storage room. If a few pizzas burned in the meantime, so what?

I went to school full time, and then worked twenty-five- to thirty-hour shifts each week. The schedule was challenging, but the fun we had went beyond merely romancing our female coworkers and customers. Bob and I often worked a weekend "close" shift until 1 A.M. When our pal and coworker Bret Muncy got off at midnight, we squirreled him away in the attic. Later, when the restaurant closed, Bob and I cleaned and locked up with night manager Phil Nuccio. Bob and I then drove around the block, waited until Phil was out of sight, and returned to Straw Hat. Meanwhile, Bret climbed down from the attic, disabled the alarm system, and unlocked the back door. At a prearranged time most of the guys on our crew returned for an all-night poker, pizza, and beer party. Since Bret was the smallest, we stuffed him through the refrigerator window and into the "cold room," where he opened all the kegger taps. We fired up the pizza ovens and cooked customized hot pies all night while running two poker games. The only thing interrupting the bash was the security guard driving by on his scheduled rounds: When he shined his flashlight inside, we grabbed the beer pitchers and took cover under the tables until he left. On one occasion, the day manager opened the restaurant at daybreak and found most of the crew groggily playing cards or sleeping in the booths. Scores of dirty mugs and pizza pans littered the place. We ignored his flustered retribution rantings, and reminded him he couldn't fire everyone and open for business that day. The manager's face melted into an expression of surrender; he pulled up a chair, and we dealt him into the game.

Straw Hat's "union shop" status meant more to me than the marginal increase we enjoyed over minimum wage (we earned about 20 cents more, though union dues ate up most of the difference). As a boy, I listened raptly to Grandpa's yarns of club-wielding strikebreakers battering his fellow blue-collar union soldiers in stories of courage, grit, and brotherhood. Mindful of this legacy, I carried my union membership card with pride. As a gung-ho union man, I studied our contract and monitored employer compliance with our bargained-for rights. When I discovered our contract allowed us a shop steward (something we never had), the employees chose me to fill the position. I accepted with unbridled eagerness, hoping to strike blows against unfair management practices on behalf of my laboring brothers and sisters. The union, however, ignored my enthusiasm: Our representative visited us only when an employee fell delinquent in dues. As I soon learned, romanticizing the value of union membership only led to harsh disappointment.

Soon after I became steward, our contract neared expiration. Our union representative was a motivating speaker who showed great indignation over our grievances against Straw Hat's corporation. I had a list of objections, like the time a supervisor (eager to save money by avoiding a plumber) told me to shove my arm down the toilet and unplug the big turd some customer dumped there; when I told him to kiss my ass, he wrote me up for refusing to obey orders. If someone dropped a pizza or sandwich on the floor, another cost-conscious supervisor wanted us to pick it up, brush it off, and serve it. We were told to keep quiet about the broken warmer that kept the spaghetti meat sauce at the wrong temperature, giving everyone who ate from it diarrhea. The union rep promised many changes and new benefits in our next contract, and if management balked, he pledged that our union would back a strike. He passed out to us a draft contract with clauses calling for higher wages, better hours, safer working conditions, and respect for seniority. He vowed that the union never would yield on these core principles, and no greedy, bottom-line-focused corporation could bully us. We cheered his boldness; surely, the modest increase in union dues which he demanded was worth his zeal. The only dark moment during our rally came when one of our crew said he had a family and couldn't afford to strike, suggesting he might cross a picket line. The rep glanced over at a big goon with him, who banged his fist on a table and sneered, "Scabs who cross picket lines might find their windshields smashed or their fingers broken." I jumped down the goon's throat for making a threat: My job was to look out for

the whole crew, not just those who agreed with our pro-strike sentiments. The rep stepped between us, chuckling to ignore his friend's
"sense of humor." Other than that tense blip, his resolve impressed us. I
trusted him, even after he pulled me aside before leaving and whispered,
"Of course, we may have to surrender a minor point or two during the
actual negotiations."

A couple of weeks later, as the contract expiration approached, the
rep grew irritated with my repeated requests to attend the contract talks.
Only when I said I'd be there with or without his blessing did he agree. I
met him and a Straw Hat corporate attorney at a local Italian restaurant.
After a friendly lunch, they got down to business, which took no time at
all. I sat stunned watching the rep present our demands one by one;
Straw Hat's lawyer rejected each summarily, and the rep rolled over on
every point—except the union dues increase. The union promised to get
us a 50-cent raise; over a few bites of sourdough they now reduced that
pledge to a mere nickel increase. Straw Hat's lawyer gave one major concession: greater union leeway to remove employees who didn't pay their
union dues. They shook hands; the rep then turned to me with a big
smile and said, "Well Jim, it looks pretty good, huh!" Now it was my
turn to uncork: I pulled him aside and called him a worthless sack of
shit for selling us out with a sweetheart deal between union and management: "I guarantee my crew will strike and shut down the restaurant,
and we'll do it without you union bastards if we have to." The rep grew
furious; he told me "troublemakers" find they have no friends in either
camp, and I had better wind up being "helpful" to settling the contract if
I valued my job. I stormed out of the meeting, drove to Bob Wyatt's
house, and told him about the startling betrayal I just witnessed.

Bob and I knew my claim of broad support for a strike was all bluff.
Actually, a big chunk of our crew would never stand up to management.
Still, we managed to hold the shaky line for a month, forcing additional
negotiations while trying to maintain a base of strained support among
the crew. Only Bob Wyatt, Bret Muncy, and a few other stalwarts remained solid with me. When the day for the contract vote arrived, we
were in trouble. It looked like the union and corporation had peeled off

enough employees to prevail. I worked a couple of fence sitters feverishly to line them up; walking into the meeting, my whip count showed we'd win by one vote. As the union and management together made their case for acceptance, I saw Bob was missing. Bret slipped away and called his house, and then returned with the bad news: "Bob's *really* sick and home in bed. He says he's got a 105-degree fever, he's puking his guts up, and can barely walk, let alone drive." I rushed to the phone and got my vomiting soldier on the line: "Listen, Bobby, we need you *now*," I pleaded. "This thing wins if you show; if you don't, we're screwed." There was an undecipherable response on the other end, and then the line went dead. When I called back, the phone rang with no pickup.

Bret asked if Bob was on his way. "He'll be here," I promised, making one of my greatest leaps of faith. If word got out that we lost Bob's vote, our fragile line would collapse in a heartbeat. When my turn to speak came, I filibustered to give Bob time to get there. As I lashed out at the contract provisions and the negotiation process, the union and the corporate managers fumed. I recounted the dirty deal I'd witnessed at the Italian restaurant, and I accused our union of being a rat's nest of sellouts and cheats. I kept one eye on the restaurant door throughout my speech, which ended when a manager told me my time was up. It was time to vote, and Bob wasn't there.

In alphabetical order, a union teller called the roll on whether to accept the union-drafted contract. My whip count proved accurate: Our crew split down the middle on whether to accept or reject. As we neared the end of the roll, like a cavalry scene in a western, the restaurant door flung open. Bob trudged in, semi-comatose, as the teller called his name to vote. His was the final name on the roll, and he cast the deciding vote to reject the contract. "Boy, am I glad to see you!" I said, "But I think you forgot something." Bob staggered over to look at his half-naked self in a nearby wall mirror. In his rush to get here, he had forgotten to put on clothes. He only wore pajama bottoms!

Bob's vote forced the union and management to return to the bargaining table; a few weeks later, we had a decent contract with a pay increase to $3.10 an hour. Although we won the battle, we lost the war. A confidential corporate memo leaked to me suggested that both management and the union wanted me fired, but they had to defer any retaliation until it wouldn't look like an unfair labor practice complaint. Meanwhile, Straw Hat fired Bob shortly after the vote for missing a day of work, even though he was in the hospital and under a doctor's care on the day of his illness. The union refused to support his grievance. I stayed at Straw Hat for a few more months before quitting and going to work at a rival pizza parlor. Once they told me they were a non-union shop, I took the job—and I never had any employment problems there.

A year later, when I went to a Labor Day picnic at the Alameda County Fairgrounds, my old union had a fund-raising booth: They sold tickets to throw softballs at a dunk tank. I saw my former union rep, dry and smiling, climbing onto the collapsible seat in the tank. I gave a $5 bill to a husky Little Leaguer who assured me he had a good pitching arm.

I turned and walked away. A few moments later, with my back to the tank, I heard a big splash, and then a familiar voice growled, "Goddamn it!" Smiling, I kept walking without looking back.

When I left Pinole, I left behind a self-destructive lifestyle and attitude. What I didn't leave behind was my old friend Frank. Tricking him into enlisting in the military didn't mean I wanted to be rid of Frank; I just wanted to entrust his care and feeding to the U.S. Navy for a couple of years. By now Frank's hitch was over; he earned an honorable discharge, itself quite a feat considering he once slugged a prissy, newly minted Naval Academy second lieutenant. Like the proverbial bad penny, Frank was back on my doorstep with no place to live or work.

To help Frank get on his feet, Bob and I got him a job with us as a bartender while we were still at Straw Hat Pizza. Frank didn't last long: His inflated sense of street pride always got him in trouble. He refused to wear part of the required uniform, a geeky straw hat, because it interfered with his Afro hairdo, which blossomed to mushroom-cloud proportions. While working, he quenched his thirst freely—and for free—at the beer taps. Frank also resented female authority, so when Sue (our domineering and disliked assistant manager) screamed at Frank for his repeated insolence, he leered at her breasts and told her, "You know what, honey, bitchy women like you make me hot. I bet you'd kick some ass in the sack." By the time Sue fired Frank for his serial rule breaking, he enjoyed near-cult status among the crew.

Frank's never-ending, stubborn code of manly honor, coupled with his equally stubborn irresponsibility streak, made him both maddening and hilarious. In Frank's pride universe, there was no room for faint-hearted men. He'd go to any length to prove his toughness, which often made him a ripe target for practical jokes, even macabre ones. In 1978, Bob's father (Big Bob) died. It was a devastating blow, and it placed head-of-household responsibilities for a large family on Bob's shoulders. A few hours before Big Bob's wake, I went with Bob to the mortuary to make sure everything was in order. Bob carried a brown grocery bag as we entered the viewing room. Big Bob's closed casket sat at the other end. Bob asked the funeral director to leave us alone for some private time. The mortician quietly backed out of the room, closing the doors behind him.

Big Bob once read that some morticians didn't bother dressing cadavers with below-the-waist clothes that can't be seen in a half-open casket; he said that when he died, he should be buried with his underwear, socks, shoes, and personal belongings. When Bob gave the mortician his dad's clothes for burial, they included his Fruit of the Looms and Beatle boots. Fearing theft, Bob kept his dad's personal treasures until now, which he carried in the grocery bag. We opened the creaky casket lid: There was Big Bob, wearing a 1970s lime green, belted-in-the-back polyester leisure suit. Bob ignored my plea not to send his dad through eternity wearing a lime green leisure suit; he said his dad liked it, and it was too late for wardrobe changes. Besides, Bob's focus now wasn't on style: He wanted to fulfill his father's desire to be buried fully dressed. "I need you to check for me," Bob said.

"Check what?"

"Come on, buddy," Bob pleaded. "This was important to Dad. I need you to check for me."

Now it's true that I loved Big Bob, but I loved him in life; I wasn't too keen about getting intimate with him in death. At first, I recoiled at touching his dead body, but Bob's pleading left me no choice. I closed and latched the casket lid, and then reopened it so the entire lid (instead of just the upper half) rose. Yes, I told Bob, the shoes were there.

"What about his socks?"

I reached for Big Bob's trouser legs. Jumping back in fright when I got an electric "carpet shock" after touching the polyester slacks, I slowly pulled up his pant leg until a glint of sock was visible. "Socks are okay," I reported.

"Now the underwear."

"Come on Bobby! If they put on his socks and shoes, they probably put on his *choners*, too!"

"We need to be sure," Bob solemnly replied. When I asked Bob who were the "*we*" he envisioned for this underwear expedition, Bob told me he already had a job: He needed to hold the brown grocery bag with his dad's things.

Standing over lifeless Big Bob, my mind replayed those low-budget, horror movie scenes from the late show: The mourner looks down into the coffin; suddenly the dead guy's eyes pop open, he springs up and grabs the victim's throat. Now I half-expected that to be my fate as soon as I groped near Big Bob's crotch: As he strangled me for the violation, the last words I'd hear would be a ghostly "*D-o-nnn't touch my underwear.*"

"Bobby, can't we just assume . . . ?"

"Do it for Dad," he replied.

Trying to suppress the heebie-jeebies, I felt around Big Bob's hips for the seam of his briefs. When I felt it, I stepped back to mop my forehead: "Okay, his bun-huggers are on him." Bob then opened the brown bag and fished around inside. "My little sister Tracy made this ring for Dad and he always wore it," Bob said as he handed it to me. "It goes on his left pinkie." Although this request wasn't as invasive as the underwear hunt, it required that I touch Big Bob's flesh, which up to now I'd avoided. I tried sliding the ring on Big Bob's finger, but I couldn't get it over his bent and frozen knuckle. When I tried to straighten it, an unmistakable sound came from within the casket: *Crack!*

"You just broke Dad's finger!" Bob yelled at me. Under the circumstances, I asked Bob to overlook the misstep and move on to the next item. To put Big Bob's wallet and comb in his left rear pocket, I had to slide my arms underneath and roll him like a log on his side; I felt the eerie cold of his body through his clothing.

Although I felt goosey at first about touching a corpse, by the time I finished my duties, I was over the discomfort, which came in handy for my Frank prank the next day. Bob asked Frank and me to go to the chapel ahead of everyone and make sure things looked right before the funeral service. In the sanctuary, Frank and I found floral arrangements with Big Bob's name on them surrounding someone else's coffin. It was a "pauper's casket," the kind used for "John Doe" county burials when no relative claimed the body. It was the cheapest casket available: rectangle pine planks nailed together, with sheets of blue felt cloth stapled to the outside. I asked a custodian why the wrong casket was here. Not to worry, he said. The cemetery workers left the John Doe while they took off for a smoke. He assured me the casket and its contents would be gone before the Wyatt party arrived.

While Frank and I waited alone in the sanctuary, he complained that being in the room with a dead body gave him the creeps. Superstitious about such things, Frank started pacing nervously. Now that I was desensitized to corpses, I decided to have a little fun at Frank's expense, and got the ball rolling by playing on Frank's well-earned pride of being a naval veteran. "Hey, Frank, take a closer look at that casket—it's a U.S. Navy casket."

"How do you know?" Frank asked.

"Because it's covered in blue to symbolize the ocean. If it were for an Army guy, they'd cover it in green. Whoever's in there is a Navy veteran, just like you. Let's go open it and make sure the funeral people did a good job for him." Frank wanted no part of that suggestion, so I challenged his nerve. Ginning him up, he agreed to stand next to me as I lifted the lid. Inside was a disheveled Asian corpse who didn't look like much thought had been given to his final appearance. "Okay, we looked. Now close the lid," Frank demanded.

Suddenly, I feigned shock: "I can't believe it! Frank, look: They put this poor bastard in the casket the wrong way! His head is where his feet should be, and his feet are where his head should be. We need to pick him up and turn him around. We can't let a Navy man get buried backward." Of course, there was no top or bottom to the rectangle box, but that point was lost on my tense friend. "You want me to do what? Are you fuckin' crazy?" Frank stammered. "I ain't pickin' up no dead guy and turning him around."

We'd been friends far too long: Frank knew if he failed to step to the plate and help me, I'd tease him as a coward for the rest of his life. Cursing a blue streak, Frank stormed to the head of the casket while I gave directions: "You lift him by his shoulders, and I'll lift his feet. Then we'll walk him around and put his feet where his head is, and vice versa." I tried not to laugh as Frank's face contorted with revulsion when lifting the corpse from his end. I grabbed the feet, and we circled around with the cordwood-stiff body. Suddenly, Frank heard a noise; panicked, he flung the body back into the casket. It landed on its side and balanced there for a second or two, and then it rolled over face down. Frank slammed down the casket lid and ran to a nearby pew. Cemetery workers came in, loaded the casket onto a cart, and took it away.

Frank trembled as he snarled at me: "*Let's pick him up and turn him around . . .* you asshole! That was a close call!" Now I administered the *coup de grace* to Frank's superstitions with this made-up factoid: "Close call? Frank, do you know what you've done? Didn't you notice that guy was Chinese? I learned about it in my comparative religions class. In the Chinese culture, you bury a dead guy face down when you want his spirit to keep watch over you. If those workers bury that guy face down, you'd better be ready for his ghost to follow you around for the rest of your life!" Frank's eyes bugged open wide, and then he bolted out the door trying to make sure he didn't spend eternity haunted by the spirit of some pissed-off dead Chinese.

Too late.

• • •

I loaded my schedule each quarter with every political science course offered. The entire poli sci department consisted of one teacher, Esther Goldberg, who also comprised half of the economics department. During my two years at Chabot, I was always in one or more of her classes. Now I not only read and learned more about politics, I had a great teacher challenging me intellectually. I couldn't wait for her class to begin each day. I think Mrs. Goldberg viewed me as a star pupil, but her personal fondness for me never meant she cut me any slack academically. She once gave a lesser student with a lower test score a better grade than me; when I griped, she said she held me to a higher standard. Although still grumbling when I left her office, I took it as a great compliment. Mrs. Goldberg demanded my best, and no amount of schmoozing on my part could undo her expectation.

As community college graduation day approached, I learned that I had been accepted to the nearby University of California at Berkeley. As long as I passed all my finals at Chabot, I would begin my junior year at Cal in the fall of 1977.

The La Bamba, that battered old Pontiac I bought from Bob for $250 when first I moved to Livermore, served me well. Aside from its being the reason Bob and I met, it also got me to work and school every day for the two years I attended Chabot. Since it was such a clunker, I never spent money on preventive maintenance. I oiled it when the dashboard "low oil" warning light illuminated; I replaced the bald tires when one of them blew, and then with retreads. Still, I attached sentimental value to the jalopy. When the day came for our final Chabot exam, I called Bob and suggested we ride to class in the La Bamba together for old times' sake. Bob hesitated, knowing the car was on its last legs. He didn't want to risk missing the crucial test. "Come on, Bobby!" I coaxed him. "The La Bamba's our lucky car! It'll make it! Trust me!"

Bob agreed reluctantly, and I drove to his house and picked him up. On the way, the engine broke free from a cracked motor mount, and it jumped and banged so hard under the hood that it dented the metal body. We ignored the clanging noise and set off on our rickety drive to Chabot. A few minutes later, just as we approached the freeway exit for the college, thick plumes of black smoke billowed from under the hood.

Flicks of red could be made out in the sudden darkness. "The engine's on fire!" Bob yelled at me. "Pull over!"

"No way," I replied. "I said this car's gonna make it, and it will." Bug-eyed but daring, Bob yelled out his frantic approval: "You crazy bastard! Let's go! Gun it!" I floored the accelerator; the glass packs screamed as we raced down the final mile-long straightaway of Airport Boulevard. Huge flames now jetted from the hood; the ominous sound of melting, buckling metal echoed through the passenger compartment. As the La Bamba raced down the road, we left behind a smoke trail resembling a NASA launch. Car passengers heading in the opposite direction stared in disbelief at the two guys rocketing past at breakneck speed and screaming out the windows, "Ohhhhhhh, shhhhhhit!!!" from a car on fire. I never braked until we turned the corner into Chabot's parking lot, when I shouted for Bob to bail out. We flung open the car doors and jumped out of the still moving Pontiac. The La Bamba rolled up the incline and into the field, where it came to rest. Soon flames engulfed the entire car. Curious spectators began streaming out of class to watch the inferno as Bob and I dropped back into the crowd anonymously.

"I told you the La Bamba would get us here!" I whispered and slapped him on the back. "It's our lucky car!"

"Hey," a campus custodian called to me, "whose car is that? Or should I say, whose car *was* that?"

"It looks abandoned to me," I replied.

"So what happened to it?"

"Sorry," I told him, "I can't stay and chat. I have to go take a final."

9

THE PARTY OF
THE LITTLE GUY

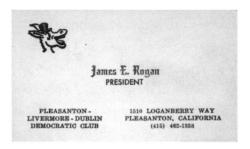

James E. Rogan
PRESIDENT

PLEASANTON -
LIVERMORE - DUBLIN
DEMOCRATIC CLUB

1510 LOGANBERRY WAY
PLEASANTON, CALIFORNIA
(415) 462-1358

The commute from Livermore to the University of California at Berkeley was laborious: It took about two hours each way by bus and train. Unlike Chabot, where I attended every day, the scheduled classes at Cal for my political science major occurred two or three days a week. At their conclusion, I would hustle back to Livermore so as not to be late for work. Between commuting, working, and a disjointed school schedule, I never felt part of campus life at Cal. Not that it mattered much: I didn't quite fit into the Berkeley social structure anyway.

Coming from a union household in 1960s San Francisco, I always believed the party line: Democrats looked out for the little guy; Republicans took care of the country clubbers and profiteers. That's why I became a Democrat: Everybody I knew was the little guy, and I wanted to be part of the team that looked out for them. Although my switch to the GOP was years away, early hairline fractures in my simplistic analysis of the political parties started showing about this time.

Just as my experience at Straw Hat soured my previously unshakable pro-union theology, I chafed under Cal's brand of liberal orthodoxy. Like most young people of that era, I saw the long-concluded Vietnam War as a quagmire. Unlike many of its protesters, I came from a pro-military, Uncle Jack–revering family—and I retained those values. I thought our mistake in Vietnam was that we ignored General Douglas MacArthur's sensible prescription for war: "There is no substitute for victory." I agreed with Uncle Jack, who fought in a world war, Korea, and Vietnam: American soldiers should "go in, kick the shit out of the enemy, and come home alive." U.S. troops shouldn't be deployed in combat unless they're sent in to win. With Berkeley's open hostility to *anything* military, my pro-military bent alienated me from the politically correct line. When I once mentioned in class that I tried to enlist post-Vietnam, classmates hissed me. While student protesters clamored to have ROTC booted off campus, I enrolled as a civilian in a few ROTC military history and military science classes as a show of support, and because of genuine academic interest. My contemporaries thought this all freakish: They questioned my liberal credentials, and I questioned their sense.

When it came to raw militancy, my classmates were mere pikers compared to some on the faculty. One kept a framed picture of Karl Marx in his office; another hung posters lionizing Angela Davis and the Oakland Black Panthers. In lecture halls, professors treated students to the wonders of the Soviet command economy, the genius of the welfare state, and the patriotism of Alger Hiss. Classroom analysis of Republicans tended to be more cartoonish than analytical: Gerald Ford? Dumb. Nixon? Crooked. Goldwater? Nutty. Reagan? Nuttier. Dead Republican presidents fared no better: Taft? Too fat. Coolidge? Too silent. Harding? Too horny. All of this sounded a bit off-kilter, but since the faculty was mostly liberal and (presumably) Democrat, to me it still meant their hearts were with the little guy. That made it easier to overlook their academic bias.

Having volunteered on every local, state, and national campaign since first getting interested, I was becoming a seasoned Democratic politico. Now I saw a chance to graduate from ringing doorbells and stuffing envelopes to the next level. It came in 1976, when the Democratic Party held caucuses around the country to elect delegates to their national convention. Former Georgia Governor Jimmy Carter headed up the list of Democratic presidential candidates; I was pulling for my old warhorse,

Hubert Humphrey. After three failed presidential bids, Humphrey announced he'd accept a draft, but he wouldn't campaign in any primary. I saw a belated chance to help Humphrey when my governor, Edmund G. Brown, Jr., made a last-minute entry into the race. I filed to run as a Brown delegate, hoping his victory in the California primary would block Carter's nomination, and then throw open the door to a Humphrey draft.

Party activists were to elect delegation slates by congressional districts at local caucuses on April 11. I paid to have small "Rogan for delegate" cards printed in time for the election. My first campaign lasted for the duration of the caucus—about 90 minutes. It was a mixture of nervous embarrassment and Walter Mitty thrill to walk up to strangers, shake their hand, pass out a card, and ask them to vote for me. Here I delivered my first campaign speech. Though scared to death as I walked to the stage, in a show of bravura, I declined the use of both microphone and podium and projected my voice to the rear of the room. Despite my painful shyness, I discovered I could speak forcefully and directly, and that I liked doing it without hiding behind a script or an obstruction. The crowd appreciated my youthful moxie: I lost the race, but I was the only speaker in a slew of them to get a standing ovation. All those spoken word record albums Aunt Della bought for me must have rubbed off just a bit.

Next, I joined the Livermore Democratic Club; it disbanded after one or two meetings. The following year local Democrats in the surrounding communities regrouped as the Pleasanton–Livermore–Dublin ("PLD") Democratic Club. Its president, lawyer Alan Grossman, ran the show with his law partner, Dave Harris. The PLD Club was the most fractious group imaginable, with its members feuding endlessly. Grossman's great antagonist was "CARD" (Committee Against Redevelopment), a group of anti-growth retirees led by Birdie Bianchi, an egg-shaped woman who resembled "The Penguin," Batman's wicked nemesis, in both appearance and temperament. A professional complainer, Birdie loathed Grossman and did everything she could to make his tenure as club president miserable.

Despite its quarrelsome reputation, I joined the PLD Club hoping to find a way to get more involved locally. I attended my first club meeting at the Pleasanton Hotel in January 1978. That night, Grossman bickered with Birdie through the entire session, using rulings provided by the parliamentarian (his partner Harris) to try to silence her. Birdie refused to relinquish the floor, shouting over Grossman and Harris, who shouted back. It was like watching a bad vaudeville act. At meeting's end, Grossman announced that the club would elect new officers next month, and that he'd seek reelection; also running was Mike Soffa, a schmoozing salesman and self-proclaimed future mayor. Birdie declared her candidacy in a bitter speech directed at Grossman, who jumped into a tit-for-tat with her. After listening to these shenanigans all night, I left the club, vowing never to return.

The next evening Birdie made a surprise phone call to me. As part of the nominating committee, Birdie said her job was to recruit candidates for club offices. "Some of us want to see you run for something," she said. I laughed and reminded her that I joined the club just last night; I didn't know a soul there, and didn't even plan to remain a member. What could I possibly run for?

"President," she replied.

The suggestion was ludicrous, but Birdie countered that the club needed a fresh face: "Grossman is unpopular, nobody likes Soffa, and I'm unelectable, but I control the CARD vote," she insisted. "I can throw the CARD votes to you, and with the uncommitted votes split between you and Soffa, you could win." Then she raised her voice: "The bottom line is I hate Grossman, and I don't want him back for another term!"

I joined the PLD Club to get involved; I didn't like what I saw at the meeting, and I was young and brash enough to think I could do better. The only thing crazier than her suggestion was the ease with which I accepted. After I hung up, my longtime college girlfriend Terri Lemke asked me about the phone call. "Well," I replied, "I decided that if I'm going to get started in local Democratic politics, I'm going to start at the top."

Grossman and Soffa rightfully thought my candidacy a joke. Why wouldn't they? Nobody knew me; I was a community college kid who cooked pizzas for a living. Though I lacked experience, I had enthusiasm. Forming a one-man campaign committee, I went to the local stationery store, bought a stencil, and fashioned a homemade letterhead. Then I typed out a message to the club membership with a brief biography, an outline of my Democratic involvement, and urged them to help me re-form the club:

> "I believe there are enough members who want a president to en-courage, not discourage, debate. The function of the president should be to preside over discussion, not to dictate it. I know there are many members who are dissatisfied with the perfor-mance of some of our club officers—and there are enough of them to send a real shock through some complacent candidates' premature expectations of victory. If you have felt 'abandoned' by your club's leadership, then join me."

I addressed a hundred copies of the letter to the club membership roster Birdie had given me, slid into the envelope a snapshot of Hubert Humphrey with me (to show my Democratic bona fides), and timed the mail delivery for the day of the vote.

Surprisingly, when my letter hit, the party establishment overreacted to my amateur effort. By noon on the day of the election, an aide to my Democratic state assemblyman (and my one-time junior college instructor) Floyd Mori banged on my door. "Assemblyman Mori asked me to come to your house and get your telephone number," she gasped. "He wants to call you from Sacramento *immediately.*" A few minutes later, Mori was on the line, saying he supported Grossman and demanded to know if I was a "free man" or "an agent of that CARD group." His questions and tone allowed me to read between the lines: Mori would be embarrassed if some young upstart beat his handpicked choice to lead the local Democratic club. Mori told me the club takes direction from Sacramento, and that Mori would decide who remained in the race. Wanting to play kingmaker, I think Mori sought my nod to his authority. He didn't get it: "I'm not an agent of CARD," I told him, "or anyone else."

"Well, I heard from Grossman that you're a tool of Birdie Bianchi," Mori shot back. I reiterated that I was my own man, and then proved it by thanking him for the call and for my Econ 101 grade in 1975, and then said goodbye.

A few minutes later there was another knock on my door: This time it was Grossman's partner, Dave Harris, who got down to business: Would I withdraw from the race in exchange for a committee appointment? When I rejected that, he hinted that Grossman might support me if I made "certain concessions." Again, I turned him down without asking what concessions he had in mind. Harris left only after I agreed to meet with him and Grossman in their office before tonight's vote. What a fuss my letter had created! Lawyers and a state legislator fretted, at least for the next eight hours, that Straw Hat's oven man threatened their power base. I loved it.

That night, just before the club convened, I arrived at Grossman's office and found him with Harris and Soffa. Grossman said he might withdraw and support me if I made unspecified concessions. Soffa objected, but my refusal to deal made the objection moot. As I got up to leave, Floyd Mori called from Sacramento and directed Grossman to withdraw and endorse me. Mori probably concluded Grossman would lose in a three-way race, and he'd have an easier time controlling this punk former student than the unpredictable Soffa.

The membership meeting began at 8:00 P.M. at the Pleasanton Hotel. Grossman opened it by announcing his withdrawal and endorsement of my candidacy. "We need some new young people to invigorate our club," he said. Jumping to his feet, Soffa complained that Grossman and I had summoned him to a secret meeting to concoct a "dirty deal." After Soffa had finished, I rose and recounted the day's events and how I rebuffed all attempts to sway me. When I finished, the audience applauded. Sensing a tide, Soffa threw an arm around my shoulder: "I'm with you, Jim," he exclaimed with a touch of insincerity. When the ballots were counted, I pulled off the upset and became the youngest Democratic Club president in California. The final vote was 0 for Birdie, 1 for Grossman, 9 for Soffa, and 39 for me. To me, this was more than my first political win: The election certified me as a party man in the party of the little guy.

Grossman announced the results, and then said, "I guess I'd better turn this whole thing over to our new president." He walked over and dumped an armful of file folders in my lap. "You're the new president," he said, "so go take over." I walked to the front of the room and took my seat in the president's chair. Before I could settle in, Harris began making parliamentary motions and raising multiple objections to confound the program and make me look incompetent, and he did a good job of it. I hadn't used *Robert's Rules of Order* since Mr. Lasley's eighth grade advanced government class. Now tag-teaming, Harris and Grossman outgunned me on point after technical point. Limping along, I tried to run the meeting in an orderly manner, but that collapsed when Grossman provoked Birdie and her group into a shrill debate. In the confusion, I saw Harris and Grossman exchange pleased glances over my predicament. Then a calm, sensible-sounding man rose and objected that the series of motions and the ensuing chaos were out of order; his motion to adjourn thankfully passed. My savior later introduced himself to me: Tim Baird, a member of the Alameda County Democratic Central Committee. Tim pledged his help during my term; in the coming months, I came to appreciate his friendship as much as I did his intervention that first night.

When the meeting ended, a laughing Harris slapped me on the back and asked me to join Grossman, Soffa, and him for a "victory drink" at the bar. "Oh, yeah," Harris chortled, "I forgot—you're not old enough to join the men at the bar!" The three of them laughed as they walked away. Later, I saw them standing near the bar recounting how they made a monkey out of me. Unaware I was within earshot, I heard one of them tell a Mori staffer, "Tell Floyd not to worry: We'll keep this kid in line!" They still were cackling when I left the hotel.

For the next month, I spent every spare minute boning up on parliamentary procedure and studying the files Grossman delivered to me unceremoniously. At the next club meeting, I was prepared for mischief. When it began, I returned fire, handling their motions and objections with dispatch, and then purged Grossman's appointees from all committee assignments. Birdie Bianchi remained in my corner for about two minutes; once I took over, she shifted her gun sights from Grossman to me.

With both Grossman's and Birdie's respective factions stirring the pot, I needed allies, so I began a membership recruitment drive at the community college. With Tim Baird's helpful guidance, we saw a huge influx of new club members. In a couple of months, I controlled a majority of votes and was able to set the agenda. I started a club newsletter and a regular speakers' program, which brought to the monthly meetings elected officials and debates on pressing issues. The club sponsored dinners, fundraisers, and a Democratic campaign headquarters for the 1978 statewide elections. When Assemblyman Mori refused to contribute to the cost of our headquarters fund, I stunned regulars by ordering all his campaign signs and brochures removed until he ponied up his portion of the cost (which he later did).

Our attendance and membership rolls swelled; by the end of the year, the PLD Club was one of the largest Democratic clubs in the state. Grossman and Harris stopped attending meetings; unfortunately, the ever-caustic Birdie never missed one. Despite some early tensions with Assemblyman Mori, my hard work began paying off. My name circulated among the Alameda County Democrats as a "can-do" up-and-comer, which is what I hoped would happen. County party leaders assigned me to committees and local organizational efforts, and I dove into each task. I became Tim Baird's alternate on the Alameda County Democratic Central Committee, and U.S. Congressman Fortney "Pete" Stark appointed me as his alternate to the California Democratic State Party Convention. As a side note, twenty years later I served in Congress with Pete Stark. During the height of the Clinton impeachment trial, I sidled up to him on the House floor and asked if my impeachment role made me unpopular among his liberal Oakland Democratic base. After getting the expected answer, I asked if he was still a millionaire, as he'd been when first elected to Congress in 1972. Perplexed by the question, Pete asked why I wanted to know that. Handing him a copy of his 1978 letter appointing me his personal representative to the California Democratic Party, I smiled and replied, "I just wanted to know my blackmail parameters before I set my price to sell this back to you!"

At the 1978 State Democratic Convention in Sacramento, I was reunited with my old boyhood memorabilia-collecting pal Dan Swanson, with whom I now attended Cal. Danny also tracked alongside me politically: He was a member of his county Democratic Central Committee and a convention delegate. One night before dinner, my PLD friend Tim Baird invited Dan and me to join him for a cocktail. "I hear you're old enough to drink now!" Tim teased, reminding me of Dave Harris's election-night dig when I snatched the club presidency from his law partner while I was still underage. We found a cocktail lounge at a nearby hotel and went in to have a snort.

Seated across the bar from us were three beautiful women. All wore shimmering cocktail dresses adorning flawless figures. Soon they gazed in our direction with eyes projecting a glint of interest. They kept looking our way coyly while whispering to each other; one smiled at me. Thinking we might hit the jackpot, Tim (ten years our senior) called us into a huddle to devise a game plan. "Okay, we send over some drinks," he suggested, "then one of us goes over and invites them to join us. Maybe we can take them to dinner and a movie." I had hung around Frank in Pinole long enough to know that dinner and a movie wasn't the end game in a bar pickup, but what the hell—it was a start. We told our waitress to send the ladies a round of drinks; they accepted, raising their glasses in thanks: "You guys are cute!" one of them called out.

Tim and Dan elected me to make the approach. When I walked over and pulled up a chair at their table, Sheila smiled and introduced me to her friends. All three were charming and receptive. "What do you guys do?" she asked. I told her Tim was a fireman, and that Dan and I were pre-law college students. I hoped the "fireman and law school" angle would bolster our respectability and chances. The ladies were impressed, but stalled at accepting my encouragement to join us. "I guess we could do that," Sheila teased, "but after the drinks, what did you have in mind for later?" I suggested Tim and Dan's preapproved dinner and movie idea. Sheila looked at her friends, and then took my hand in hers. "Well, we'd love to date you tonight, but why don't we just skip the preliminaries? You see, college boy, we date for a living."

When I returned to our table, Danny's eyes filled with hopeful anticipation: "What did they say?" he asked.

"They said we're doing the movies alone tonight."

As the end of my year as club president approached, it appeared that my newly forged political reputation and alliances would be short lived. In May 1979, one month before my graduation from Cal, I received notification of my acceptance to the UCLA School of Law for the fall term. This meant I'd have to say goodbye to all my political contacts and relocate to Southern California. It meant starting all over.

It amazes me that I got into a "top ten" law school. I knew nothing about the admissions process, and didn't even know that the school one attended might make a career difference. I assumed it was the lawyer, and not the pedigree, that counted. My formula for choosing the schools to which I applied wasn't based on their Ivy League reputation. If the application fee was no more than $5 for an out-of-state school, and no more than $10 for an in-state school, I applied; if it cost any more, I didn't. Nor did I know one was supposed to prepare for the law school admissions test. I took no review course; I worked at my pizza job until 2 A.M. the night before the test, got up a few hours later, and groggily sat for the exam. Not surprisingly, my LSAT score was awful, but my grades at Chabot and Cal were decent, and I guess my life story intrigued someone at UCLA's admissions office. They decided to give me a chance.

Before graduation I dropped in on my friend, retired San Francisco Mayor Elmer E. Robinson, who served two terms in that office as a Republican before I was even born (1948 to 1956). Robinson was lonely and forgotten when I looked him up some years back and asked to come by and talk politics with him. The old man appreciated having a young devotee wanting to soak up his war stories, and I became a regular visitor.

Now he was enthusiastic about my pursuing a career in law, and spoke proudly of his sixty-four years of practice. When I went to say goodbye before leaving for UCLA in what turned out to be our last visit, his parting words of advice surprised me, especially considering our mutual San Francisco roots: "If you want to run for office down the road, don't come home to San Francisco. Get established in Los Angeles. All the money and political power are heading south, anyway. Besides, San Francisco has changed so much. It used to be the crown jewel city in my day, but now it's the moral garbage dump of the world."

Knowing of my political autograph and memorabilia collection, Robinson surprised me with a special gift: He took off the wall his prized photograph bearing the handwritten inscription "To Elmer E. Robinson, with best wishes, John F. Kennedy" and handed it to me. "President Kennedy signed this picture for me about two weeks before he was assassinated," Robinson said. "I want you to have it for your collection. Someday, when you're a congressman, hang it in your office, and when you look at it, remember me." True to my promise, that picture hung in my congressional office, and hangs in my office today. Each time I look at it, I recall yet another public servant I met who took the time to encourage a kid along the path.

In closing these recollections from my Berkeley years, I remember another kind man. One of my Cal professors was William "Sandy" Muir, a personal favorite of mine even though he (like Elmer Robinson) was a Republican. Professor Muir didn't know or remember me from school; I was one of two hundred students in a large lecture hall taking his course. I got a good grade in his class, and when I later applied for law school, he met with me when I wanted a letter of recommendation. After our interview, he came through with a gracious letter.

Almost twenty years later, when I became Majority Leader in the State Assembly, one of my staff said a Mr. Sandy Muir came by the office earlier in the day. He was running for the state assembly from Berkeley and wanted to know if I would consider giving him my endorsement; he had no clue I had once been his student. I called him on the telephone and explained my policy: I couldn't endorse anyone I didn't know without hearing where they stood on the multiple issues of the day, like tax cuts and abortion. He apologized for making a presumptuous request, saying he should have known better. I cut him off, saying I'd make an exception for him. "Feel free to use my endorsement any way you want," I said, "and I don't care how you stand on any of the issues." This caught him off guard; after thanking me, he asked why I'd do this for him.

"Because," I replied, "when I applied to law school and asked my professor, Sandy Muir, for a recommendation letter, he gave it to me without needing to know where I stood on tax cuts and abortion."

10

LOVING THE NIGHTLIFE

The nightlife ain't no good life, but it's my life.

—WILLIE NELSON

On June 17, 1979, I became the only member of my family to graduate from college, earning my bachelor's degree from Cal. There was no time to rest on my laurels, since this milestone marked only the midpoint on a much tougher journey. On graduation night, Bob Wyatt and I loaded all our belongings into a U-Haul. Bob joined me in the move to Los Angeles, where he would finish college while I attended law school. At the last minute we picked up another passenger for the trek: the ever-present Frank, who said he'd come on a temporary basis just to help us get our Southern California bearings. Bob was still naïve enough to believe that when Frank said "temporary" he meant it. Still, Frank brought some value to the expedition since he once lived briefly in L.A. A year earlier, Bob and I visited him and Rocky at their Southern California digs—a flophouse motel. They had no lock on their door, and their drug addict and biker neighbors wandered the parking lot all day and night seeking dope and booze. The boys slept in rickety single beds; Bob and I drew straws for the remaining sleeping accommodations—nothing more than a folding cot on one side of the room and a pile of dirty laundry on the other. Bob won the cot, but with victory came the responsibility of keeping the gym socks stuffed into the gaping wall holes used by a platoon of roaches.

With our rental truck packed, we hugged and kissed our families goodbye. It was midnight when the three of us pulled away into the darkness. We drove until noon the next day, when we reached the Summer Wind apartments at 19609 Sherman Way in Reseda (an L.A. suburb in the San Fernando Valley). We had no choice but to live in the valley, almost twenty miles from UCLA. The nearby campus rents of $1,200 a month (in 1979 dollars!) for a shabby studio apartment gave new meaning to the phrase "sticker shock." Home was now apartment #208, a two-bedroom unit that included a fireplace in the living room that blew heat from underneath the plastic logs while a rotating red light illuminated the artificial inferno. For our bachelor paradise we paid $325 a month split two ways (it should have been split three ways, but occupationally challenged Frank made up the third wheel).

We arrived in Southern California with no friends, no family, and no connections. After paying our first and last month's rent, we found ourselves broke and without job prospects. Our first priority was eating regularly. Luckily, the local McDonald's had a giveaway promotion: Customers received a card with two scratch-off trivia questions; if the customer guessed right on the first question, the prize was a Coke. He could redeem the Coke, or take a chance and scratch off the second question. If he guessed wrong on the second question, he forfeited the Coke; if correctly answered, the prize was a Big Mac, fries, and a large Coke. Seeing there was free food to be had, I shared our plight with a perky young cashier. She snuck me a whole bag of scratch-off cards, and got me handfuls more of them when our supply ran low. Bob, Frank, and I rationed the game cards: We each got two a day. Every few days we took a stack of the cards to the Reseda Public Library to research the answers. We adopted two rules: No matter how sure the guess, nobody scratched off an answer without getting written confirmation from a library reference book. Second, if anyone broke the first rule and got it wrong (voiding the card and wasting a free meal) the offender went without dinner that night. After missing a Big Mac or two, I wouldn't answer the question, "What is your name?" without first checking my birth certificate. During the summer of 1979, McDonald's and my cute cashier friend provided three hungry guys with high-fat manna from Heaven.

Bob and I combed the want ads looking for night jobs so that we could attend school during the day. One of the few occupations that fit this schedule was bartending, but neither of us knew how to mix drinks. We cured that by attending a one-week bartender's college, promising the owner we'd pay the tuition when we found employment. Once I nailed down the drink repertoire, I called or visited almost every nightclub, lounge, disco, hotel, corner bar, and tavern in the San Fernando Valley. I filled out job applications by the score, but soon I learned a diploma from bartender college wasn't worth the paper on which it was printed. Owners wanted experienced bartenders, not greenhorns. Since Bob and I couldn't remedy that hole in our resume legitimately, we cured it by lying. I told potential employers that I used to be the head bartender at a nightclub in San Francisco called Reflections, but they couldn't call there to verify it because the cops shut it down for being a bookie joint. However, if they wanted to speak to my ex-supervisor, Mr. Bob Wyatt, I would provide a number for them to call ("Jim Rogan? He was the best bartender we ever had."). Of course, Bob's Reflections reference was a Mr. James Rogan ("Bob Wyatt? Why, he was the best bartender . . .").

I got lucky one Saturday afternoon when I called Our Place, a small corner bar in nearby Northridge. Willie, the owner, said her bartender had just quit and she needed immediate help. "You can do the shift tonight; if it works out okay, then you're hired." This chance couldn't have come at a better time: Our McDonald's trivia card supply was getting thin, and my cashier girlfriend had gone back to college.

I showed up at Our Place shortly before my 6:00 P.M. shift began. An immediate problem presented itself when I met Willie and Vi, the two black women who co-owned the bar. Embarrassed, Willie apologized to me: "Honey, when I talked to you on the phone you had this touch of a drawl. You sounded, well, *black*. I guess I should have asked. You see, this is a bar with an all-black clientele. I just don't think this will work. I'm sorry to disappoint you." The hard-nosed Vi insisted that a white bartender would not do, so I made my appeal to Willie. "Listen," I pleaded, "you need a bartender, and I need a job. Why not give me a crack at it. I'll work free tonight. If it goes all right, then give me the job. If not, it didn't cost you anything, and it gets you off the hook for tonight." The two women huddled near the jukebox. I could hear Vi insisting it was a bad idea, but Willie had a gambler's heart and made the final decision: "We'll give it a try, but are you sure you'll be okay in here by yourself? Some of our clientele might not be very friendly to you." I assured her I'd get by on raw Irish charm. With great reluctance, Willie and Vi gave me the keys, wished me luck, and left me alone behind the bar.

Despite my enthusiasm, Willie and Vi were right. As soon as the weekend regulars started coming in, I got a cold reception from the male patrons. Snickers and wisecracks continued through the night as the music played and the drinks poured. I brushed them off with a smile or a joke. I needed this job badly and I couldn't afford to blow it.

One guy couldn't be charmed or ignored. "What the hell is wrong with Willie and Vi!" he kept grousing, saying he didn't like having whitey behind the bar. As the evening wore on, he kept drinking and complaining while the amused crowd egged him on. He peppered his hours-long monologue with racial epithets against me while I kept working and ignoring him. Then, after another shot of courage, he threatened me: "I think I'll come behind that bar and bitch-slap you," he said amid the laughter.

This was the last straw: It was time to shut down my first barroom asshole. I reached behind the sink for my walking stick—an ash cane with a solid brass knob anchored to withstand a 1,000-pound pull (a twenty-first birthday gift from Bob). I raised the cane over my head and slammed the brass knob down onto his cocktail resting atop the bar. Shards of flying glass and the loud report from the blow got his and everyone's attention. The startled customers jumped from the explosive noise and I leaned toward the troublemaker while brandishing my cane: "Listen to me, you son of a bitch. I've had enough out of you. You can sit down and shut your mouth, and I'll buy you another drink, or you can get the hell out."

I half expected a customer rebellion against me, but to my surprise, most of the patrons started telling the guy to do what I told him. Maybe they appreciated my boldness, or else they were as tired as I was of listening to his yap. It didn't matter: I tossed down the gauntlet before a mouthy guy who had been drinking and bragging all night, and he couldn't back down now. "I'll kick your ass!" he thundered, and then rained a cursing mouthful on me.

"You're 86'd," I told him. "Get out."

"Throw me out!" he replied. "You're pretty bad standing behind the bar with your fancy stick. Let's see what you got without that stick in my face!" The crowd watched silently as I tossed down the stick and went to eject him physically. As I rounded the bar, he reached into his pocket, pulled out a switchblade, and clicked it open. Pointing the blade at me, he growled, "Now I'm gonna cut you, motherfucker."

A few weeks earlier, the owner of the bartender college gave me this parting advice: "If you're going to work in L.A. bars, don't start until you buy a gun. I promise you'll need it." Here, on my very first night, I learned how prescient he was. Once I saw the knife, keeping a job was my priority no more. Showtime for this punk was over: I stepped back, reached inside my heavy brown Pendleton shirt that concealed a breakaway shoulder holster, and grabbed the butt of the snub-nose .38 special I bought for ninety bucks. I yanked out the gun, cocked the hammer, and raised the barrel to his head.

"Oh, my God! He's got a gun!" people started screaming. The guy with the knife dropped his weapon immediately and put up his hands, shrieking a combination of begging, crying, and cursing. I could make out random phrases only, like "Don't shoot me!" and "You're crazy!" People were yelling at him, at me, and each other. A sense of panic and confusion erupted.

"*Shut the fuck up—everybody!*" I hollered.

The room quieted as I paced toward the troublemaker with my gun still raised to his head; he kept retreating with his hands up until his back bowed across the top of the bar. Grinning so I'd look crazy (I learned from guys like John Cutlip and Frank that nobody wants to mess with a crazy man), but struggling inwardly to make sure my voice didn't crack and betray my fear, I spoke very slowly: "I gave you a choice a minute ago, and I'll give it to you again. You can sit down and shut your fuckin' mouth, and I'll buy you a drink. Or you can leave. But if you ever threaten me again, I'll blow your goddamn head off before you finish your sentence. What's it gonna be?"

There was a lengthy silence before he answered: "A C-C-Courvoisier and C-C-Coke. *Please.*" I picked up his knife from the floor and slid it into my pocket, went back behind the bar, and holstered my pistol. When I served the free drink, the guy's hands trembled so badly he spilled part of it; he downed the cocktail in one gulp, and then mumbled a polite goodbye.

Willie and Vi returned to the bar a few hours later, just before last call for drinks. The earlier trouble was ancient history. The owners returned to find their customers laughing and dancing to the jukebox. The liquor flowed; I lit cigarettes for the ladies and joked with the customers. Vi shook her head: "I guess I was wrong. I was sure there'd be trouble." There was no more trouble, racial or otherwise; in fact, the next day I convinced Willie and Vi to hire white Bob as their second bartender.

I liked bartending and discovered I had a knack for dishing out both drinks and banter. When I cranked up the jukebox on weekends the women argued playfully over who got to dance with me. It was a fun job; the hours fit my schedule, and there was plenty of action. More important, I honed my ability to "read" customers, learning to know by instinct why people came. Some wanted advice or a joke; some came to remember, others to forget. One might be seeking companionship, another solitude. I learned how to tell the difference, and that skill paid me dividends in every later occupation, from prosecutor talking to juries to congressman talking to constituents.

Working at Our Place gave me some needed experience, but the salary came to only $1.50 an hour or so and the tips turned out to be almost nonexistent. Customers offered to buy me drinks aplenty, but when a customer buys you a drink, you just end up drinking the tip. Since I bartended to earn money for school, and not to party, I almost always declined politely. A shot of whiskey doesn't go far in paying tuition. I hoped that the customer would leave a tip instead, but that exchange rarely occurred. Willie felt sorry for me: "I hate to tell you this, honey," she said. "My clientele will buy you drinks all night, but they're not good tippers." Since I needed to bank money so I wouldn't have to work full time during school, the job wasn't working out.

About this time, a guy who owned a bar across town told me he liked how I handled myself. "Why don't you work for me? I need a new bartender. My shack isn't much of a tipping bar either, but I'll double your salary." I broke the news to Willie, and we parted as friends. For a long time afterward, I returned to moonlight for her on nights when I was off and she was shorthanded.

I got the new bartending job at The Tarzana Inn, near the intersection of Reseda and Ventura Boulevards in the San Fernando Valley. On my first night, I learned why the owner needed bartenders so badly: They would all quit when they encountered the regulars. The owner neglected to mention before I started that the Tarzana Inn was a hangout for the local chapter of the Hell's Angels motorcycle gang. When their screaming bike engines roared into the parking lot, the rest of my customers fled.

On my first night, about an hour into the shift, a dozen or more raucous Angels arrived. I called the owner at home to tell him there might be trouble. "Throw them all out," he barked, "and then call back when you've done it." The day-shift bartender quickly gulped his nightcap and got up to leave; on his way out the door he asked me what the owner had said. When I told him my orders, he advised me to ignore them: "Do you know why he told you to do it, and he didn't volunteer to come down and help? It's because once *he* ordered them out. After they beat the shit out of him, they threw him on the ground and started bouncing the balls from the pool table off his head. He won't ever come down when the Angels are here."

I served the bikers their drink orders.

Since the Tarzana Inn operated as a one-man bar, that made me the only employee in the club each night. This made my shift more menacing: If trouble started, I had no backup. With the Hell's Angels, I concentrated on getting through the night in one piece, walking the fine line of treating them respectfully yet still doing my job. It got hairy every time I tried to explain why I couldn't serve alcohol to one of their underage runaway girlfriends with a fake ID. Serving a minor would cost me my job and earn me a possible prosecution; refusing service risked a brawl. I tried to avoid the latter, but a joke and a smile rarely assuaged some pride-stoked biker. Threatened many times, I started carrying a second gun in an ankle holster, along with the one in my shoulder holster. My pockets rattled with speed-loaders for both pistols, just in case. If ever I shot one of them, I knew I'd have to shoot them all: Their outlaw creed forbade ignoring an assault on a brother.

It was almost impossible to study while serving a swarm of bikers. Still, I tried gamely to read my casebooks under the bar whenever there was a lull in the drink orders. One night I was pouring drinks while trying to absorb my Civil Procedure text. A big ugly biker asked me what I was reading; I told him it was a law book. "What the fuck are you reading a fuckin' law book for, you fuckhead?" he asked. (I found bikers had a limited but universal vocabulary.)

"I'm in law school," I replied.

The biker next to him asked what I just said. My inquisitive customer shared what he learned about me, and that guy passed along the information to the next, who passed it to the next, and so on down the line. A while later, three Hells Angels followed me into the men's room; one threw me against a wall while another pulled a knife and held it to my throat. "So, we hear you're a fuckin' narc!" my assailant charged.

Somehow, through the Tarzana Inn version of the "telephone" parlor game, the bikers mutated the occupation of "law student" into "undercover narcotics cop" as they relayed my avocation down the bar. He put away his knife only after I took out my student ID card to prove my claim.

"Hey," one of them suggested optimistically, "maybe when you finish law school you can defend bikers in court!" I told him nothing would please me more than, one day, to see him and all his friends in court.

"Yeah, that'd be pretty fuckin' cool," he said with a nod.

As scary as these marauders acted, they paled in comparison to their molls. Some biker chicks were drop-dead gorgeous; others were a small step above the bestial. One night, two in the latter category entered dressed in black leather and chains. One woman (closing in on three hundred pounds) sat at the bar and shouted to me, "Hey, bartender, get your ass over here!" She demanded to know my name, and then told me hers: "I'm Faith," she said as she raised her upper lip toward her nose with her fingers, revealing a smattering of rotting teeth and a gum line bearing a homemade tattoo of her first name. "Listen," she said in a husky voice, "I know you bartenders get off work at 2:00, so that's when I'll be back to pick you up. You're coming home with me tonight."

Faith made it clear this wasn't a solicitation for sex: It was a command performance. When I treated it like a joke, she grew angry and smashed a beer bottle on the floor. That got my attention: This two-ton bitch looked like she could mop the floor with me if riled. "Don't get me wrong, Faith. You're, uh, *very* attractive, and your offer is tempting, but I can't—you see, I'm, uh—I'm married." That one sentence contained no less than three separate lies.

"So what?" she blustered. "Hey, I got an old lady, too." With that Faith pointed to her fat lesbian girlfriend seated at a corner table, smiling at me through another mouthful of patina-green teeth. "You're coming home with me, or I'm gonna have your skinny ass killed. Take your pick. I'll be waiting for you later tonight outside in the parking lot." With that pledge, Faith and her companions left.

Given a choice, I preferred the throes of death to the arms of Faith. Hoping to avoid both, and not knowing what else to do, as my shift neared its end I called the police and spoke with the desk sergeant. To describe him as unsympathetic would be an understatement: When I finished explaining my predicament, he laughed at me. "Let me get this straight," he said. "You're reporting that you want LAPD to protect you from some fat biker chick with her name tattooed on her gums that wants to take you home and screw you?" He put me on the speakerphone and asked me to repeat the story. As I began, I heard his fellow officers guffawing on the other end. I told him to forget it and hung up in frustration.

I closed the bar at 2:00 A.M. and locked the doors from the inside. I was afraid to walk to the parking lot, not knowing if Faith was out there waiting, and how many more Faiths she'd recruited for her proposed love fest. I spent the night curled up in a corner booth. When the morning bartender opened the tavern, I had him scout the parking lot to make sure it was Faithless. As I drove away at sunrise, I was grateful that Faith gave up hope on getting some coerced charity.

Another night I heard a loud commotion coming from the men's room. "He's in there raping that bitch!" one biker told his friend as he motioned with his head toward the noise. I rushed from behind the bar to investigate. Pushing open the bathroom door, I walked in and saw a pretty blonde on the filthy floor. Her jeans and panties were down below her knees; she cried and struggled underneath a large bearded hulk, who had her pinned down by the wrists. He never looked up until I shoved the barrel of a cocked .38 into his temple.

"Get off her. *Now.*"

Unbelievably, the woman started screaming—at me: "Don't shoot him, you asshole! *It's my father!* Get the hell out of here! Leave us alone! What's your fuckin' problem? Get out!" With my gun still drawn, I tried making sense of the macabre scene. The biker got off her slowly and raised his hands, pleading with me to stay calm; the woman jumped from the floor and pulled up her pants, still screaming for me to get out. Shaking my head in disbelief, I backed out of the restroom. A few minutes later, they emerged, still calling me names for pulling a gun and breaking up their toilet tryst. They collected their friends and left.

A week or so later I had a rare night with no customers in the bar. Toward midnight, a man and woman entered, ordered beers, and went to shoot a few games of pool. They looked like older bikers; they were quiet and kept to themselves. When the woman tired of the game, the guy asked me to shoot a couple of games with him. While we played, we talked about my law school efforts, and my continuing troubles from the Hell's Angels. "They won't bother you anymore," he said. "I'll take care of it."

With an air of cynicism, I asked my pool partner what he could do about it. He chugged on his beer bottle and then replied, "My name's Sonny Barger. I'm the founder of the Oakland chapter of the Hell's Angels. They'll listen to me."

For the rest of the time that I worked at the Tarzana Inn, no biker threatened me.

A lasting memory of the Tarzana Inn has nothing to do with bikers: It has to do with the disease of alcoholism. The owner asked me to work a morning shift to cover for a sick bartender, and told me to open the doors at 6:00 A.M., the legal hour for bars to serve in California. That morning I was only a minute or two late; to my amazement, there were a dozen middle-aged, professional-looking men and women outside banging on the door. Another left to call the owner from a pay phone to complain about the bar's not being open. When I unlocked the front door, the griping crowd made a beeline to the barstools. Their fury over my inconsequential tardiness baffled me. When one of them still complained long after I served his drinks, I asked him what was the big deal about being two minutes late.

"You don't understand, do you?" he snapped as he quickly polished off two straight double vodkas. "We're alcoholics. We *need* the stuff, understand? The next time you work mornings, don't you be even a second late."

My last night at the Tarzana Inn was like so many others: a cluster of Hell's Angels causing their usual ruckus. I poured drinks and in between tried to study, but it was so noisy that I didn't hear the first few rings of the telephone. It was the owner calling; he sounded drunk.

"Goddamn you," he slurred. "I just drove by and saw all those motorcycles outside. Get those Hell's Angels out of my lounge. You throw them out or you're fired." I told him I wasn't going to 86 a dozen bikers all by myself; if he wanted them bounced out, he needed to come down and help me do it.

"You're fired!" he screamed, and then hung up in my ear.

Picking up my walking stick, I rapped on the bar for silence. With everyone's attention, I announced, "Gentlemen, we're running the bar on the honor system tonight. The owner just fired me, so I'm leaving. Be sure you leave the correct amount of money in the till for any drinks you pour for yourself after I'm gone." I could hear the bikers laughing as I drove away.

I felt no great disappointment at being fired from the Tarzana Inn: That dump gave me nothing but trouble. Still, I had no time to enjoy my liberation. I was unemployed again, with the rent due in a few days. On Halloween Night 1979, I wandered into a Hollywood nightclub and talked my way into a bartending job. My new gig was at Filthy McNasty's, owned by German immigrant brothers Filthy and Wolfgang McNasty (they changed their given names legally). The brothers had two Mc-Nasty's nightclubs: one on the Sunset Strip, and another over the hill in North Hollywood on the corner of Victory and Lankershim. They hired me to work the North Hollywood club each night, and to cover the Strip on an as-needed basis.

Their bar on the Strip enjoyed quite a legacy. During its incarnation as the Melody Room in the 1940s, it was a favorite hangout for mobsters like Bugsy Siegel; in the 1960s, it was The London Fog, where Jim Morrison and The Doors made their debut; today, the old haunt is world renowned as The Viper Room, owned by actor Johnny Depp. Back in my day, there wasn't much to it: just a single-station bar and a small dance floor made smaller by the band's instruments. Filthy's North Hollywood club was much larger, with a bandstand and sizable dance floor, back-stage dressing rooms, pool tables, DJ booth, a room-length bar with two stations, and an attached building that housed upstairs apartments and a separate full cocktail lounge. The Sunset Strip bar was open to the public; North Hollywood operated as a private club, meaning only members could enter. Filthy's had pretty fluid standards for allowing people to get a membership card. Gorgeous women always got one for free; homely women paid a sliding-scale fee depending on subjective criteria, such as how much cleavage or leg showed. All men paid to join: If they looked normal, they paid $10 or $20, depending on the doorkeeper's mood. The doorman sent geeks and undesirables packing with a lengthy preprinted form: He told them not to come back until they filled it out, had it notarized, attached a passport photo, and paid a $100 nonrefundable application fee. When business boomed, higher standards for membership were enforced; when receipts were low, the benchmark relaxed considerably (i.e., membership cards went to almost anyone with a purse or wallet).

My first night at Filthy's was a revelation. As I set up the bar for my shift, I paid little notice to the waiters, all of whom wore tight black slacks and went about shirtless except for a black vest and black bow tie. When the doors opened, I was too busy making drinks to see that there were no waitresses or to focus on the clientele scattered throughout the hazy lounge. At 8:00 P.M. the floorshow began: A guitar-strumming emcee told dirty jokes and sang sexually explicit lyrics to an appreciative, hooting audience while I cranked out trays filled with cocktails at maximum speed. Then the DJ turned on taped bump-and-grind music. From behind the curtains danced a troupe of homosexual men dressed in Village People costumes, each of whom did a striptease down to their G-strings.

"Oh, shit," I muttered.

I walked over to Wolfgang, who manned the second bar station, and complained that he hadn't told me this was a gay bar when I took the job. I said I'd finish the shift, but I didn't want to be stuck working in some queer joint and fending off guys each night—that wasn't going to cut it. Wolfgang looked at me like I was nutty: "What are you talking about?" he snapped in his thick German accent. "Do these customers look queer to you?" For the first time I peered hard into the dim, smoky lounge. Except for the waiters, there wasn't a man in sight. Young, pretty, drinking, dancing, screaming women filled the club.

"This is Ladies' Night," Wolfgang said. "We have Ladies' Night every Monday through Saturday. From eight until midnight male exotic dancers do strip shows for the women. We don't let any men in the club until after midnight!" Wrapping his arm around my shoulder in a paternalistic way, Wolfgang continued: "Let me tell you how it works: All of these dancers, and most of these waiters, are fags. So the dancers get the women hot and the liquor gets them drunk. That means there's no competition for the bartenders."

"What kind of shows do you have on Sunday nights?" I asked.

"Oh, that's when we let in the men," Wolfgang said with a smile, "for our female mud wrestling night! And the female mud wrestlers love the bartenders because they know we protect them from the drunks who get out of line."

I returned to my station and went back to work—for over a year.

The McNasty brothers were a study in contrasts. They looked nothing alike: Filthy was tall, blond, and buffed from a rigorous weightlifting routine. Wolfgang was short, dark, and bearded. Filthy was the showman who entertained the customers both in personality and in fact. On nights when a hired band failed to show, Filthy climbed on stage with his all-girl band and performed the song he recorded years earlier (it still plays on underground FM radio stations): "You're Breakin' My Heart, You Tear It Apart, So Fuck You." Filthy cut quite a figure driving around Hollywood in his modified antique hearse or in a black stretch limousine, both of which bore vanity license plates bearing his name.

Wolfgang was quiet, sometimes brooding, and didn't view entertaining customers as part of his job description. Sometimes, if he had a few drinks, he'd get into an argument with the customers. To break it up, I'd drag my unhappy boss to the back room as he shouted that I was fired.

"Wolfy, I'm not fired. Go upstairs and go to bed."

"Don't you tell me to go to bed, you little bastard!" he'd growl. "You're fired! Get out of here!"

The second "you're fired" was my cue to tower over my boss with a jabbing finger in his chest and mock anger in my voice: "Wolfgang, I'm not fired. So go upstairs and go to bed, or I'll kick your ass, carry you upstairs, and put you to bed. And if I do that, I'll kick your ass so bad that tomorrow you won't remember firing me, and you also won't remember who kicked your ass." Wolfgang always went upstairs and to bed without any more fuss. Besides, I knew he and Filthy wouldn't fire me: A couple of times Wolfy emptied the cash registers' contents into a Seagram's Crown Royal felt bag, put it down somewhere carelessly, and walked away. I found it, brought it home for safekeeping, and then returned it intact the next morning. No matter how mad Filthy or Wolfgang got at me over something, they wouldn't can an employee who drank rarely, never took drugs, and didn't steal.

Although Wolfgang gave me more day-to-day headaches, I liked him tremendously. He was a tough and loyal friend with his own style behind the bar. One busy night I stood at his station when a waiter ordered a strawberry margarita, a strawberry daiquiri, and a strawberry piña colada from him. Wolfgang whistled as he grabbed the blender and started packing it full of ice. I marveled at his patience; I hated multiple blended drink orders and did all I could to discourage them—they took too long, the blender had to be rinsed for each drink, and it hampered my efficiency. "Doesn't it bother you to have to make three different blended drinks for this one order?" I asked my nonchalant boss.

"No," replied Wolfgang with a grin, "it's easy—watch." He dumped a pile of strawberries into the blender, splashed in some rum and triple sec, hit the switch, and then poured the identical contents into all three glasses. Wolfgang then carefully pointed to each cocktail glass while telling his rookie waiter, "This one's your strawberry margarita, this one's your strawberry daiquiri, and this one's your strawberry piña colada." Winking at me, Wolfgang barked to his perplexed waiter: "And don't fuck up the order by forgetting which drink is which. I don't want to have to remake them."

Filthy McNasty's rocked with loud bands and crowded dance floors seven nights a week. When the North Hollywood club became an "after hours" bar, my weekend shift expanded to twelve hours. I arrived for work at 6:00 P.M.; under California law, we ended alcohol service at 2:00 A.M. (serving after hours could cost a bar its liquor license). However, the dance band revved until 6 A.M., catering to those who didn't want their party to expire with the liquor curfew. Between 2:00 and 6:00, we served the most expensive coffee and soft drinks in Hollywood, yet we always had a packed house. Besides, customers sometimes gratified their after-hour desires with smuggled liquor bottles in their coat pockets, or by secretly taking drugs in the bathroom.

On many Saturday nights Filthy had me work the 6 P.M. to 2 A.M. shift at the Sunset Strip bar, and then work the after-hours shift in North Hollywood. Whenever I worked the Sunset Strip/North Hollywood double shift, the same late-night sequence played out. Following "last call" on the Sunset Strip, I put away the liquor bottles while Filthy announced to his disgruntled patrons with great flair, "People! The night is young! Let's get into my limousine and hearse! We'll take you out to my after-hours club in North Hollywood! Come on! The party's just beginning there! The ride's on me!" Filthy and I then stuffed as many customers as would fit inside his two cars, with the drunks stacked like logs in the back of the hearse. Remaining stragglers squeezed into my little Vega, and our caravan barreled across Laurel Canyon to the North Hollywood club. There the revelers drank and danced until sunrise while I worked behind the bar. At 6:00 A.M. the next morning, Filthy turned on the lights, proclaimed the party over, and ordered everyone to leave. When the Sunset Strip customers asked for a ride back to where they parked their cars, Filthy scoffed: "Do I look like a fucking taxi service?" he'd bellow while kicking everyone out. Despite this, I could count on most of these same stranded, drunken jackasses to pile into Filthy's hearse a week later for another one-way ride to North Hollywood.

Many nightclub owners enforce "no fraternizing" rules, where employees aren't allowed to date waitresses or customers. At Filthy's, employees fraternized *in extremis*. On one of my first nights there, a waiter who ordered a tray of drinks from me disappeared without picking them up for delivery. As the ice in the glasses melted, I asked another employee where he went. "I saw him heading upstairs a while ago with one of his customers," he told me. "He's probably gone up there to screw her. He might be gone for a while, so I'll deliver the drinks to his station." He explained that bartenders and waiters often abandoned their shifts to spirit a female customer to an empty room. "However," he added, "If you bring a girl upstairs and bang her, when you come back make sure she's smiling and spending money."

Not all the acts playing at Filthy's were like Kiss, Richard Berry ("Louie Louie"), or the Coasters ("Yakkety Yak"), even though they sang there, too. Most of our live entertainment came from local grunge bands. In the late 1970s, with The King now in his grave two years, the proliferation of Elvis Presley impersonators was in high gear. Most of the crummier ones beat a path to Filthy's door. We saw them in all sizes and colors: We even had black and Japanese Elvises play the club. The worst of the lot was Mike, whose bulging gut and flabby glutes strained the seams of his polyester jumpsuit. Mike took the Elvis thing far too seriously, as I learned the night he rehearsed his opening show. He walked to the bar and ordered a beer. "Here you go, Mike," I said as I popped off the bottle cap and handed it to him.

The enraged entertainer grabbed me by the shirt, screaming, "You bastard! Don't you *ever* call me 'Mike' when I'm getting ready to perform. I'm *Elvis*, do you understand?" His eighty-year old bodyguard/manager/roadie calmed him down and then explained Mike's sudden violent outburst: "To get ready for his show, he doesn't just impersonate Elvis. He *becomes* Elvis. Elvis's spirit dwells in him, and he dwells in Elvis's spirit. Their thoughts become one, and they become one. . . ." As the old man rambled on about his client's supernatural metamorphosis, I thought it best to humor them both.

Mike/Elvis refused to wait in the entertainer's dressing room for the show to start. Instead, he sat in full costume in a rented limousine parked outside. When it was showtime, his three-piece combo band played the theme from *2001: A Space Odyssey*—Elvis's concert intro music. On cue, the old roadie threw open the stage door, stepped out on the empty dance floor, and looked both ways doing his "security check." Then he called out, "All clear, Elvis, you can come do your show now." Out waddled the overstuffed performer, who jiggled his way through the repertoire. During the show, Mike/Elvis mopped his brow and chest with polyester scarves, tossing them to his audience of homely, middle-aged women. Their joyful squeals were lost on Wolfgang and me—we thought Elvis's estate should sue this guy. Worse yet, when the show ended, the "bodyguard" came out and demanded back the sweaty scarves! We laughed as the old man played tug-of-war with fans who expected a permanent souvenir: "Come on lady," he pleaded with these tubby gals, "Elvis needs his rag for the next show."

At the end of the last show, and after the bar emptied, Mike/Elvis came over and ordered yet another beer. When he asked me how I enjoyed the show, Wolfgang (off to the side and out of Mike's view) began tittering and making faces. I couldn't resist: "Mike . . . I mean *Elvis*. Listen, I've seen a lot of Elvis impersonators in my day, but you are without doubt the most convincing."

"Hey, thank yah' baby," Mike said in his best curled-lip Elvis snarl. "It's always nice to hear that from mah' fans."

"Yeah, you're the best Elvis we've ever had," I continued. "You've perfected an impersonation of Elvis Presley—during the last week of his life!"

Wolfgang laughed at my wisecrack. As I turned to laugh with my boss, through the corner of my eye I saw Mike/Elvis lunging across the bar at me. I stepped back just in time; Mike/Elvis belly-flopped on the bar, which knocked the wind out of him. As the bodyguard pulled on his legs to help him up, Wolfgang fanned the flames. Picking up a Kleenex, Wolfgang blew his nose in the tissue, and then waved it over his head: "Hey, fat Elvis! Don't you want your scarf?"

There were many times the McNastys ordered their employees into service beyond the call of duty. One such time happened on Female Mud Wrestling night, where swimsuit models wrestled and tore off each other's bikini tops in a makeshift ring filled with mud. It was a guaranteed moneymaker for the McNastys: Each Sunday evening beer-swilling frat boys, or the drunken remnants of some bachelor party, filled the seats. The highlight came when the referee "auctioned" three-rounds with Red Snapper, a curvaceous, Amazon-proportioned redhead. Unbeknownst to the customers, it was a phony auction: There was a shill in the audience employed by the models' troupe to top any bid and "win" the role of muck combatant. When I asked about the sham, the troupe's manager said he couldn't risk an aggressive drunk getting in the ring and injuring one of his girls.

One night Wolfgang received a telephone call before the show began. Bad news: The shill had been in a minor traffic accident and couldn't get to the club before the auction. "Hey," Wolfgang asked me after hanging up the phone, "do you know anything about wrestling?"

"A little. Why?"

"Because," he said, "you have to mud-wrestle Red Snapper tonight."

Although the prospect of climbing in the ring with the scantily clad, auburn-haired beauty sounded exotic at first blush, I had bigger fish to fry: I didn't think letting near-naked Red Snapper roll me in the mud for nine minutes would be a good career move politically. I told Wolfgang that if I ever ran for Congress, some compromising Polaroid photo from the match would pop up in a newspaper and finish me off. That was that.

When Wolfgang's appeals to loyalty, friendship, and outright begging proved unmoving, he enlisted a more persuasive advocate. I was restocking the bar a few minutes later when I heard my name sung out in a seductive tone: It was Red Snapper. A loosened white terrycloth robe barely covered her provocative costume. She asked to speak with me in private, and then walked around the bar and draped her arm through mine. Throwing me a pouting-lip gaze, she said, "You know, Jimmy, the auction is the main part of our show. If you don't do it, then my greedy manager will have a real auction, and one of those drunken men might win me—and maybe hurt me." Her eyes half-closed as she leaned forward as if to kiss me; her lips brushed my ear as she whispered, "You wouldn't want to see anyone hurt me, would you, Jimmy?" I felt a slight nibble on my earlobe; the scent of her Opium perfume filled my senses. Somehow, my hands found their way around her tiny waist as she pressed against me.

The next thing I knew, Wolfgang was throwing me a pair of swim trunks.

My instructions were simple: whatever bid a member of the audience made to wrestle Red Snapper, I was to top the bid until I won. Meanwhile, Red Snapper took me in a back room to teach me a few moves and holds designed to give everyone what she called "a good show." From my spot, I didn't know how the show could get any better. Anyway, I decided that if I had to be scandalized for mud wrestling, Red Snapper was the girl with whom to be shamed. After all, future voters might understand and forgive my chivalry in protecting her from harm; if they didn't, well, maybe Congress wasn't all it was cracked up to be.

As I poured drinks awaiting show time, I wondered whether or how

Red Snapper would show her gratitude after work for my sacrifice. By auction time, I caught myself looking forward to the romp. Just as the auction was to begin, the bruised-up shill came limping into the club. He took a taxicab from the accident scene and made it in time to wrestle Red Snapper, so I was off the hook. A tinge of disappointment overcame me as I handed him back the swim trunks.

At the end of the evening, as I wiped down the bar, Red Snapper came over to thank me. Flashing that blinding smile, she cooed, "Hey, Jimmy, thanks again. Maybe next time, huh? You seem like the kind of guy I'd really enjoy rolling in the mud."

Bartending at Filthy's was never boring, but like the other places, the wages and tips in rowdy joints never compared to what bartenders made in nice restaurants. I continued to moonlight occasionally, doing private parties to earn extra money. One deceptive opportunity came from a group of East Coast entrepreneurs with smooth manners and flashy clothes. They hired me to set up their newly purchased nightclub on Ventura Boulevard in Reseda. I worked round the clock during my week's vacation from Filthy's to get them ready. On opening night, the club threw open its doors and was jam-packed. Rock music star Joe Cocker made a surprise appearance and sang all night with headliner Rodney Crowell. The owners raked in thousands and thousands of dollars that weekend. I returned the next day and found the doors locked, the bar closed, and the partners gone with my week's pay and promised bonus. The club never reopened. I'd grown used to such chicanery: In the sleazy world of liquor, hustlers, and fast times, not all risks were physical.

One night another bartender invited me over to see where he worked: the Palomino Club, a world-famous country-western landmark that had been a North Hollywood fixture since the 1940s. Located just up the street from Filthy's on Lankershim Boulevard, the Palomino was a huge, barn-size nightspot and winner of the Academy of Country Music's Nightclub of the Year award fourteen years in a row. Country music circles considered the Palomino second only to Nashville's Grand Ole Opry.

Legends like Hank Williams Sr., Patsy Cline, Johnny Cash, Tammy Wynette, Waylon Jennings, Marty Robbins, Willie Nelson, and countless others all played the Palomino; stars like Glen Campbell and Linda Ronstadt got their start at the Palomino's weekly Talent Night contest.

I sat at the Palomino's long bar and watched the hard-working bartenders stuffing wads of cash into their large tip jar all night long. It looked like hundreds of dollars were in there by the end of their shift; on a good night at Filthy's I was lucky to clear $30 in tips. By comparison, the Palomino looked like a gold mine for bartenders. Later that night, I met owner Tommy Thomas, who told me he needed an experienced bartender and offered me a job. I needed more money for law school, so it was goodbye to rock and punk at Filthy's, and hello to hillbilly.

On my first night at the Palomino, I went to Tommy Thomas's office, which was not much bigger than a walk-in closet. Tommy looked annoyed when I reported for work: His first words had no semblance of welcome in them. "Look around in here for a W-4 tax form," he barked, "and when you find one, fill the damned thing out. And remember: If I ever catch you stealing from me, you're fired. Also, we shot-glass pour here [measure out the ounces of alcohol before dumping it in the customer's glass]. If I ever catch you "free-pouring" [pouring the alcohol directly into the customer's glass without measuring], you're fired."

As I scavenged about looking for a W-4 form, a pretty cocktail waitress entered the office to bring Tommy a drink. Her giddy presence ended Tommy's brusqueness. Surly Mr. Hyde suddenly became charming Dr. Jekyll. Tommy's eyes lit up as he bantered playfully with her before telling her to come and meet the new bartender. Joanne extended to me a warm hand. She was a petite brunette with a shy smile, but there was nothing petite or shy about her mountainous breasts unconstrained by a bra and pouring out of a low-cut, undersize tank top shirt emblazoned with the Palomino's horse logo.

"Hey, Joanne," Tommy urged, "why don't you give Jim a real Palomino welcome on his first night here? Go ahead and show him, honey! Oh, yeah, and tell him about how you're a witch!" Joanne placidly complied with the vague request by raising her tank top and thrusting forth her bare breasts, proudly displaying them as if they were new acqui-sitions (which they probably were). As she stood there holding the pose, Joanne told me she was a practicing witch, but I needn't worry—she was a "white" witch, and never did bad ("black") witchcraft. While she lec-tured on these occult nuances, Tommy motioned with his thumb to Joanne's still-exposed treasures and asked me, "Well, what do you think?"

"Tommy, I don't think I'm going to find any W-4 forms in there."

There was quite a collection of characters working at the Palomino. The bar manager, Mike, was there more than twenty-five years. A short man with greased-down hair, perennial beard stubble, and stumps for where two of the ten fingers on his hand used to be, Mike had all the charm of a guy selling dirty pictures from a trench coat at the bus station. He had an indefinable accent, spoke in sentences without punctuation, and laced them heavily with the invented word "onna-counta," which was his own hybrid for the phrase "on account of" ("Hey, Jim, onna-counta gimme a beer onna-counta I'm thirsty onna-counta I've been working hard onna-counta I really need a beer . . . "). Mike was an early poster boy for the importance of sexual harassment laws. He thought it proper to skulk behind new cocktail waitresses and goose them with his finger stub, and then run up and down the bar holding up the stump while yelling to the customers, "Onna-counta her ass ate my finger!" Mike was just one reason why, in our crew of some forty waitresses, half of them turned over every two weeks, and many never made it through their first shift. Tommy Thomas ran employment ads for cocktail waitresses in the *Los Angeles Times* seven days a week, 365 days a year.

The head bartender, Tom, provided another compelling reason for waitresses to quit. Tom watched them with an eagle's eye, and filled a scratch pad each night with dozens of "write-ups" (slips of paper on which he detailed every minor flaw he found in a waitress). Often, he made things up in his unending effort to curry favor with Tommy. Notes such as "Violet's hair was messy," "Regina didn't call her drinks in the proper order," "Marsha took too long counting her change," "Carla was rude to a drunk," and other misdemeanors were noted and stuffed into his cash register drawer for Tommy's later review. In no time the waitresses all came to love me as much as they hated Tom: When Tom ended his shifts early and I covered his station, I took his snitch notes from the drawer and handed them back to the waitresses to throw out. When I started at the Palomino, Tom mentioned offhandedly that he could recommend a great cocaine supplier. When I told him I didn't do drugs, his jaw slackened and he looked at me with amazement. "I don't mean to stare," he said, "but I thought everyone used cocaine." In his universe, everyone did. Now and then, customers left small paper bindles of the powdery drug on the bar, intended as my tip for an evening of good service. I always thanked them for thinking of me and then dumped it down the sink without any fanfare when nobody was looking.

Head waitress Carmen, who started at the Palomino during the Truman administration, was a nasty old hag. In her time, she saw thousands of waitresses come and go. So had Doorman, the hulking, dim-witted security guard who forever sat under a huge cowboy hat on a stool watching the entrance. I once asked Doorman how long he had been at the Palomino. "About twenty-five years," he said, "not counting the ten I spent in San Quentin for second-degree murder." Though he was dumb as a post, Doorman's brute strength was legendary. Each night he sat quietly on his stool, but he could flip from docile watchdog to vicious bouncer in the blink of an eye.

One busy Saturday night Doorman caught some guys sneaking in by climbing over the wooden fence on the club's back patio. He roughed them up unnecessarily before throwing them out. Later that evening, as Doorman stood outside, he saw a pickup truck slow down as it approached. One of his earlier beating victims sprang from the bed of the truck and leveled a crossbow at him. As Doorman broke into a slow plod for the club, the guy in the truck fired, hitting Doorman with an arrow in the buttocks. Blood seeped from the wound as Doorman walked inside the busy nightclub with the arrow protruding from him. Thinking it a gag, the customers howled with laughter: "Hey, look! He's got an arrow in his ass!" Doorman pointed to the arrow and said he'd been shot, but with his dull, monotone pronouncement, nobody took him seriously. Growing frustrated, he walked to Tommy's office, where the boss counted the receipts and didn't want to be disturbed.

"Hey, Tommy, I got shot with a arrow." Tommy looked at the arrow protruding from Doorman's rump, and then snarled, "Get out of here, you jackass. Can't you see I'm counting the money?"

"Oh, sorry," Doorman said. Not until he collapsed and knocked over the coffeemaker did people figure out this wasn't a joke. Tommy called the paramedics; they couldn't carry Doorman to the ambulance because he was too big. They stood over him and asked him to get up and walk. A surgeon removed the arrow; then Doorman walked out of the hospital and returned to finish his shift. Only toughness eclipsed Doorman's dumbness.

The owner, Tommy Thomas, was a piece of work. He had a split personality that made employees fear him: One minute he was everyone's best friend; the next he was firing a longtime employee for some trivial reason. He once told me his diet pill addiction caused his mercurial mood swings. Obsessed with the belief that every employee stole from him (some did, but rarely the ones he suspected), he hired spies, and then hired a second layer of spies to watch the first group of spies, because he thought the first spies might be in cahoots with his thieving employees. It grew quite complex.

Whenever Tommy blew up at me, I diffused his abusive temper by acting too stupid to know I was in trouble. Once in a back storeroom he caught me in the clinches with Lynne, a hot blond waitress. Of course, this violated Tommy's cause-for-termination "no fraternizing" rule. Screaming for all the waitresses to gather around, Tommy sought to make an example of me before an audience. With the crowd assembled, he asked if it was true that he just caught me making out with a waitress. Trying to look as confused as possible as to why that would get me in trouble, I admitted the conduct: "Sure I was! I'd still be there if you hadn't interrupted!" He jabbed his finger at the bold "NO FRATERNIZING OR YOU'RE FIRED" sign prominently displayed near the time clock. "Read this sign to the waitresses!" he shrieked. "Go ahead! Read this sign!"

I squinted at the words, pretending to silently struggle with the vocabulary. Turning to Tommy with a faux puzzled look on my face, I replied: "So what's the problem, Tommy? I wasn't smoking."

Tommy stared at me in disbelief, and then doubled over in a belly laugh. "You stupid bastard! You can't even read! Hey, girls! He thinks the sign says "No Smoking!" Can you believe it? And he tells all you waitresses he's in law school! Law school! That must be his pickup line for you dumb broads to get into your pants! Ha ha ha . . . !" Tommy guffawed all the way back to his office, forgetting to dispense with me. I laughed, too, and then resumed my date with Lynne after work.

Until lightning struck at the Palomino, I never took dating very seriously in Los Angeles. Why would I? For nightclub bartenders, women were a dime a dozen; the job didn't make for serious relationships. Only once did I fall in love, and when I did, it wasn't with some barfly: It was with my longtime college girlfriend Terri Lemke. We planned on marrying when I finished law school, but our relationship didn't survive my move south to UCLA. All my dating after that was casual and indifferent. Then at the Palomino I started working alongside Gay Hahn. She was a chestnut-haired professional ice skater who once trained for the U.S. Olympic Team. Her heart wasn't in competing, so she dropped out to turn pro, working around the world in the Ice Capades before moving to California. Gay took a part-time job at the club while waiting to begin teaching at a new ice rink when it opened in the valley. Unlike my other waitress merry-go-round dates, Gay was elegant, charming, and smart. She outmatched me in every way. We became serious from the start and soon fell in love. Gay kept encouraging me to see in the shadowy distance the outline of a future bigger than stacking tires, selling vacuum cleaners door to door, and bartending. At twenty-four, I had found everything I wanted in a woman, and I found her in the ramshackle Palomino Club. We not only defied Tommy's "no fraternizing" rule, but we took it a step further and became engaged.

Gay and I dated while Bo Derek was the hottest name in movies. Back then, Bo's face beamed from multiple magazine covers stacked in every news rack. To tease Gay, I told her that Bo Derek came into the Palomino and tried to pick me up. When Gay stood nearby as I answered the phone at work, I'd admonish the confused caller: "Listen, Bo, I told you before not to bother me. I'm in love with another woman." Gay just shook her head at my silliness, and of course never believed my tall tale for a minute.

One night Gay and I went to dinner at Hampton's, a popular Toluca Lake restaurant owned by Paul Newman that specialized in gourmet hamburgers. Near the kitchen stood the "hamburger bar," where customers added their own condiments. After Gay dressed her burger and returned to the table, I went to the burger bar. From across the room I saw Bo Derek approaching the counter to do the same. Bo and I met while passing condiments to one another; I told her my fiancée (seated with her back to us and unaware of Bo's presence) was a huge fan. "Today's her birthday," I said. "Maybe you could wave to her after I get her attention. She'd get a big kick out of it."

"Why don't I just come over to the table and say hello?" Bo asked.

"Oh no," I responded. "She's very shy. She'd kill me if I brought you over. Just wave to her! That would be fine." I returned to the table while Gay remained oblivious to my encounter. As I settled into my chair, I managed a stern expression on my face, grumbling about how "that woman won't take no for an answer."

"What are you talking about?" Gay asked as she took a bite out of her burger.

"Like I told you before. It's that pesky Bo Derek. She won't let up on me. I can't even come to dinner without her stalking me." Gay rolled her eyes. "Well, if you don't believe me, just turn around and look." Gay turned in her seat. There was Bo Derek, who on cue smiled and waved. With Gay's back now turned toward me, I pointed at Gay and blew a kiss to Bo, who reciprocated the gesture. Gay turned slowly and faced me: a look of disbelief seized her face. "Oh, my God!" Gay sputtered. "That was—that was Bo Derek! Why is she waving and blowing kisses to you? I don't understand. . . ."

"Like I've been telling you, babe. Do you think I make this stuff up?"

Of course she thought I made this stuff up. Still, that night, Gay paid for dinner.

There was another major benefit to working at the Palomino: the outstanding impromptu entertainment served up by showbiz stars who wandered in to catch a show. On any given night Willie Nelson, Elton John, Bernadette Peters, Chuck Berry, Linda Ronstadt, or Bette Midler might take over the stage with the house band, Jimmy Snyder and the Palomino Riders.

A founder of rock and roll—"The Killer," the legendary Jerry Lee Lewis—often played at the club. A Jerry Lee performance had nothing predictable about it except that it guaranteed a sellout crowd. One night Jerry Lee took the stage in a packed house for his first show; he banged out a few notes, and then shoved the piano off the stage, sending it smashing on the floor below. As the audience hooted, Jerry Lee yelled at a stunned Tommy Thomas, "The next time I play your fuckin' club, have a piano that's in tune!" The audience cheered as Jerry Lee stalked off to his dressing room, refusing to do the show. Tommy somehow managed to find another tuned piano in time for the second show. After that, every time Jerry Lee played, a piano tuner sat underneath the stage for each show and retuned the piano before and after each performance.

Crowds who came to see Jerry Lee Lewis proved as rowdy as their idol. Once, when he played on my night off, I came in to catch his opening show of a three-night run. Tommy filled the old barn above legal capacity; by the time he went on, the whooping cowboys in the audience had been drinking for hours. Tanya Tucker, seated in the front row, joined Jerry Lee on stage, mounted the piano, and sang a couple of torch songs as the fiery pianist pounded on the keys. One excited cowboy climbed atop a table for a better view. An arm reached up from the crowd and jerked him backward. Soon tables overturned, fists and beer bottles flew, and a melee erupted. When one drunk tried to climb on the stage, Jerry Lee kicked him in the head and sent him flying backward into the audience, never missing a note on the piano. A hysterical waitress working her first night ran up to me in a panic: "Do something!" she screamed.

"I am," I replied. "I'm watching the show."

When Hoyt Axton came to play, he kept his repertoire of songs taped to the side of his acoustic guitar to remind him which number came next. Hoyt rehearsed one night before we opened for his first show. When his manager ordered a tray of beers from me, I popped off the bottle caps and rang up the $10 sale on the cash register. "Put it on Hoyt's tab," the manager replied. My boss Tommy had a simple rule: *Nobody* ran a tab unless Tommy personally authorized it, and Tommy didn't pre-approve a Hoyt Axton tab. The manager fished through his pockets and came up empty, and then cursed me when I took back the tray of beers.

"You know," I said, "I'm sure when Tommy gets in tonight he'll let me start a tab for Hoyt. I'm willing to risk my job as a personal favor. By the way, that's a great looking 'Hoyt Axton on Tour' baseball cap you're wearing. . . ."

"You no-good, Arab-trading bastard," the manager sputtered as he swapped me the cap for the tray of beer bottles. Later that night, the manager came to my bar and tossed to me a "Hoyt Axton on Tour" baseball jersey. I asked why he was giving this to me: The manager replied, "Hoyt told me to give it to you. He says if you're gonna fuck him out of his hat, you might as well fuck him out of his shirt, too!"

Hoyt Axton may have needed to tape a list of songs to his guitar to know what next to sing, but at least he knew what to sing when he sang it. This was in contrast to country star Jerry Jeff Walker, who often had no idea what he was singing on stage because he was so plastered. He forgot lyrics and made up words as he went along. His unruly fans couldn't care less: The more disorganized the show, the more they loved him. Jerry Jeff came in drunk one night, put his head on my bar, and cried like a baby. When I asked if he was all right, he looked up and sobbed, "American Express just took away my credit card because they say I owe half a million dollars." I was startled: "Jerry Jeff, how did you run up half a million dollars on a credit card?"

"Well," he said, scratching his head, "our tour bus broke down one night. We were drinkin' and partyin'. One thing led to another, and I charged a Lear Jet!" I don't know if his story was true, but it was good enough to buy him a drink.

Many of our performers used drugs or alcohol backstage. On the day we announced that country music star Charlie Rich would perform there, both shows sold out immediately. I worked the back service bar the night he played; half an hour before his performance, Charlie sidled up to me and made small talk before asking me to whip up a dozen margaritas. I made the drinks and sent them back to his dressing room, assuming they were for his band. Later, Rich staggered to the stage when introduced. He was so drunk that he twice fell off the piano stool, never completing his first song. The audience booed and demanded a refund. Tommy was livid: He walked around the club shouting, "Do you know how much I paid this son of a bitch? Do you know how much this act cost?" Later, Tommy stormed out of Rich's dressing room after seeing a dozen empty margarita glasses. The veins in Tommy's neck throbbed so hard that I thought he might have a stroke. "Who served Charlie Rich twelve margaritas?" Tommy screamed. Pointing an accusing finger at me, he charged toward me. "Did you do it? Well, did you?" I looked over at the doormen carrying the unconscious Charlie Rich from the stage. Seeing he was in no condition to talk, I deflected the question: "Tommy, just because I'm illiterate doesn't mean I'm stupid." Tommy cursed and fumed as he marched around, swearing he'd find the culprit. Later that night, Tommy said the IRS was garnishing Rich's entire salary for back taxes owed. "No wonder the poor bastard drinks before he sings," Tommy lamented.

When comedian John Belushi came in to watch a Jerry Lee Lewis show, Tommy invited him into the back office. I brought them drinks before Belushi went to Jerry Lee's dressing room to visit between shows. The waitress serving them later complained to me, "Belushi's stuffing so much cocaine up his nose that even Jerry Lee's warning him to be careful." Coming from Jerry Lee Lewis (no faint heart himself when it came to partying), that spoke volumes. "What can you do?" the waitress shrugged. "These guys love the nightlife."

She was right: These guys loved the nightlife. When I moved to L.A.

and started bartending in Hollywood, I loved it, too. Each sunset promised another evening crowded with action; the stream of women (whether band singers, waitresses, or customers) never ran dry. This mirage of never-ending fun can eclipse the knowledge that overindulgence isn't cost free. Viewing each night through a kaleidoscope makes it easy to overlook changes so subtle as to be almost imperceptible. Regular customers, so filled with youth and energy at night, looked strangely pale and haggard when bathed in sunlight. At shift's end, when I turned up the house lights after last call, otherwise jolly people grew surly. They didn't want the party to end, and had no purpose in life beyond its resumption. Everything between now and tomorrow night acted as mere filler until their next fix. Like Dorian Gray's portrait, the faster people chase the nightlife, the faster their painting ages in the attic.

When John Belushi died of a drug overdose some months after partying with Jerry Lee Lewis, I thought about how much he loved the nightlife and what it cost him. I thought about what it cost so many others I met along the way; then I took a hard look at what it had started costing me.

11

THIRD WHORE FROM LEFT

Despite its early lure, in time I learned bartending wasn't all playtime. It could be hard, dirty, laborious, and sometimes demeaning work. I spent innumerable nights pouring drinks while listening to depressing stories, dragging comatose customers to cabs, wiping some drunk's vomit off the bar, mopping up poorly aimed urine streams, listening to earsplitting music that caused me some permanent hearing loss, ducking from thrown glasses, facing down threats, breaking up or getting into fistfights, and tossing out troublemakers. Crawling into bed at night, my back and shoulders ached from long hours of stooping over the well and sink; my eyes hurt from reading law books in near-darkness, and my clothes and hair reeked of cigarette smoke. When I tried to sleep, I couldn't get the sound of clinking glasses and bottles out of my head. Clocking in for each night's shift, the potential for tragedy lingered in the back of my mind.

One Saturday night in 1980, I was eight hours into my shift at Filthy's North Hollywood club. At the 2:00 A.M. alcohol curfew, I started locking up the liquor bottles and preparing for the after-hours segment. A customer at the bar told me of a fight at the pool table across the room. I grabbed my walking stick and rushed over to break it up. There I saw a crowd watching Filthy kick out a well-dressed man with a bloody nose;

the man brushed by me as he left the bar. I recognized him from earlier in the evening: I had served drinks to him and his three companions.

With the disturbance over and the liquor put away, I asked Wolfgang to watch the bar so I could go outside and take my break. Leaning against the wall in front of the club, I lit a cigar given me by a customer, and prepared to enjoy a few minutes of quiet. The streets were empty; I savored the fresh outdoor air as I watched the glowing ash grow. Then I heard a sudden commotion coming from the parking lot. Rounding the corner from the lot and running toward me was Brett Fortune, a young guy I had earlier thrown out with his friend because they looked underage and had no ID. Right behind in pursuit was Willie James Russell, the guy with the bloody nose Filthy tossed out a few minutes earlier. As Fortune came within a few feet of me, he spun and faced his pursuer. Russell struck him repeatedly in the head and upper body with what appeared to be a closed fist. Fortune did not swing back; curiously, he hung on to Russell's shoulders with both hands, swinging around in a circle with him.

Earlier in the evening, I took a punch breaking up a fight between the drummer and the bass player in the band. Now I was angry that I had to wade into another fight, and do it on my break to boot. Tossing my cigar to the ground in disgust, I lunged between the two brawlers and threw my elbows into them: "Break it up, you assholes," I ordered. Russell pivoted toward me and swung at my head; I ducked and the blow missed. As he drew back to strike again, I cocked my fist and began stepping forward to land a haymaker to his jaw. Suddenly, I saw a glint of light bounce off metal in his hand. It was the first time I realized he hadn't been swinging a closed fist at Fortune or me.

It was a knife. Russell hadn't been punching Fortune; he was stabbing him.

I dove out of the way just as Russell thrust the blade at me again. While still in mid-air, I reached for the gun in my ankle holster. As I rolled out of the way and jumped to my feet, I heard screaming next to me: Two women leaving Filthy's walked inadvertently into the middle of a murderous assault. I shoved them out of the way and toward the entrance of the club with such force that one woman tripped and dented a plaster wall with her head; the other left a huge clump of her hair and scalp stuck inside my flexible watchband.

Fortune still maintained a death grip on his attacker's shoulders; Russell again raised his blade to strike him. I leveled my pistol a few inches from Russell's head, turned it upward a few degrees, and fired a round right next to his ear. My hand jerked from the recoil; I brought the gun down and level with the bridge of Russell's nose. When I ordered him to drop the knife, Russell froze and stared at me, his knife still raised above Fortune. His face contorted and he frothed at the mouth. I'd never seen anything quite so hideous.

Panicky people rushing out of the club created pandemonium. My peripheral vision picked up Russell's three friends near the parking lot, shouting frantic and indecipherable instructions to him. While holding Russell at gunpoint, now I had to worry about his pals in the shadows. I warned all of them to freeze and keep their hands where I could see them. Meanwhile, Russell ignored my command to drop the knife. With my gun still pointed at his head, I said, "Drop that knife *now*, or I'll blow your fuckin' brains down Lankershim Boulevard." He just stared wild-eyed at me and didn't comply. I pulled back the hammer with my thumb until it cocked into place, and I gave him a final warning: "I said drop it, you son of a bitch."

His friends were screaming; the crowd was screaming. Fortune was still standing, clutching Russell's shoulders, while his knife remained frozen in the air above the victim's chest. Russell's head turned from side to side frantically; he had a crazy look in his eyes. Whatever was going through his mind, he refused to obey my command to drop his weapon.

I decided to kill him.

I lowered the gun barrel slightly and aimed for his sternum. With .125-grain hollow-point bullets loaded in my revolver, a blast to the chest would knock him out of his shoes. Just as I started squeezing the trigger, Filthy ran from out of nowhere directly in front of my gun and charged Russell. My boss didn't know he had come within half a heartbeat of my killing him instead. Russell now swung his knife at Filthy, who tried bravely to disarm him with his bare hands. Filthy shouted at me, "Jim, shoot this bastard!" but I couldn't get a clean shot with both Filthy and the victim rotating madly in my line of fire. Russell broke free and ran south on Lankershim; his white disco suit was covered in Fortune's blood. Filthy screamed for me to shoot him as he fled to prevent his escape, and then he tried to wrestle the gun from me to do it himself when I refused. Knowing I couldn't let Filthy start capping a cheap handgun (with marginal accuracy at anything less than close range) down a commercial street, I pushed Filthy away. Meanwhile, Russell's three friends ran to their car and sped off.

Holstering my gun, I rushed to Fortune, who staggered onto the front steps and collapsed. He was conscious and crying, saying he was dying and that he couldn't breathe. I tried to calm him as I opened his shirt to see how badly he was injured. Meanwhile, after going hand to hand with the knife-wielding killer, I thought Filthy was going to strangle Fortune's friend, who watched the assault but didn't intervene. "You yellow bastard! You stand there and watch your buddy get knifed and you don't even try to help him!" The friend sobbed as he sank to the ground, his head in his hands, while Filthy kept berating him for cowardice.

The more Fortune gasped for air, the more he panicked. Fortune asked if he was going to die; I told him his cuts looked superficial and that he'd be all right, but I was lying. He had multiple stab wounds in the chest, stomach, and throat. I tried giving him mouth-to-mouth to force oxygen into his lungs, but I heard my breath come out of the gurgling wounds.

At the sound of approaching sirens, Fortune's eyes rolled back in his head and his body convulsed. Then he was still. I think he was dead before the ambulance arrived. While paramedics assessed the scene, I slipped back into the bathroom and washed his blood from my hands, arms, and face. I rolled up my sleeves to hide the blood smears, and then went back behind the bar to finish the last four hours of my shift. Most people in the club remained ignorant of what happened and the party continued unabated. Throughout the night customers saw blood smears on my white shirt and asked merrily: "Hey, Jimmy, did you have a fight or something?"

"Yeah—or something."

The LAPD captured Russell hiding in some bushes an hour later. I learned that the trouble started after I told Fortune and his friend to leave the club. They'd snuck back inside and hung out at the pool table. He and Russell then quarreled over whose turn it was to shoot a game; a shoving match ensued, and Fortune hit Russell, which accounted for the killer's bloody nose. Filthy threw both men out: Fortune through the back door and Russell through the front. They'd met again in the parking lot, where Russell brandished his knife, and Fortune fled around the corner to the front door where I was standing.[10]

I returned to my apartment the next morning after dawn. When Bob Wyatt saw my bloodstained clothes, he asked, "What the hell happened to you?" I tossed him the expended shell casing from the round I fired next to Russell's head. Bob raised it to his nose; when he smelled the sulfur and gunpowder, and saw the indentation made from the firing pin, his eyes opened wide. "Oh, my God," he asked. "You killed someone, didn't you?"

No, I didn't kill anyone; but for many years thereafter, the memory of Willie James Russell brutally murdering an unarmed kid made me wish I had.

It didn't take long in my bartending career to figure out there was a right and a wrong way to approach law school. The right way is to live on campus and have no outside job or financial obligations, thanks to generous parents or student loans. The right way enables one to do nothing but focus on one's studies.

I definitely did law school the wrong way.

From the moment I walked into my first class, I felt as though I was in hell. On a typical day, I left Reseda at 6:00 A.M. and commuted in heavy traffic to make my 8:00 class; my last class ended at 4:00 P.M., which

---

[10] The District Attorney subpoenaed me as a witness a few times, but he never called me to testify. The DA and Russell plea-bargained the charges down to voluntary manslaughter, and Russell went to state prison for a few years.

meant I hit the same traffic going home. I couldn't get an on-campus parking permit; this added extra time trying to find a place to park near school. Since I rarely found one, I parked illegally, and the daily tickets quickly ate into my bartending income. Sometimes I tried to recycle my previous parking tickets by placing an old one on the windshield to avoid getting a new one, but that old trick rarely fooled the meter maids of Westwood. From school I hurried home to Reseda, changed clothes, and rushed to get behind the bar for the start of my 6:00 P.M. shift in North Hollywood. I worked until 2:30 A.M., grabbed a late dinner at an all-night chiliburger stand, and then went to bed about 3:30 A.M., often too exhausted to sleep. Less than three hours later, the grueling cycle began anew. All night long I mixed drinks, washed glasses, stocked shelves, lit cigarettes, entertained my customers, and broke up fights—while trying to study a law book propped in a wire bookstand and illuminated by the bar sink's dim red light bulb. I tried to sleep and study whenever a spare moment came: At break time, I curled up for a few minutes and snoozed atop the Coors and Budweiser cases in the storeroom.

I should have known that these circumstances diminished the chances of succeeding at law school. By the first month's end, I stopped attending lectures regularly. I couldn't stay awake in class, and I feared having a professor call on me to expound on a case 200 pages ahead of where I had read. The results of my first semester examinations were, not surprisingly, a disaster.

After the school posted my grades, Assistant Dean Fred Slaughter summoned me to his office. He explained I was on the cusp of being dropped from law school because of my low first-semester grade point average. He produced my "blue book" criminal law examination essay on which Professor Abrams penciled, "This student has no conception of criminal law." Reading less than half of the assigned casebook, and attending only a fraction of the professor's lectures had a lot to do with his evaluation of my potential. Dean Slaughter now leaned forward, looked me in the eye, and uttered perhaps the harshest sentence anyone ever spoke to me:

"You know, Jim, law school isn't for everybody."

"The admission process is very competitive," Slaughter continued. "When we admitted you, we gave you a seat that could have been given to another applicant. There's no shame in it not working out." Slaughter tossed the blue book on the table before me, leaned back in his chair, and then stared at me in silence. Slaughter assumed I was a goof-off; his deportment made his opinion and objective clear: I couldn't hack law school, and I should make a graceful exit.

His words presented a clear vision of my vaporizing future. My throat felt so constricted that I thought I might hyperventilate. I looked down at my bluebook exam, tossed like rubbish on the table. It was as if Slaughter had stuffed it in a symbolic toilet and now wanted me to flush it, along with all my dreams.

I'd been here before. My mind flashed back to that time when the boy's dean called me to his office and kicked me out of high school. That was different: I took the blame for being an intentional screw-up with Frank, and we both deserved expulsion. Now, daily, I almost killed myself trying to juggle work and school. The material wasn't too hard, and I could do it if given the time. None of that mattered now: Slaughter wanted to make room for someone else. A swelling anger boiled over my initial surge of panic. My jaw tightened in defiance: "Dean Slaughter, at what grade point average does UCLA involuntarily drop a student?"

"65.0 percent," he said.

"Any what is mine right now?"

"About 65.7 percent," he replied.

"Then as far as I'm concerned, there is a 'point-seven' difference between us ever having this conversation again." I refused to quit.

To his credit, when I told Slaughter of my personal situation, he grew far more sympathetic. He suggested I take a leave of absence and try to save enough money for school, and apply for student loans. It was either that or take the upcoming second semester finals and risk losing my seat forever if my grades flat-lined. I had no choice: I was too far behind to catch up with my studies in time for test week. I signed the request for a leave of absence, and he approved it on the spot.

For the second time in my life, I found myself out of school when I wanted to be in.

As I discovered again, when things go wrong, they go wrong all at the same time. I'd taken up bartending so as to attend law school in the day; now it looked like bartending might cost me my law school chance. It made me grow resentful; instead of fawning over big spenders, I grew irritated with their blowing on drinks in one night more money than I needed to finance my entire legal education. My nights seemed even more occupied with loud-mouthed drunks and fistfights; the clientele didn't change, but I guess my toleration level did. Bartending stopped being fun; the kicks were gone. Now it was just hard work.

Gay was my one remaining ray of sunshine; she never ceased to show me love and encouragement. Then one morning while I was at her house, she began sobbing as she hung up the phone. Her mother had called; she said doctors diagnosed both of Gay's parents with terminal cancer. She needed to move home to Palm Springs to care for them. We decided that I'd keep working in Hollywood, awaiting my return to UCLA. However, as the months passed and her parents' condition deteriorated, I was only a distant comfort. When Gay asked me to move to the desert and accelerate our marriage plans, my answer was no. I had been through too much to quit school, but Gay needed me now, not at some uncertain graduation date. One night she called and tearfully broke our engagement. Because I loved her I understood, but understanding didn't lessen the ache.

While out of school I moved from bar to bar searching for that larger tip jar, but I never found it. Good money wasn't to be had in the rowdy joints where I worked, and the elegant restaurants had no openings. Even that fat tip jar I saw on my first Palomino visit proved to be an illusion: The front bartenders collected the tips and then divided them with five unseen service bartenders working in the back. On a busy night at the club, I cleared maybe $30 in tips. I barely made ends meet with my earnings. My hope of bankrolling cash for law school wasn't happening.

I was in between bartending gigs when Frank quit his job as a bouncer at the Pussycat Theater, a local porno movie house in Canoga Park. He recommended me as his replacement, and I took the job. I couldn't afford to be too particular about a paycheck when I wasn't working. If I had to be a porno theater bouncer to finish school, then the porno theater would have to do. Still, replacing Frank at the Pussycat was the nadir of my working experience. My job involved walking up and down the aisles, shining my flashlight on customers I suspected of masturbating and shouting at them: *"Hey—No mas! Vamanos!"* At the end of the night, the manager collected the used popcorn and drink cups thrown on the floor; the next day he reused them, cheating the owner out of concession stand receipts (inventory was kept based on the number of containers used). Then he'd scrape hardened grease off unsold hot dogs from the night before and throw them back on the rotisserie the next day. When rats in the storage locker chewed open unsold candy boxes, he'd dump the remaining candy into used boxes and glue it closed. We got into an argument over it; I can't remember if I quit or he fired me. I lasted there about a week.

I was tired, angry, increasingly bitter, and brokenhearted by Gay. I tried to ease the pain by shuffling between cocktail waitresses, band vocalists, models, and struggling actresses I met behind the bar, but I ended up showing them all the emotional attachment that General Sherman showed the people of Atlanta. I knew how far I had slipped from Gay's classy standard when my latest fling invited me to a preview of her movie, a dungeons-and-dragons-genre film called *The Sword and the Sorcerer.* Lori was a wanna-be actress who had earlier jump-started her career with a multipage nude photo spread in *Penthouse.* As we sat in the darkened theater, I waited for Lori to make her debut on the silver screen. Ten minutes went by, then twenty, then forty-five, but still no girlfriend sighting. "My part's coming up!" she giggled excitedly at the inevitable Roman orgy scene. As the camera panned the morning-after coterie of drunken lechers, Lori called out, "There I am! There I am!" I couldn't pick her out from the cluster of castle trash shaking off the cobwebs from their night of debauchery. "Which one are you?" I asked.

"Right there!" she replied excitedly. "I'm third whore from left."

Sometimes we make life out to be much tougher than it really is; that was certainly true of me at this juncture. When I tired of wallowing in self-pity, I took stock of my situation and found it to be difficult, but not hopeless. Yes, I was on the verge of being kicked out of law school, but be-ing *on the verge* is very different from being *kicked out*. It didn't take a rocket scientist to figure out how to correct the problem: Quit working full time and at night for the sake of my grades, and dump the nightlife for the sake of my stability. I decided that if I took any more side jobs while in school, they'd be part-time and law related.

As my leave of absence neared its end and the time came to resume my studies at UCLA Law School, I poured my last drink behind a bar. This time, I wised up and took out as many student loans as I could grab. Instead of living far from campus, I sold all my furniture, put the rest of my stuff in storage, and gave up my apartment. I traded the long freeway commute from the San Fernando Valley for the trashy, bohemian student co-op only a few blocks from campus. The five-story concrete co-op was populated by students who either didn't win a room in the UCLA dorm lottery, couldn't afford private off-campus housing, or who were leftover hippies longing for their free love and pot-smoking days of yore. I fit into the first two categories; the third category comprised the "professional students" evading life's responsibilities by triple-majoring in valueless courses and remaining well beyond the standard duration of four years—while the government they despised and ranted against subsidized their education and indolent lifestyle. What a place.

My second-floor co-op room overlooked the trash dumpsters, which gave off a constant aroma to match the ambience. The sickening smell suppressed my appetite, which suited me perfectly under the circum-stances. Co-op food made Army K-rations look gourmet by comparison:

The cook made meals from whatever he hashed together. Dinner might be a pot of peanut butter soup, or a mushroom-and-onion sandwich; our fruit came rotten and badly bruised, purchased for pennies-on-the-dollar at the local farmer's market. Despite all this, the co-op was really cheap: $400 for room and board for the entire semester, and *cheap* was what I needed.

I had mixed luck with co-op neighbors and roommates. My first roommate ranked among the worst—a guy who cut out magazine pictures of women's bare feet and taped them inside his locker to gratify his toe fetish. I kicked him out after a couple of days when I caught him staring lustily at my date's sandaled and pedicured foot. Psycho Roy came in a close second. He lived upstairs; his idea of a practical joke was to shove the communal Kenmore dryer off the co-op roof, or to ship to his despised father on Christmas a blender stuffed with feces. Then we had George, an Elmer Fuddish student who kept trying to get me kicked out of the co-op because I criticized its socialist structure ("I hate woo, Wogan. Why won't wu moow away, and won't wum wack?") There was Montwid, a harmless but terminally stingy kid who gobbled as many slices as he could of the large pizza that everyone chipped in to buy, then happily bragged to daddy that he always got more than his money's worth. Montwid lacked social grace and common sense so badly that his name became an adjective for dumbness ("You poked yourself in the eye? What a montwid thing to do.")

Not everyone at the co-op fell into the caricature category. You had to respect my baseball-ace friend Mari Nelson, a woman who could throw a fastball like Sandy Koufax. After a game of catch with Mari, I needed to ice my swollen hand. Another of my roommates, Mitch Hanlon, turned out to be a refined, cultured undergrad whose choirboy innocence belied a devilishly sarcastic wit. One of the best guys I've ever known, Mitch was an accomplished musician studying to be a doctor; in time, he gave up pre-med and followed his heart. Then there was Raffi Kuredjian, a roommate who, like Mitch, became a lifelong friend. Raffi embodied the bull-in-a-china-shop personality. He was loud and brassy: If my rough edges needed smoothing, Raffi's needed dynamiting. When we went to a nightclub looking to meet women, he thought nothing of elbowing me aside, interrupting my pickup lines, and blaring: "Hey, *bay-bee*! Don't dance with this guy! Why don't you let the best lookin' man in the whole bar show you how it's done! Come on, *bay-bee*!" Raffi then would grab her hand and yank her onto the dance floor without awaiting her reply. However maddening his ultra-rude encroachment seemed, it worked far too often. To add insult to injury, after poaching on my intended date, Raffi would come back to bum twenty bucks off me so he could buy her more drinks.

Raffi and I had no shame in trying to one-up each other in the pickup department, but most women found our childish antics more entertaining or annoying than date-worthy. One was Daphne, a pretty brunette we both competed for unsuccessfully. Daphne was our neighbor in the co-op; whenever we saw her in the dining area we shoved and wrestled our way to her table, and then dominated the conversation by acting like jackasses, alternatively complimenting her and playfully insulting each other. Daphne always laughed at our jousting for her attentions, but in the end, we both struck out. Besides, Daphne spent all her free time at acting classes. Avoiding Raffi's and my romantic interests didn't do her any harm: Not too long afterward, she landed a big movie part and went on her way to Hollywood success: actress Daphne Zuniga.

Raffi was fearless. One night we heard a woman scream that two guys just stole her car. "Come on, Raf!" I called as the stolen car careened in our direction. Raffi took my invitation to good citizenry too literally. As the car screeched by us, I positioned myself to get the license number. Raffi didn't waste time with such details: He dove through the driver's open window, grabbed hold of the thief's neck, and pummeled him with his free hand as the car dragged him up the street.

Friendships such as these made the otherwise dilapidated co-op a tolerable, and at times wonderful, memory.

My initial law school experience had been so harsh that I dreaded returning. That battering first semester had left my confidence shaken, and this festered during my hiatus out of school. As it turned out, my fears proved unfounded. Once I reentered the classroom and watched professors tie fellow students in intellectual knots, I felt perfectly at home. Also, it made a huge difference that I lived near campus instead of commuting, that I studied in the law library instead of reading by the bar's sink lights, and that I didn't exhaust myself with fifty-hour workweeks on top of a rigorous class schedule. Calmer diversions now replaced my earlier distractions: Instead of breaking up fistfights and knifings, my after-class hours might find me helping Laura Birkmeyer shop for a melon-ball spoon for her school party, or trying unsuccessfully to beat Jeannine Gallant at the co-op's Pac Man video game tournament. This time, nobody threatened to kick me out of school. This time, I knew I'd make it.

If anything, boredom replaced intimidation. Much of law school study focuses on the theoretical rather than the practical. I liked the law, and later came to love it, but years of working and struggling left me dissatisfied with mere abstract learning. Ready to be done with the preliminaries, I just wanted to get on with the real world. Still, I did what I needed to do, and even achieved a modicum of academic excellence, earning a coveted slot on the prestigious *UCLA Law Review*. Having this on my resume assured that I could get a top legal job upon graduation.

I couldn't help but notice how many of my formerly fun classmates started to adopt a stiffer corporate persona as they approached graduation. That didn't work for me. Still too much a Mission District kid, I couldn't pull off that personality makeover and never wanted to try. Besides, my irreverent sense of humor always percolated to the surface. When I tried to punch occasional lighthearted holes in otherwise serious classroom discussions, it left some of my more staid professors scratching their heads about me. In one class, we discussed *ad nauseum* (Latin for "the subject was so talked to death that all the listeners felt like barfing") three ancient English criminal cases (*Regina v. Charleston*, *Regina v. Cunningham*, and *Regina v. Stanley*). In the United Kingdom, the state brings cases against criminal defendants in the name of the King (*Rex*) or the Queen (*Regina*). Tiring of a particularly dull discussion, I got a laugh when I raised my hand and jokingly asked the professor a politically incorrect question: "If this *Regina* chick is such bad news, then why do they keep letting her out of jail to commit more crimes?" In another class the professor discussed a concept called "the prisoner's dilemma": Should an innocent defendant plea bargain and accept one year in jail, or risk trial against strong circumstantial evidence and face life in prison upon conviction? While debating the issue with his students, the professor kept categorizing the first option as "only" a year in jail, and insisting such minimal time did not warrant the risk of lifetime incarceration. When he sucked me into the debate, I challenged his perspective with one of my own: "Professor, your opinion might change if you didn't view it as 'only' one year in jail; try thinking about it as 365 individual visits to the prison shower."

My subtle rebellion against the stuffiness of the legal world seeped into my on-campus job interviews with law firms—sometimes not so subtly. One particularly officious prospective employer sat across the interview desk from me weighing my worthiness to clerk for him. He started the interview by telling me he read only the first page of my two-page resume: "Resumes should be only one page," he huffed in his snottiest tone. "When someone gives me two pages, I only read the first page and throw the second page away." With that, he crumpled the second page of my resume and threw it at me, bouncing the wadded-up paper off my chest.

"The reason my resume is two pages," I told him as I threw the page back, "is that I've led a two-page life. You seem like a guy who's led a half-page life, and probably would be more comfortable with a quarter-page clerk." I didn't get a callback on that one.

In another interview, some incapable-of-improvising lawyer read his canned list of pre-employment questions to me. Near the end of the ordeal, he asked me to identify my three weakest points. I politely explained the silliness of his question, suggesting that anyone with truly "weak" points wouldn't reveal them in competitive interviews with a prospective employer. Unable to veer from his script, he again read to me the question from his checklist. "Well, let me think," I said as I tapped my forehead. "Okay, I've got it. I'm an alcoholic, I sell nuclear secrets to the Soviets, and I crack under pressure. Other than that, I'd make a hell of a lawyer." I watched him copy dutifully my answers onto my resume so he wouldn't forget them when considering my application. Alas, another lost callback!

My wise-guy cracks got some laughs, but an impertinent sense of humor had its social consequences. I kept asking my hottie classmate Laura Birkmeyer for a date; although we went out many times, Laura always clarified at the start of the evening it wasn't a "date." The first time she told me that, it left me confused: "But Laura, I asked you out. We've gone to dinner and a movie. If that's not a date, what is it?" Laura stared at me for a moment, and then she replied: "It's—*it's an appointment.*" Laura and I had many *appointments* during law school, but she drew the romance line in the sand at each one. At a law school party, I tried to tee up yet again with Laura, but without success. Later that night, I overheard classmate Janice Orenshein tell her, "You know, Rogan would probably be fun for you to date, but he sure has some *rough edges.*"

I may never have gotten past the appointment stage with my still-dear friend Laura, but at least I salvaged from the rejection a great future book title!

Though I now was free of the Hollywood nightlife, I never shook loose from my old friend Frank Debrose. The summer before graduation, I received invitations from some prestigious firms to join them for a law student rite-of-passage: the coveted summer clerkship. Wanting to experience a change of pace, I eschewed my Los Angeles and Honolulu offers and selected an Atlanta firm simply because I thought it might be fun to live for a while in the South. Meanwhile, Frank needed a home again: After he bankrupted his now ex-girlfriend's family business, she kicked him out. Making the mistake of feeling sorry for Frank, I let him come with me to Atlanta.

I drove from California to Georgia in my old 1971 Chevy Impala; Frank followed behind in his '73 Impala. Our beat-up junker cars looked like "probable cause to search" on wheels: Driving across Alabama, we were stopped and our cars searched by every single state trooper whose path we crossed on the highway. Whenever a trooper pulled me over, I invited him to search my car at his leisure. In contrast, jackass Frank always took a different tack: "Hey, Smokey, I wasn't speeding. What's the roust? I'm a taxpayer and a veteran. You work for me. This is America! What's your problem?" That speech always guaranteed we'd be detained an extra couple of hours; I grew accustomed to sitting on the curb and watching Frank's interior seats and hubcaps being tossed onto the side of the road while the dope search intensified.

Once we made it to Atlanta, we shared an apartment near Emory University. While I summer clerked at Powell Goldstein Frazier & Murphy, an old-line firm with blue-chip clients, Frank found an evening bartending job at a strip joint on Cheshire Bridge Road. Because of competing work schedules I saw little of Frank, but I always knew when he was home: Some stripper left a trail of bejeweled bras and panties strewn on the floor leading to his room. I kept warning Frank to be careful of the company he kept, since the Cheshire Bridge neighborhood had a seedy reputation. However, Frank's edginess more than matched Cheshire Bridge's notoriety. Near the end of summer, with a few days left on my clerkship, I returned to the apartment one evening and found a pale, trembling Frank trying to cover a still-smoldering shotgun hole blasted in the ceiling. He wouldn't tell me how it got there; he only insisted we needed to get out of town *now*. When I refused to leave before my clerkship ended, Frank spent his last sleepless days in Atlanta peering out the window through a crack in the Venetian blinds, nursing his secret concern. The day we packed the car to head home to Los Angeles, I never saw a chubby guy move so fast.

Not long before graduation, I took my daily jog around the perimeter of UCLA. As I ran down the dirt trail bordering Sunset Boulevard, I approached a fork in the road. Through the corner of my eye, I saw another jogger, an older man, nearing the intersection at the same time. At first I sped up, and then I slowed down: I wanted to be either ahead of him or behind, but not shoulder to shoulder when our paths intersected on the narrow path. He must have had the same instinct, because he mimicked my speed changes at the same time. We chuckled and nodded a greeting when we ended up alongside each other on the dirt trail despite our mutual attempt to avoid it. Since we jogged at the same pace, we struck up a conversation. It turned out we were both native San Franciscans, so the bulk of our conversation centered on hometown interests.

As we passed the row of sorority houses on Hilgard Avenue, the jogger studied a bevy of coed beauties sunning themselves on a porch before letting out a sigh of envy: "Man, you single guys today have got it knocked. Look at all those gorgeous girls! Today young guys get it all. Back when I was your age, we never got anything before marriage beyond copping a feel on the dance floor. All we ever got was the promise of much more once you put a ring on the girl's finger and tied the knot. But, hey—we all learned how to be pretty good dancers!" I asked where he used to dance during his youth in the city; his casual reply almost rocked me back on my heels: "We used to hang out at a club called the Cable Car Village."

The Cable Car Village? I halted in my tracks. This was the bar where my mother worked as a cocktail waitress when bartender John Baroni impregnated and then abandoned her a quarter century earlier. "My mother used to work there," I told him, trying not to let my jaw slack open. "Her name was Alice Kleupfer. Did you ever know her?"

"Oh, Christ!" he exclaimed. "I knew Ali! A cute platinum blonde with a long ponytail. I dated one of her friends! Ali was a hell of a dancer. What a small world. So that's your mom, huh? How's she doin' these days?" My heart pounded from both the run and the news. I brushed off his questions with one of my own: "Did you also know a bartender there named John Baroni?"

"Sure!" he said, still beaming at the *small world* nature of our conversation. "Jack was one of my good friends growing up. We went to school together." I took one more breath, and then asked the jackpot question: "Is he still alive?"

"Well, I hope so!" the jogger chuckled. "I just talked to him last week."

Bingo.

My face must have lost color, because suddenly the jogger stopped smiling. He looked concerned: "Hey," he asked, "Is everything okay? How do you know Jack?"

"You better sit down on the curb," I suggested breathlessly. "I have a story you need to hear."

By the time I finished my account, the jogger looked dumbstruck. "Look," he told me, "Jack's got a family now. I don't know how he's gonna feel about all this. Why don't you write him a letter and seal it. Send it to me, and I'll mail it to him. If he contacts you, well, that's up to him." I got the jogger's name and address; we shook hands and he wished me luck as we parted company.

In my letter to John Baroni I got straight to the point. I told him who I was, and that I would soon finish law school. I gave him my address and telephone number in case he wanted to contact me; if he chose not to, I wouldn't disturb him again. For days thereafter, each time the telephone rang, I wondered silently if it was him. Each time it wasn't, I felt the competing emotions of disappointment and relief. Then one afternoon I was at my part-time law clerk job at the California State Bar when the receptionist paged me: "You have a call from a Mr. Baroni." I closed the door and sat at my small desk. After staring at the phone for a moment, I lifted the receiver. A nervous voice on the other end asked if he was talking to Jim Rogan.

So many times in my life I thought of him and wondered how he felt about having a child somewhere in the world. I didn't know what to expect when he called, but I knew what I wanted to hear. I wanted him to be a man, accept responsibility, and give me the chance to connect with the other half of my biology.

I didn't hear that speech.

"This is Jack Baroni," he stammered. "I got your letter. I don't know what to say. I know you think I'm your father. Well, uh, maybe I am, and maybe I'm not. Who knows? Anyway, what do you want from me?"

What do you want from me?

For a moment, I couldn't breathe. I spent fifteen years looking for my father, wondering about his health, his family, his well-being. Now we were speaking, and his first question was *what do you want from me?* I felt nauseous.

Trying to shake off the blow, I replied in the most measured tone I could muster: "I don't want or need anything from you. I'm graduating from law school soon, so my future's set. I looked for you all these years to make sure you were okay, and to let you know I was, too. If I had a kid out there, I'd want to know him. I thought you might feel the same way. I'm not trying to cause you any trouble. This won't happen again. I'm sorry—I've got to go."

"Well, wait a minute, don't hang up," he interrupted. "We can talk for a few minutes. That won't hurt anything."

He spoke without emotion, telling me that he and my mother had dated. When she became pregnant, she said he was the father. "Your grandfather came to see me and told me to marry her," he said. "I told him what I'm telling you," he continued. "How do I know I'm the father? Maybe I am, and maybe I'm not. It could be me, or it could be someone else. I don't know. After all, she worked in a bar. I was in love with another girl at the time. We got married. This was all a long time ago."

Putting aside his suggestion that my mother was a young slut rather than a girl who lost her innocence to the wrong fellow, I tried masking my simmering anger: "She says you were her first—and only—before she became pregnant."

"But how do I know?" he insisted. "Maybe I was, and maybe I wasn't."

"We can find out if you really want to know," I replied. "There's an easy ways to do it. We can take a paternity test. We can put this question to bed." The suggestion of a paternity test made him uncomfortable, and he changed the subject.

In a firing squad, there is an ancient tradition: One rifle is loaded secretly with a blank round. This practice grants each of the executioners the psychological possibility that he did not fire the fatal shot. The man whose name appeared on my birth certificate now sought the same comfort: He wanted deniability, not truth. As he continued in this vein, a wave of disgust came over me. I hoped he wasn't my father.

Senator Edward Kennedy with me and my two boyhood buddies and fellow political junkies, Dan Swanson *(left)* and Roger Mahan *(center)*, May 1971. Almost thirty years later, on the last day of President Clinton's impeachment trial, I pulled this picture out of my briefcase and showed it to Ted Kennedy as we chatted on the Senate floor. Ted got such a chuckle from the old photo that he took it around to show his colleagues in the Senate chamber.

HARRY S TRUMAN
INDEPENDENCE, MISSOURI
August 19, 1970

Dear Mr. Rogan:

I was glad to autographed your engraved picture of the White House and it is being returned to you herewith.

The "S" in my name stands for the first letter of the first name of each of my grandfathers. In order to be strictly impartial in naming me for one or the other, I was given the letter "S" as a middle name. It can be used with or without a period after it.

I appreciate your very kind comments and send you best wishes,

Sincerely yours,

Harry Truman

Mr. James Rogan
25 Poncetta Drive
Apt. #110
Daly City, California 94015

President Harry S Truman helped me to settle a score with my obnoxious seventh grade teacher, Mr. Puhr.

Former vice president Hubert Humphrey took time to greet me at the KGO radio studio in 1971. Later he shared with me this advice about politics and life: "Work hard, study hard, fight the good fight, and my friend, be of good cheer."

Shaking Governor Ronald Reagan's hand, Walnut Creek, California, June 1973. This was the day I talked Reagan into giving me his handwritten speech note cards *(below)*.

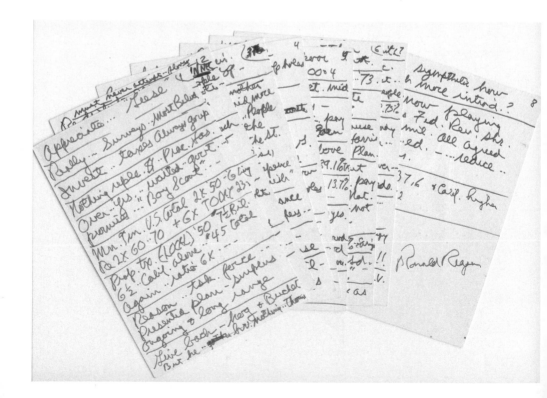

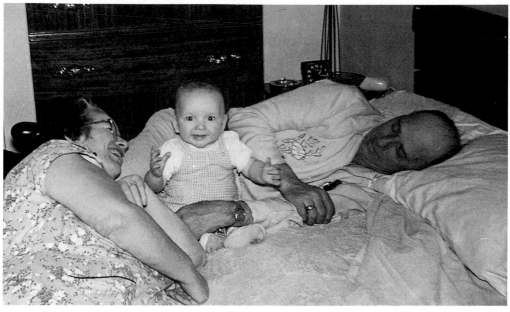

My grandparents, Jimmy and Helen Kleupfer, doting over me, 1958.

My legendary Uncle Jack. Every kid I grew up with wished he had an Uncle Jack!

Here I am as a first grade student of Sister Mary Clarence. Note the cockeyed bow tie, which I twisted as a silent act of defiance to my fearsome nun.

My mother, Alice Rogan,
at her high school graduation, 1953.

My biological father, Jack Barone,
bartending at San Francisco's
Bimbo's 365 nightclub, 1956.

The incomparable Frank Debrose *(left)* and Rocky Iaukea, my two Pinole pals.

Working the 525-degree oven at Straw Hat Pizza in Livermore, 1977.

I was a delegate to the 1978 Democratic midterm convention in Memphis; the youthful Arkansas attorney general I met there would make more than one important appearance in my life.

Frank Debrose, Bret Muncy, Yours Truly, Dan Swanson, and Bob Wyatt at our "Farewell to Northern California" party, 1979. Later that night Frank, Bob, and I drove a rental van all night long to our new life in Los Angeles.

Bartending at the world-famous Palomino Club in North Hollywood, with our immigrant bar-boy from Eastern Europe, Tzonko. The only English poor Tzonko knew was what he had learned while working in this hell-raising, two-fisted cowboy bar.

With my mother Alice, sister Teri, and brothers John and Pat, 1986.

Judge Barbara Lee Burke swore me in as a new judge while Christine held the Bible, December 14, 1990. Christine later said she looked so stern from trying not to weep with pride; I think it's because someone just told her I was taking yet another pay cut!

Talking to the press after arraigning a murder suspect, 1988.

Holding our newborn twin daughters, Claire and Dana, 1992.

Christine, the twins, and I spent the morning of Election Day 1994 relaxing and unwinding from my roughhouse campaign for the California State Assembly.

With former presidents Richard Nixon *(above)* and Gerald Ford *(below)*. Ford gave me his autograph when I was a boy; twenty-five years later, he campaigned for me for Congress.

With former president and Mrs. Jimmy Carter *(above)*; introducing Ronald Reagan to my family *(below)*.

With Presidents Bush: George H. W., the forty-first president, and George W., the forty-third.

With my family and President Bill Clinton in happier times; a year later, he and I were combatants during his impeachment and trial before Congress.

The thirteen house managers who prosecuted President Clinton's impeachment trial, 1999.

After blanketing himself with more disclaimers, he pivoted and asked questions about my life and family. To me this was useless chatter. "If you're not my father, then what do you care where I went to high school?" I wondered privately. Still, I kept my temper in check and answered him. Since I expected this first conversation to be our last, I tried to glean as much information about him as possible. When I asked if he was still bartending, he exclaimed, "Oh, hell no! That was part-time work while I did construction. I've been a general contractor most of my life." He said he married Bev, the woman to whom he was engaged while he dated Mom on the side, and they were still married. Bev had not been able to bear children; her adopted son from a previous marriage was about my age.

I also learned why I never found him: When they dated, Mom knew him as "Jack Baroni." When I was born, Mom entered his name on the birth record; she assumed his formal first name was "John." Not only did she have the first name wrong (his given name was *Jack*), she spelled his last name phonetically (and incorrectly), using an "i" instead of an "e." So, while I spent all those years searching telephone directories and records for *"John Baroni,"* I never thought to look for *"Jack Barone."*

He asked if I ever visited San Francisco; I told him I made frequent trips there to see my family. "Well, give me a call when you're up here. We can go have a drink and meet each other."

"As a matter of fact, I'll be there in two days," I replied.

After another bout of stammering, Jack suggested we meet for lunch. Now it was my turn to balk. "If you don't acknowledge me as your son, what's the point of meeting?" I asked.

"Well, you just sound like a good kid and I'd like to meet you." When I begged off, he persisted: *"Please?"* I agreed reluctantly to meet.

A week later, I was the first to arrive at Joe's of Westlake restaurant in nearby Daly City. I waited for Jack near the cocktail lounge, his designated rendezvous spot. We had no photographs to ease identification; we had only a general physical description of each other. Waiting for him was a wrenching exercise. Each time the front door to Joe's swung open and a middle-aged man entered, my heart jumped. I studied the face, searching for some glint of familiarity while wondering, "Is *that* him? Is *he* my father?" I saw my "father" enter a dozen or more times, only to have the man walk past me and greet a waiting friend. It was awful.

When Jack Barone did arrive, he knew me right away. It was a good thing: I wouldn't have picked him out of a lineup. Unlike me, he was short, with an olive complexion and black wavy hair. We shook hands; he ordered a round of drinks, and then we sat at a corner table. The encounter became increasingly awkward; the wine glass in Jack's hand trembled as I endured more of his strained paternity theories. Mostly he showed a clear lack of enthusiasm to determine the truth. Strangely, when he treated me to this litany during our telephone conversation, I grew angry. Now I just shrugged it off: "He doesn't look like me," I thought. "He's probably not my father after all."

Jack asked a favor: Would I drive with him to his home in Marin County and meet his family? I said no—what was the point? If he didn't admit I was his son, I didn't want to be on display for his relatives and neighbors like a sideshow attraction. He pleaded with both his voice and his eyes. I gritted my teeth and relented.

An hour later, we headed up his private, tree-lined driveway in Kentfield. His wife Bev was warm, gracious, and welcoming as she ushered me to a seat in their kitchen. Bev said she knew about me before her marriage to Jack. "In fact, I was pushing my baby's stroller in Golden Gate Park when I saw your mother pushing you. My girlfriend pointed you out and said, 'There's Jack's other son.'"

After Bev served coffee, she stepped back to size up Jack and me visually. "You know, I definitely see the resemblance," she said. "Your faces look very similar. You have the exact same smiles and eyes. In fact, both of you squint your left eye when you smile. Oh, yes—I definitely see the resemblance!" Jack scowled at her, but she ignored him and continued: "My feeling is this: If you're Jack's son, then that makes you my son, too. And I think we need to find out." Jack cleared his throat and shot her yet another dirty look. Meanwhile, Bev volunteered information about Jack and his roots while pulling out old family photo albums to show me. One particular picture caught my eye: It depicted Jack doing his Al Jolson impression. "Jolson was one of my favorite singers," he said, "but you're too young to know him." Jack didn't know that from the time I was a kid, nobody could explain why I fixed on Al Jolson (who died in 1950) as one of my favorite singers. As a teen, I had a collection of Jolson records and tapes. Now I kept the Jolson connection to myself: "He was before my time," I replied, and then turned the album page.

When it came time to leave, Bev made me promise to write. She pulled me aside and whispered, "Jack will need to resolve this. Give him some time. He'll come around." Jack then drove me home. We suffered another awkward moment as we sat in the car looking for the appropriate parting words. He tried to stuff $150 into my pocket, telling me "Here, go buy your pals dinner tonight." I know he meant it as a kindness, but it rubbed me the wrong way. I kept remembering that first phone call. I left the money on the front seat. "Well, let's keep in touch. You're a good kid," he told me as I stepped from his car. As he drove away, I saw him watching me in his rearview mirror until the car pulled out of sight.

As promised, I wrote to Bev and him over the next dozen years. She replied to each letter; he never wrote once. During my youth, I wanted to know the truth and let the chips fall where they may. I got my wish: The truth was that my father didn't care that he had a son.

There was only one way for me to deal with the ancient ghost of Jack Barone. I returned it to the grave and moved on.

I turned in my final law school examination one blustery day in December 1983 and walked back to the co-op for the last time. With enough credits to graduate six months before the formal cap-and-gown ceremony, there would be no pomp to commemorate my milestone. The chaotic adventure that began years ago came to an anticlimactic, private end. Without a moment to lose, I packed my belongings, threw them into the back seat of my old Chevy, and drove away. It was time to begin a new journey—and a completely new life.

That evening I drove to San Francisco, where, for the next ten weeks, I lived in the basement of my brother Pat's home while studying for the California Bar Exam. I followed a very strict regimen: For two months I studied eighteen hours a day, allowing myself no entertainment except a daily workout at a local gym. I concentrated on studying and nothing else: I didn't intend to suffer through this grueling bar exam ordeal twice. After taking the three-day test, I again packed my car and returned to Southern California, where I had previously accepted an associate attorney position with a prestigious, one hundred-year-old Los Angeles law firm.

As it turned out, Frank lived in a small rental apartment in Glendale, a suburb of Los Angeles. For once, he reciprocated my hospitalities by inviting me to sleep on his couch until I found a permanent place to live. Because I intended to find an apartment about twenty miles away and close to the ocean, I viewed Glendale as a temporary shelter.

Frank's unchanged, raucous lifestyle simply accelerated my plans to find an apartment as soon as possible. I couldn't sleep amid the all-night partying romps with his revolving-door girlfriends. After a few nights like that, I went for a walk one morning, determined to rent the first available unit I could find just to get some rest. I didn't have to go far: Half a block away, I saw a sign on a building advertising an available apartment. I signed the lease on the spot, and the next day moved into apartment #136 at 245 West Loraine Street.

Glendale ended up being more than a place where I just "passed through." And although I'll tell you about it later in the book, my walk down Loraine Street that morning to get away from Frank's craziness proved to have the single greatest impact on my life.

I saw it all: illegitimacy, abandonment, death, alcoholism, jail, welfare, food stamps, drugs, bartending, bikers, knifings, and heartbreaks too numerous to count. It all came back to me on June 1, 1984, when I received a letter notifying me that I passed the California Bar Exam on the first try. Now it was James E. Rogan, Attorney at Law. On the day I took the oath of admission to the bar at San Francisco's Scottish Rite Temple, there was Frank Debrose, reminding me of my roots: "Hey, not bad for a Mission kid Grandma used to whack with the pancake turner!"

If getting my law license was *a* milestone, it wasn't *the* milestone. Attorney General Bill Clinton told me years earlier that a law degree made a great fallback position for someone who wants to run for Congress. With Washington as my true goal, a law degree moved me just another step toward the goal. Still, going in so short a time from bartender to lawyer made a big cultural difference. Now I'd wear suits to work instead of an ankle or shoulder holster. After bartending for Hell's Angels, how hard could lawyering be? I'd much rather be called an attorney than be called a porno theater bouncer. For me, that comparison alone made it easy to indulge the notion that, no matter what happened next, I had made it.

At least I thought I had.

As a new first-year associate at Lillick McHose & Charles, I earned a near-astronomical starting salary of $40,000 a year. Coming off so many below–minimum wage jobs, I'd never seen so many zeros before. The firm gave me my own wood-paneled office on the 43rd floor of a Wilshire Boulevard skyscraper; I had a secretary, dining privileges at some of L.A.'s swanky private clubs, and a staff of law clerks and paralegals to handle much of the grunt work. Despite all this, my satisfaction with practicing corporate law hit a wall almost immediately.

As my first attorney assignment, I defended a company that owned a cargo ship. The plaintiff was an old longshoreman whom my client disfigured severely through sheer negligence. After studying the file and researching the law, I filed a motion to dismiss the case based on a legal technicality that I uncovered. Two of my firm's partners came with me to court and watched me argue the motion; I won, and the judge tossed out the injured stevedore's claim.

While the partners slapped me on the back and congratulated me for doing such a fine job, I looked across the courtroom and saw the longshoreman, his head hanging low, listening as his lawyer tried explaining the legalities of his loss. The old man and his wife understood only the bottom line: The shipowner crippled him, the owner was at fault, but he'd get nothing. "I don't understand," he kept saying. "I got hurt. I can't work no more. What's gonna happen to us?"

It was too much to bear. Feeling guilty, I walked over and told him I was sorry. It was nothing personal, I said—I was only doing my job. As I made this little *mea non culpa* speech (another useful Latin phrase I learned in law school: it means "It's not my fault I just screwed you over"), I never looked up from my new pair of corporate-looking wingtip shoes: I couldn't look the old man in the eye. At the end of my sputtered explanation of the advocate's obligations to a client, the old man's wife took him by the hand. "Come on, honey," she whispered tear- fully, "let's go home." I watched as they walked silently down the hallway and out of view.

Later that day I returned to that fancy new office I worked so hard to earn. I closed the door and stared out the window at the L.A. skyline try- ing to sort through my confusion. Is this what it meant to be a lawyer? Had I really worked all these years to feel miserable about winning? That old man was a longshoreman just like the man who raised me. What if this had been Grandpa? Would some pants-wetting rookie lawyer telling him "Sorry, just doin' my job" provide for his family? Who'd have taken care of Grandma, Lynn, and me?

As the months went by, when I looked beyond the freshly minted law degrees hanging on the walls of my contemporaries at the firm, I saw my fellow young associates gaining weight, drinking, and developing marital problems. Very few felt joyful about their lot. We were happy to have graduated, to have passed the bar, and to be in the club. We just didn't like what we did for a living. One of the partners picked up on my troubles. When I told him what bothered me, he tried cheering me up: "Being an associate sucks," he said, "but there's light at the end of the tunnel. Keep your head down for seven years, do what everyone tells you to do, and then if you make partner, it's all been worth it." When I asked what was the payoff in being a partner, he replied, "Because then you get your own new associates to shit on."

"Let me tell you about our DA loan-out program."

These words convinced me to join Lillick right out of law school. I had solid offers from other prestigious firms, and yet more had flirted with hiring me. But Lillick found a way to sweeten the recruitment pot. Knowing I wanted to learn how to be a courtroom lawyer, the partner assured me that if I would come to Lillick, I'd be eligible for their special training program. He promised they'd loan me to the Los Angeles County District Attorney's office for three months, where I would receive a wealth of trial experience while receiving a law firm paycheck.

"Our DA loan-out program was made for you, Jim," the partner told me. "It's good for you, because after three months of trying back-to-back cases, you'll become a skilled trial lawyer. And it's good for us, because you'll be more valuable to our firm. We'll make that investment in you, because in so doing we're really investing in the firm." With this promise dangling before me over designer pizzas at Hollywood's trendy Spago restaurant, I reached across the table, shook his hand, and accepted the position on the spot.

Soon after starting at the firm, I told the partner I was anxious to begin the DA loan-out program. "Well, we do have that program," he said, "but now that you mention it, we haven't sent anybody through it in about ten years." He promised to put me "on the list," so that when my turn came we could discuss it further. I felt snookered.

Knowing from experience that squeaky wheels get oiled, I started a yearlong, unrelenting campaign of pestering the partners about sending me. Finally, just to get me out of their hair, they agreed to send a small training class to the DA program, including me. However, they modified the original recruiting promise: They would send me for one week, not three months. I'd also be required to make up the billing hours. Having no bargaining position, I agreed.

In mid-January 1985, I began my DA training class at the Los Angeles County Traffic Courthouse. I listened that first morning as our DA instructors explained the ethical obligations of a prosecutor: Strike hard but fair blows; never charge a suspect or proceed to trial unless the evidence shows beyond a reasonable doubt—and you personally believe—that the defendant is guilty. Before starting the first mock trial exercise, the instructor asked for a volunteer and my hand shot up. I was hooked the first few minutes of the drill. The excitement of the courtroom as an arena, coupled with the high standards for prosecution, made me want this legal job more than any other.

I spent that lunch hour at the County Hall of Administration, filling out an application to be a Deputy District Attorney for Los Angeles County. A few months later, after a background check and three interviews, Assistant District Attorney Curt Livesay called and offered me the job.

The next morning I turned in my notice at Lillick. That started a stream of partners flooding into my office, trying to talk me out of quitting. One asked how I could go from now making $44,000 plus bonus, to $29,000 and no bonuses ever; another knew how to hit me where it hurt: "You want to go into politics, right? Our firm has big-money corporate clients. That's who you need if you want to run for office, not cops and crooks. You could be a partner in five years, with a beautiful home and driving nice cars. Don't throw this away for a job that will *always* be out there if you ever want to leave once you've made it."

I listened politely, but I wasn't persuaded by the arguments. "*Once I've made it?*" "Making it" to me didn't mean keeping my head down for seven years and sucking up to partners. *Making it* didn't mean apologizing for winning, and being unable to look my adversary in the eye when I did. *Making it* sure didn't mean longing for the day when I'd get my own flunky upon whom to dump.

Funny, but all my life I wanted a secure, prestigious job. As soon as I had it, I wanted to pitch it over the side. I learned it was more important to enjoy the psychic income of doing something in which I believed, and now I knew where to get it. On Monday morning, April 29, 1985, I raised my hand and took the oath of office as a new Deputy DA for Los Angeles County.

When my two-week training period ended, I got my first assignment: the Pasadena Courthouse. Reporting for work, I assumed there would be a "shepherding" period, where an experienced prosecutor would assist me until I developed a level of competence. After all, I had no trial experience and knew almost nothing about criminal law, criminal procedure, or the rules of evidence.

Wrong.

"You're the new DA in Division 4 of the municipal court," the stern head deputy said as he welcomed me aboard. "The judge takes the bench at nine, so don't be late." I was shocked to learn that the office's on-the-job training consisted of sinking or swimming. A sense of panic developed: "I don't know anything about trying cases! I don't know how to plea bargain or what a case is worth if the PD [public defender] offers to settle it. I don't know the law, and I'll be up against experienced guys on the other side. Shouldn't we get a senior DA to sit with me for a week or so until I get the hang of it?"

"Oh, you'll figure it out," my new boss told me as he handed me a stack of about thirty files set on the calendar for that day. "Here you go. Good luck, and don't do anything stupid."

Walt Lewis, the assistant head deputy of the office, overheard my plight. He called me aside and handed me a piece of paper. "Here's my office phone number," he said with a reassuring smile. "Call me from the courtroom if you have any questions." I took Walt up on his offer, calling him dozens of times that first day alone ("Walt, the PD wants 90 days in jail for his client with credit for time served if I dismiss the ADW charge and let him plead to disturbing the peace. Does that sound right to you?"). It almost never sounded right to Walt, who knew shrewd defense attorneys wanted to take advantage of my ignorance. Walt transitioned quickly from teacher-supervisor to teacher-friend.

Bartending for Hell's Angels was nothing compared to the intimidation of walking into court for the first time as a DA. The savvy public defender assigned to the same courtroom moved around with such confidence: He knew the bailiff, all the private counsel, the staff, the judge, and he knew the ropes. I didn't know anybody, and had never seen a jury trial before.

"What have I gotten myself into?"

Everything inside me clamored to run to Lillick and beg them to take me back. When I introduced myself to Joanie, the veteran court clerk, she was like a yard dog smelling fear on the mailman: "Is this your first DA assignment?" she snapped with an air of irritation. When I faked a smile and nodded yes, she rolled her eyes in frustration. "Oh, God!" she sighed, calling out to the stenographer, "We've got to break in another baby DA! This is gonna be a long week." The PD's mischievous grin let me know he planned to roll me.

That morning I bumbled my way through arraignments, pretrial conferences, sentencing hearings, disposition negotiations (lawyer talk for *plea bargain*), evidence suppression motions, and felony preliminary hearings. It was terrible to be so inept publicly. At my continued begging, the boss had a senior DA sit with me for an hour or so while I did a few preliminary hearings. She wasn't a comforting presence: She yelled at me each time I made a mistake and kept telling me how frustrating it was for her to watch someone so stupid.

By the time we broke for lunch, I wanted to climb under a large rock, but there was no time to boulder-shop. When the head deputy saw me in the hallway, he tossed me another file, captioned *People v. Bellhouse*. "This deuce [drunk driving case] is set for jury trial at 1:30. You came here to try cases, right? So go try one." When I reminded him I'd never seen a jury trial before, he gave me a blank stare before telling me, "Well, you're about to see one now."

"The PD goes first," he said. "Watch and do like him, only try to do better." Skipping lunch, I sat at my desk and used the hour trying to sort through the police reports. When I went upstairs for showtime, the same public defender who worked me over that first morning now opposed me in the Bellhouse trial. Earlier, Walt told me that since the defendant's blood alcohol level was right at the bare minimum illegal limit, it would be okay to offer him a chance to plead to a lesser charge. The defense lawyer, however, didn't want to strike a deal; he knew easy pickings when he saw them.

Before calling in the prospective jury, the very patient Judge Gary Klausner suggested to both sides that a disposition to a lesser offense might be appropriate: "The defendant's charged with driving with a point-one-zero [0.10 percent] blood alcohol level," he told me. "That's the bare minimum for a DUI conviction. Because of the calibration margin of error on the intoxylizer machine, the jury will find him not guilty on that count because they won't have a belief in his guilt beyond a reasonable doubt. I'll buy you a hot dog if you can win this case." Any microscopic shred of confidence I might have had flew out the window.

When the prospective jurors entered the courtroom and jury selection commenced, I studied the PD's sloppy approach and didn't feel quite as intimidated as before. When my turn came, I took a deep breath, forced a broad smile, and stepped before my first panel. Happily, my nervousness eased up; I felt comfortable asking questions and bantering with the jurors. It wasn't until later that it dawned on me why: I had been a bartender! In many ways, this was no different than working the clubs in Hollywood, only now I had a bailiff to handle troublemakers. Sure, I drew lots of objections when I made procedural errors, but I just accepted the court's rulings and plowed along.

On the third day of trial, the defendant took the stand confidently, but his boldness proved to be his undoing. I caught him in a lie during my cross-examination, and that's when I saw the jurors' faces change. They looked annoyed at him for trying to pull the wool over their eyes. This was his big mistake, and the jury punished him for it. Later, they found him guilty on all counts. That day I won my first trial, and also a hot dog from Judge Klausner!

The next morning, I was tossed another case set for trial in Division 4. Outside the courtroom sat a new jury panel waiting for the trial to begin. Two grandmotherly women in the group chatted together; one of them had been on my Bellhouse jury the day before. As I walked into the courtroom I greeted her; when I passed by, she turned to her friend and said excitedly:

"Do you know who that young man is? *That's the District Attorney!*"

12

FINDING A PURPOSE

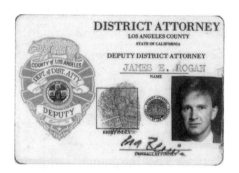

Unlike the drudgery of answering interrogatories and summarizing depositions at Lillick, each day in the DA's office brought new adventures. My colleagues and I thrived on the challenge of piecing together puzzles to create a true picture of what happened on the streets. The police investigators' shoe leather meant nothing if the DA didn't put in the necessary hours to prepare the case for trial properly. The DA's efforts—*my* efforts—ultimately determined if the bad guy walked free or got dunked.

In the months that followed I handled every imaginable type of case: strong-arm robberies, burglaries, dope peddlers, assaults, arsons, and rapes. I might see a "keeping geese without a permit" case in the morning and a "pill case"[11] that afternoon. I handled my first gang murder case with only a few weeks under my belt. Two members of the Black Urban Guerilla gang kicked the front door off the hinges at a Pasadena flop-

---

[11] "Pill Case": DA slang for a death penalty case. The phrase came from the manner in which California's lethal gas chamber operated. After guards strapped the condemned into a chair and sealed the death chamber, they dropped a cyanide pill into a bucket of acid. As the acid broke down the cyanide pill, it emitted the deadly gas. Prosecutors always studied the record carefully when deciding whether it merited "dropping a pill" on the killer.

house apartment. They shot a rival dope dealer as he sat on the couch begging for his life, and then laughed as they fled. Had they bothered looking down during the murder, they'd have seen the woman pinned underneath the door and peering up, etching into memory the killers' faces for her later in-court identification.

Every day, terrific camaraderie flowed freely between the prosecutors. I shared a small, windowless office (nicknamed "the pit") with three other deputy DAs: In the early morning we read our case files while bouncing ideas, strategies, and legal precedents off each other. We attended and critiqued each others' arguments. We went with our IOs (investigating officers) to crime scenes, autopsies, and county jail interviews, and to track down rabbits in the wind (fleeing or missing witnesses). We lectured at police departments on new search-and-seizure laws, went on late night "ride-alongs" with patrol cops to learn about their jobs and to teach them evidence collection practices to help with courtroom admissibility. We attended lineups and interrogations, and became experts on everything from fingerprints to rigor mortis.

This courthouse fellowship went beyond cops and fellow prosecutors. I developed deep respect for, and friendships with, many of my public defender and private defense counsel opponents. They had the tougher jobs. While I might spend lunchtimes sitting in my office reviewing case files, most PDs spent theirs huddled in the smelly lockup, interviewing through a wire mesh screen their never-ending supply of newly arrested clients. At day's end, I went home while the PDs did more interviews at the downtown county jail. When the case ended, the police, witnesses, victims and their families lined up to thank me; when the PD lost a case after breaking his or her neck to help a guilty defendant, often the crooks called them a "dump truck" who sold them out. When the PD won, the now-free defendant sometimes didn't bother to say thank you.

Contrary to the uninformed notion that both camps are personal enemies, DAs and PDs would commonly engage in courtroom battles in the morning and then grab a quick burger together at lunch before returning for an afternoon of more combat. During breaks, I'd find an empty jury room with my PD to negotiate pleas while we munched on the stale cookies from the basement lockup. In between plea bargains, we'd talk about our families and the judges and lawyers we liked and disliked, and share war stories. Walt Lewis, my early mentor in the job, had a theory about why these bonds were common in our offices and rare in private law firms: "In civil cases," he said, "it's about how much money people will pocket, so that makes it personal. In criminal court, it's about how much jail time some bad guy will do."

Looking back, it's funny how surroundings can change, but the basics stay the same. I traded a hardscrabble background for a law degree and a dignified job, but I found that life in the DA's office could be as crazy and colorful as life in the Mission District. And when my thoughts turn to courtroom craziness, I think of the public defender I learned the most from, fought the hardest against, and had the most laughs with: Leonard E. Read III.

A talented flamenco guitarist, Lenny Read doubled as the Peck's Bad Boy of the Los Angeles County Public Defender's Office. Looking more like a rocker than a barrister, Lenny never allowed personal appearance concerns to bedevil him. His shock of uncombed dark hair offset his shaggy beard; as courtroom attire he preferred an ugly patterned sport coat, askew neckties that coordinated with nothing, denim shirts, casual corduroy pants, and sneakers. Perpetually irritated with lying clients, everyone could hear Lenny yelling from the lockup at the newest defendant that his alibi was "full of shit," and that he'd better fess up right now. Lenny had both great instincts and a knack for getting the straight skinny on the first try.

Despite his talents as a trial lawyer, Lenny *always* found himself in trouble with his supervisors for making some off-color joke or disrespectful crack. A seventeen-year veteran of the defense bar, Lenny must have held the PD record for career punishment duty: His bosses kept shipping him to the municipal courts, normally the training ground for new prosecutors and public defenders.

Thanks to some new misstep, Lenny drew me as his rookie DA in Division 6 of the Pasadena Municipal Court, Judge Samuel L. Laidig presiding. Although Judge Laidig was honest and fair, he had grown old and cranky after spending over two decades on the municipal court. Each year he wrote and asked the governor to elevate him to the superior court, but it never happened. Forever consigned to the world of arraignments and drunk driving trials, Laidig didn't seem to take much joy in the job.

When the public defender's office shipped Lenny off to Laidig's court, I breathed a big sigh of relief. Laidig ended up yelling so much at Lenny that he was too tired to yell at me. Lenny inflamed the situation by showing little deference to the impatient jurist, and once Lenny saw how easily he could get under Laidig's skin, Lenny made a game of it. This only intensified Laidig's irritation, which in turn intensified Lenny's enjoyment of the sport.

Lenny had long ago mastered the art of using double entendres to show disdain for someone in court, while leaving nothing on the written record but an innocent-seeming transcript to avoid State Bar discipline. One day Lenny and I were litigating a dope sale case before Laidig when suddenly Laidig went off on Lenny for some minor infraction. I saw that "waiting in the weeds" look in Lenny's eyes, and I knew he would find some way to get back at the judge. It didn't take long.

In my direct examination of the undercover cop who purchased the dope from Lenny's client, I elicited testimony that went something like this:

> **Q: So after you gave the defendant money for the heroin, what happened next?**
> **A: I handed the defendant the previously marked, department-issued currency to complete the sale. Then the defendant motioned with his head over to a brown paper bag resting atop a nearby concrete wall.**
> **Q: As the defendant motioned with his head toward the bag, did he say anything?**
> **A: Yes.**
> **Q: What did he say?**
> **A: He said, "The shit's over there."**

Q: In your training and experience as an undercover narcotics officer, did that phrase have any significance to you?

A: Yes. To me it meant the heroin was inside the brown paper bag, and the defendant was inviting me to retrieve it to complete the sale.

Q: Thank you. No further questions.

Now it was Lenny's turn to cross-examine the witness, and he saw his chance to strike back at Laidig without leaving any fingerprints at the crime scene:

Q: So officer, you claim my client said [Lenny now motioned to the judge with his head and raised his voice] *"The shit's over there,"* is that right?

A: Yes.

Q: And when he said [Lenny again motioned to Laidig with his head and stared at the judge while shouting the key phrase] *"The shit's over there,"* could you hear clearly?

A: Yes.

Q: When he said [repeating the conduct] *"The shit's over there,"* how did you really know [again making the head motion] *"the shit's over there . . ."?*

This went on and on. Each time Lenny motioned with his head to Laidig and used that phrase, the judge scowled but said nothing. Laidig was annoyed that Lenny kept using a profane word, but I think he was oblivious to Lenny's purpose. If Laidig missed Lenny's intentions, nobody else in the courtroom did.

Lenny's hazing went beyond grumpy judges. Lenny disliked one police officer because he felt this cop always stretched the truth, and sometimes lied outright, whenever he took the witness stand. One day, Lenny and I were trying a case with that particular cop as a witness, and Lenny suspected the cop of making up testimony again. When he heard the cop on my direct exam mispronounce the word "asked" as "axed" repeatedly,

Lenny amused himself (and most everyone else in the courtroom) by ramming home, on cross examination, my witness's malapropism:

Q: **What did you say you did with my client after you handcuffed him?**
A: I *axed* him his name.
Q: **Did you** *axe* **him one time?**
A: No. I *axed* him many times.
Q: **I'm sorry—did you just say he** *axed* **you?**
A: No, I said I *axed* him.
Q: **Why did you want to** *axe* **my client?**
A: Because it's standard procedure.
Q: **Do they teach you in the police academy to** *axe* **suspects like this when you handcuff them?**
A: Yes. We always *axe* them when they're cuffed. . . .
Q: **And you think it's all right to** *axe* **a suspect before a jury has determined guilt or innocence?**
A: Yes, it's standard procedure.
Q: **So when he was handcuffed, that's when you just felt like** *axing* **him again and again, right?**
A: That's right.
Q: **And you felt no threat to your personal safety as you repeatedly** *axed* **this defenseless, handcuffed man, did you?**
A: No.
Q: **Your Honor, I move that the case be dismissed for police brutality. . . .**

Of all the defense attorneys I could have drawn when I prosecuted the Ding Dong Burglar, wouldn't you know it would be Lenny! In this case, a retarded looter broke into someone's home in the middle of the night. Instead of sneaking in, grabbing the booty, and fleeing, my crook grew hungry after he collected the silverware. As the victims slept upstairs, the defendant went to the kitchen, ransacked the refrigerator, sat at the table, and then ate their leftover bucket of Kentucky Fried Chicken and drank their bottle of Ocean Spray CranApple juice. The defendant made so much noise that he awoke the sleeping wife, who walked downstairs to investigate. When she saw the defendant gorging at her kitchen table, she screamed and ran nude from the house. Hearing his wife's shriek, the husband also jumped from bed and fled. Unperturbed, the defendant made no effort to escape: He returned to the cupboard, opened a box of Hostess Ding Dongs, and started munching on the individually wrapped snacks.

Within minutes, squad cars surrounded the house and a police helicopter hovered overhead. The police used a loudspeaker to order the suspect from the house with his hands up. The defendant stuffed the one Hostess snack he hadn't finished into his pants pocket and ran from the house in a feeble escape attempt. The arresting officer (my witness) tackled him to the ground, handcuffed him, patted him down for weapons, and seized the pastry in his pocket as evidence. I had the cop tell his story on direct examination. The smirk Lenny wore when he stood to cross-examine him signaled that he planned something unexpected.

Buried in the archives of the Los Angeles County Courts is an official transcript of Lenny's cross-examination, and it reads something like this:

Q: So let's go over the story one more time. After my client was handcuffed, what did you do to him?
A: For officer's safety I patted him down for weapons.
Q: And during your patdown search, did you feel anything suspicious?
A: Yes.
Q: Where was your hand when you felt the suspicious item?
A: Outside his right front pants pocket.
Q: That would be near his groin, right?
A: Yes.
Q: With your hand near his crotch, could you feel the outline of anything suspicious?
A: Yes.
Q: Describe what you felt.

A: It was a long cylindrical object.

Q: Did you grab the long cylindrical object to better identify it?

A: Yes.

Q: Did you squeeze the long cylindrical object to better identify it?

A: Yes.

Q: Did you yank on the long cylindrical object to better identify it?

A: Well, I pulled it out, yes.

Q: You eventually pulled out the long cylindrical object to identify it?

A: Yes.

Q: What was the long cylindrical object you felt and grabbed and squeezed inside my client's pants?

A: It was a Ding Dong.

Q: Can you describe his Ding Dong's appearance?

A: Yes. It was wrapped in tinfoil.

Q: Did you ever remove the tinfoil from my client's Ding Dong to inspect it further?

A: Yes.

Q: What color was my client's Ding Dong?

A: Black.

Q: Your Honor, let the record reflect my client is Caucasian, not black. This is a clear case of mistaken identity. I move to dismiss the charges.

Most people view as meritorious a prosecutor's claim never to have lost a case. I was still too green to know that seasoned prosecutors scoff at such boasts: The DA who "never lost a case" most likely is ducking the tough ones, "cherry picking" the easy ones, or simply not trying many cases. Lenny disliked trying issueless cases and wanted to plea bargain them when appropriate. By now, I had a reputation as an up-and-coming young DA, and I often reminded everyone that I had never lost a case. This string of luck left me feeling cocky with Lenny, especially since he prefered to settle his cases. The day came when, on one particular case, Lenny and I couldn't work out a deal. This one had to go to trial.

When the jury first entered the courtroom, Lenny, his client, and I sat at counsel table. The two lawyers presented a study in contrasts: I looked every bit the part of the clean-cut, bright-eyed, respectful, eager beaver fighting for justice. The slovenly Lenny looked at the jury as though they bored him, and his Superfly client did little to spruce up the picture: The defendant wore dark sunglasses, a broad white Panama hat that the bailiff kept ordering him to remove, and platform-soled acrylic-heeled pimp shoes with gambler's crap dice embedded in them. During the trial, Lenny and I teased each other privately: He called me Clark Kent and snickered at my goody-two-shoes image; I mocked him for looking like a sluggard who interrupted his homeless stay in the park to come in and try a case. As the days wore on our private joke escalated: If I caught Lenny looking at me, I'd stiffen in my chair just a little more straight at counsel table; Lenny responded by slumping just a little more in his chair. At breaks when the jury exited the court, I rose as a sign of respect for them; Lenny (still slumped in his chair) would swivel around and turn his back to them. I wore neatly pressed pinstripe suits; I think Lenny started sleeping in his unmatched clothes to give them a more authentic "thrift store" look. If I held the door open for a juror, Lenny would close it in his face. Each time I taunted Lenny that I'd eat his lunch at verdict time, he'd just smile and say, "We'll see, young man, we'll see."

When the jury sent out a note from their deliberations advising the court that they had reached a verdict, I leaned over to Lenny and whispered in advance what a pleasure it had been to kick his ass. The defense lawyer gave me a silent, paternalistic nod. The judge asked the clerk to read the verdict; several jurors smiled and nodded to me; Lenny yawned at them.

Lenny still yawned after the verdicts were read on all counts: *not guilty*.

When the judge adjourned court and I stumbled outside scratching my head in bewilderment, I ran into the jury panel. They all told me what a wonderful prosecutor I was. "You were so much better than that other guy! You were so polished and elegant! Of course, we didn't think you proved your case. But, oh, your argument was so beautiful!"

A few days later, when a fresh jury panel came in to begin a new trial pitting Lenny and me against each other, I looked over and caught Lenny's eye. This time, I ran my hands through my hair to mess it up just a bit, and then slumped into my chair. Lenny leaped from his seat and made a chivalrous bow from the waist to the entering panel. We both cracked up so hard that an annoyed Judge Laidig admonished us to shut up and stop fooling around.

Yes, my friend Lenny Read was a character in the courtroom. He was slovenly, quirky, and a comedic riot. But if you sized him up for how he looked rather than how he thought, at the end of the case you'd wake up to find him wearing your pants. I had a lot of fun and learned a lot from Lenny; mostly he showed me how to take my job seriously, but not myself.

Lenny wasn't the only colorful defense attorney whose path I crossed in the Pasadena courts during my early days as a prosecutor. Charlie Lloyd comes to mind—a flamboyant trial lawyer who kept more than one murderer out of the gas chamber by making his signature closing argument: Charlie would drop to his knees before the jury, fold his hands as if pleading, and sob crocodile tears as he repeated ten, fifty, a hundred times, "*I beg you! I beg you! I beg you! I beg you . . . pl-e-e-e-e-ease don't kill this poor boy!*"

Dapper Harry Weiss, a lawyer since 1941, cut a dramatic figure in court: He wore pastel suits and ties and a white straw boater, and carried a walking stick. Harry insisted that his chauffeur park his stretch limousine in the red zone right outside the courthouse and accept a parking ticket (Harry didn't believe in public parking lots). Although Harry often changed chauffeurs, they looked indistinguishable—all young, blond, blue-eyed, muscular men whom he hired as his valets. Harry was famous for continuing cases endlessly before pleading his clients guilty. Nobody I knew could remember ever having seen Harry in trial, although I'm told that in his day he could be masterful before a jury. Harry came into court one morning and asked me for yet another continuance on an already ripe file. I told Harry that the case had no defense, that his client was guilty, and it was time to plead him or go to trial. "Oh, I'm going to plead him guilty," Harry said jokingly, "but I need a couple more continuances before I do. If I don't collect my fees, how else do you expect me to pay for all those parking tickets?"

Once I told Walt Lewis I was about to start a trial against some lawyer I hadn't met named Homer Mason. Walt balked: "*Nobody* goes to trial against Homer," he warned me ominously. "Maybe you ought to cut a deal and give him what he wants." Walt's words cemented the challenge for me: I'd battle this trial god and find out whether I measured up. Walking into court, I saw my "formidable" opponent waiting: An old, stoop-shouldered lawyer sat at counsel's table fumbling through a disorganized folder. When jury selection began, old Homer appeared so confused and disoriented that I feared he might have Alzheimer's disease: He couldn't remember the city where our courthouse was located, the name of his client, or the charges filed against him. Seeing that even the jurors began to shift uncomfortably in their chairs, I feared Homer's apparent incompetence would give my defendant grounds to appeal an inevitable conviction. Remembering Walt's earlier warning to be wary of particularly bad attorneys (because a sympathetic jury might bend backward to help them), I tried removing the sting from Homer's performance. I began my portion of jury selection like this: "Ladies and gentlemen, I know that people often think prosecutors and defense attorneys are enemies. Although it's my job to try this case, I want to begin with a personal observation. No matter what happens with your verdict, I will always count it an honor to try a case against a living legend of the bar, Mr. Homer Mason. Homer fought for civil rights and justice in our community long before I was born. He is an honored and respected lawyer who has forgotten more about the law than I will ever know. This is a special privilege for me, and one I will not forget."

As the trial wore on, Homer got worse. He bungled direct and cross-examination, did a horrible job on jury instructions, and seemed oblivious to his surroundings. The coup de grâce came on the morning of closing arguments. Homer showed up for court wearing a dingy, wrinkled plaid coat, and a food-stained, threadbare necktie. Over the right shoulder of his jacket you could see a huge white splatter of bird droppings: It looked like every Pasadena pigeon had dive-bombed him intentionally. When it was Homer's turn to address the jury, he shuffled over to the witness box, positioned the American flag behind him, pulled out a tattered, yellowed transcript of some closing argument he had made in another case from the 1950s, and read it word for word—even the parts where the charges and the defendant's name differed. Poor old Homer: This was more painful to watch than a mugging.

Unbelievably, Homer tapped a sympathy vein in the panel: He hung the jury (ten for guilty, two for not guilty). When I submitted my retrial recommendation to Walt, he asked how Homer did. As I recounted the experience and got to the part about Homer's coat being splattered with bird droppings, Walt howled with laughter:

"When you saw that, how did you feel? You felt sorry for him, right? Let me tell you something—you aren't the first one! And do you know why? *Because Homer was wearing what he* always *wears to closing arguments: his bird shit suit!* I think he spreads that bird shit on the coat himself! I can just imagine him telling his wife this morning, '*Oh, honey, today's another closing argument for the jury. Will you go to the closet and get me my bird shit suit?*' Listen, Jim, Homer will always find one person feeling too sorry for him, and he'll hang your jury forever. You can't beat this guy."

With Walt's special Homer Mason dispensation in my pocket, I offered Homer a plea bargain that I knew would be too good for him to refuse.

In another case, my DA colleague Tony was taking quite a drubbing from the defense attorney in a rape trial. For a week, as things went badly for him, Tony moped around the office. As the end of the trial neared, Tony turned chipper suddenly: "Last night I found the silver bullet to saving my case!" he said as he brushed his teeth in the bathroom. Tony claimed the defense had tarred his victim as a drunken barfly willing to have sex with any guy who bought her a drink. Tony wanted some evidence to prove that the Irish pub where she met the defendant was a respectable place. He thought he found just the right witness to say so, and he was about to call her to the stand. When I asked how this mystery woman might rehabilitate his case, Tony let me in on his bizarre theory: A few months earlier, the judge presiding over Tony's trial had gone to drink at that very bar and picked up this woman! "When I put her on the stand," Tony explained, "and the jury finds out that our judge also hangs out in that bar and dated my witness, it'll make them think the place is respectable."

I waited for Tony to laugh and say he was kidding, but the yuks never came. "Tony, you can't be serious," I said. "You're going to call some woman to the stand and have her testify that your judge picked her up in the same bar? Are you nuts? How do you think that's going to go over with your judge? He's gonna kill you!" Nothing I said could dissuade Tony.

Well, if you can't stop a train wreck, you might as well go watch it. I walked around the office telling everyone what was about to happen. When word got out, a large delegation of DAs rushed upstairs to see Tony's self-immolation. When the judge took the bench, he saw most of the District Attorney's office tittering in the front row. The unsuspecting judge chuckled at the sight. "What's going on?" he asked. We all looked at each other and said nothing; I bit my lip. The judge shrugged his shoulders, picked up the file, and resumed the trial.

Moments later, the judge told Tony to call his next witness. A buxom floozy in the audience stood and marched to the witness stand, looking like what she was—a barroom pickup. She had big hair, oversized costume jewelry, a loud-patterned, low-cut, sequined sweater exposing ample cleavage, with spike-heel sandals and stretch pants pulled across her even more ample hips and thighs. The judge's face at first showed a look of semi-recognition, and then his mouth dropped open.

"*Counsel, approach the bench*," he commanded. "*Immediately!*"

Tony sauntered to the sidebar with the defense attorney and the court reporter; the witness gave the judge a nod and a knowing smile. The judge said something to the court reporter, who then stopped transcribing the discussion. We couldn't hear what the judge said at the bench, but you couldn't mistake his body language. As Tony explained what he intended to do, the judge's face and ears turned beet red. Then the judge jabbed Tony in the chest with his index finger. Everyone returned to their seats except Tony, who stood and announced, "Your Honor, I have no further witnesses. The People rest their case."

Just as in the Mission District, other oddball characters kept popping up in my supposedly dignified practice of the law. A coroner's employee was working with me on some homicide issue. While meeting in my office, he admired the framed photos of presidents Nixon, Ford, Carter, and Reagan standing alongside me. "Hey!" he said, "I've had my picture taken with some famous people, too!" Rummaging through his wallet, he said, "I've got one in here somewhere. It's me with Natalie Wood."

"Oh, Natalie Wood!" I replied. "She was a great actress. You know, not too long before she drowned in that boating accident, she almost hit me with her car one night in Reseda in front of Lanny's Inn. She stopped and asked if I was okay. She sure was a beauty. So, where'd you meet Natalie Wood?"

His eyes darted and he grew evasive: "Well," he stammered, "I didn't exactly *meet her*." Shaking my head in disgust, I kicked the ghoul out of my office just as he started to produce a dog-eared Polaroid from his wallet.

In one of the first drunk driving cases I tried as a rookie, my main witness was the arresting officer who used his nightstick at the scene to beat the defendant into submission. Naturally, the defense argued police brutality. After I questioned the cop about the arrest on direct exam, the PD pulled out his client's bloody shirt from that night and waved it in front of the jury as the cop explained calmly why he billy-clubbed the defendant silly. I didn't know enough yet to avoid asking "why" questions unless I knew the answer in advance, so I asked my cop on redirect exam if he meant to split open the defendant's head with his nightstick.

"Oh, heavens no!" he insisted to the jury.

"Then *why* did you hit him on the head with your billy club?" I asked stupidly.

"Well, I arrested him for drunk driving and tried to handcuff him, but he resisted. So I tried to hit him in the ankles with my nightstick to get him to comply, but each time I swung at his legs, damned if he didn't keep blocking my billy club with his head!"

During breaks, sometimes I'd go down to the courthouse lockup in the basement and hang out with the sheriffs running it. Our in-jail defendants cooled their heels there while awaiting their court appearance. The lockup was a square concrete room equipped with concrete benches, an exposed aluminum toilet, and a sink. At noon, the deputies passed out the usual lockup lunch to the hungry inmates—a dry bologna sandwich, an orange, and a cookie. One day I stood near the lockup when I overheard a deputy calling out the lunch order to his backup partner: "We need twenty-three lunches and four foodballs." I paid no attention to the word "foodball" at first, but after hearing varying numbers of foodballs ordered each day, the deputy piqued my curiosity. "What's a foodball?" I asked finally.

"That's what we feed troublemakers," the grinning cop replied. "The sheriff says we have to feed them a sandwich, an orange, and a cookie, but he didn't tell us *how* to feed it to 'em!" With that, the deputy took an orange, a bologna sandwich and a cookie, smashed them together, rolled them into a wet, lumpy glob, and then tossed it across the aisle to his waiting partner.

"One foodball," he yelled, "coming right up!"

Another bailiff with most of his teeth knocked out kept inviting me to the "street fighting" class that he taught after work. He said his classroom had a concrete floor; when I asked if they used pads on the floor, he looked at me as if I were stupid and asked his own question instead: "Do the streets have pads on the floor when you fight?" When I asked what the rules were, I got the same foreign look: "Do the streets have rules when you fight? The only way to learn how to street fight is to do it. We get together a couple of times a week, roll up our sleeves, and take turns kicking the living shit out of each other. Come tonight—we won't start until you arrive." As far as I know, they're still waiting for me.

Deputy DA Jim Grodin told me the story of when he worked in the Special Investigations Division the day a panicky security agent reported a possible kidnapping of a very senior DA. One afternoon, the senior DA signed out the official car (equipped with an antitheft homing device) for lunch and failed to return for a prearranged meeting. The agent grew concerned after a check revealed the DA wasn't at his usual noontime haunts. Jim Grodin got a heads up that the agent traced the car, and the coordinates pointed to a downtown flophouse motel. Fearing a hostage situation, the eager agent brushed aside Jim's warning not to overreact and sent an army of gun-toting investigators to the location. Sure enough, they found the missing car; the hotel manager identified the room rented by the driver. The investigators evacuated the other rooms and surrounded the front and back of the motel. Using their bullhorns, they ordered everyone to come out of the room with their hands up or be tear-gassed. Everyone in the room—all two of them—came out: the senior DA and a young rookie female deputy DA wrapped in a bed sheet.

Not all DA lore dealt with offbeat people. Some stories involved fabled prosecutors like L.A. County Deputy District Attorney J. Miller Leavy, who tried and won the first reported "no body" murder case. Mrs. L. Ewing Scott, a wealthy socialite, disappeared one day without a trace. The police investigation concluded that the unemployed Mr. Scott (who mooched his way through life on his wife's money) murdered her to inherit the fortune. All the evidence was circumstantial, and police never found her body. Leavy charged the defendant with murder without any direct proof of Mrs. Scott's death. The defense attorney stung the prosecutor's case in closing argument with a powerful demonstration that went something like this:

"Gentlemen of the jury, I am here to announce today the so-called crime has been solved. Mrs. Scott has been located. She is alive and safe, and she's waiting in the hallway now."

Turning to his associate, the defense attorney called for him to bring in Mrs. Scott. The associate walked to the door and held it open while the stunned spectators awaited her entrance. The seconds clicked by; nobody came through the door. The cagey defense attorney then finished his closing argument:

> "No, gentlemen of the jury, Mrs. Scott isn't out there. We don't know where she is. But you all looked at the door and waited for her to enter. That means you have a reasonable doubt as to whether she is alive or not. Under the judge's instruction, you legally cannot convict Mr. Scott if you have a reasonable doubt about his guilt. Because you expected Mrs. Scott to enter, you cannot now say you have a reasonable doubt that she is dead. You must acquit."

It was the second most brilliant argument ever made in a murder trial. The *most* brilliant came moments later from the quick-thinking Leavy in his final summation: "Yes, gentlemen of the jury, every person in this courtroom turned and looked at that door. Every person looked— except one. The defendant didn't look, because he knew Mrs. Scott wasn't coming through it." The verdict: guilty of first-degree murder.

When Deputy DA Aaron Stovitz prosecuted one particularly vicious murderer, the defense attorney camouflaged the killer for trial like a high school civics teacher: sport coat with patches on the sleeves, fake horn-rimmed glasses, slacks, necktie, haircut, manicure. They even got a "Rent-a-Grandma," an ancient trick where the defense hires some old woman (wearing a shawl and her white hair in a bun) to sit in the front row. During trial, Granny knits, holds her Bible, and smiles lovingly at the killer she's never met. Stovitz knew the trial wasn't going well; he wanted to get the defendant on the witness stand where, under needling examination, he hoped the violent killer would flip out and give the jury a real glimpse of his true character. The defense didn't bite: They rested their case without calling the defendant, who exercised his right not to testify under the Fifth Amendment. Stovitz saw his case slipping away.

Then Stovitz grabbed an opening during the defense attorney's closing argument. With everyone's attention diverted toward the killer's lawyer, Stovitz looked across counsel table and made eye contact with the defendant. Stovitz pulled on his own necktie as if it were a noose, while making his eyes bug out and his tongue hang from his mouth. It was Stovitz's unsubtle way of showing the defendant that he should be executed. The previously docile defendant jumped from his seat in a rage, threw himself on top of Stovitz, and pummeled him. As bailiffs rushed to pull the crazed defendant off the prosecutor, Stovitz lay on the ground looking at the jury, nodding his head and pointing his index finger at his attacker in a silent message: "Now you just saw what an animal this guy really is!" Many years later, I saw Stovitz at our annual DA alumni dinner. When I asked if this old story was true, Stovitz smiled, patted me on the back, and walked away. It was easy to read his eyes: If it wasn't true, it ought to be!

Normally, it took a few years for misdemeanor prosecutors to graduate to felonies. I looked forward to the day when I'd be assigned to superior court and start playing in the big leagues. I lucked out when, after just few months on the job, we got a new boss in Pasadena, Beverly Campbell. Bev was one of the first women in the DA's office to earn a Grade Five management position. Her experience and abilities mattered little to two old-school male deputy DAs: When they bitched about not wanting a woman telling them what to do, Bev busted them back to misdemeanor traffic court. This left two openings for felony DAs, and a shortage of experienced lawyers in Pasadena to fill them.

Walt Lewis lobbied Bev hard on my behalf, assuring her I was ready for superior court. To the extent he was right, I owed my preparedness to him. Walt was one of the few DAs I knew who maintained a massive up-to-date card file of relevant criminal appellate court decisions, and from my first day he taught me to do the same. Mimicking his efforts, I spent nights and weekends poring through the latest advance sheets (the freshly printed newspaper versions of just-published appellate court decisions, which are binding legal authority on the trial courts). I read and copied the relevant cases for my own growing collection of cross-referenced and indexed note cards, and soon I carried a briefcase full of them into court each day. In time I became a walking encyclopedia of

criminal law, procedure, and evidence, with thousands of cases at my fin-
gertips. Judges relied on my research; even opposing defense lawyers
asked me for help: "Hey Jimmy, we're doing a prelim this morning in a
dope case. Your coppers stopped a car where my guy's the passenger, and
they searched the car without a warrant or permission. You got any cases
I can look at?" I always helped opponents with such requests: Walt taught
me that being a prosecutor was the only lawyer job in the world where the
advocate's sole obligation was to do the right thing. Walt hammered away
on the theme that we were officers of the court and ethically bound to ac-
complish justice, not convictions. That meant making sure the judge
knew *all* the relevant cases and laws, even the ones that hurt the DA's case.
Unlike my experience in civil practice, my legal obligation was to do justice. It was a great framework in which to spend my professional life.

I had another angel in my superior court corner: Terry Green, our top
gun prosecutor in the Pasadena office. A fifteen-year veteran, Terry looked
like a DA from central casting: bright, earnest, clean-cut, and tough as
nails. Like Walt, Terry had an unimpeachable sense of ethics and tolerated
no prosecutor's failure to abide by the rules in both letter and spirit. In my
first days on the job I'd sneak up to Department E and study how Terry
demolished the false alibi of some soon-to-be-on-death-row defendant.
At the end of one of those presentations, I pointed to Terry and whispered
to another rookie DA, "That's what I want to be when I grow up."

I helped Terry on a couple of his murder cases, and he liked my work.
Although "troubled" by my UCLA pedigree (Terry was an alumnus of
our football archrival USC), he also pushed hard for Bev to ship me upstairs as one of his "slaves," as he referred jokingly to the junior lawyers in
his charge. Finally, Bev surrendered to this Walt–Terry lobbying axis. One
day she called me into her office and gave me a battlefield promotion, as-
signing me to Department E under Terry's authority. No better teacher or
DA role model existed: I tried to clone into my genes TG's sense of fairness, and well as his bulldog approach when chasing the baddies. Before
long, Terry allowed me to run the daily court calendar and try the cases
ready to go to the jury, while he focused on his back-to-back string of
high-profile capital murder defendants.

My love for the job showed in my performance evaluations: Promotions came rapidly, and always with the highest scores. After handling felonies for a couple of years, I was recruited to join the elite DA unit specializing in prosecuting murderous Los Angeles street gangs like the Crips and the Bloods. I did two tours of duty in the Hardcore Gang Murder Unit alongside a powerful assemblage of tough DAs who lived routinely with death threats as a reward for their successes. We joked that in our unit if you didn't get at least one death threat a week, you hadn't met your quota—or else you were just soft on crime.

Many of my colleagues who prosecuted gangs (including me) carried a gun to work illegally. California law does not include prosecutors among the law enforcement professionals authorized to be armed. How ironic: those of us sworn to uphold the law to protect society from violent criminals had to break the law to protect ourselves. On my first day there, I saw that one of my colleagues had a pistol in his briefcase. I asked if we had the right to carry guns; he told me no.

"Aren't you worried that you'll get in trouble, or get fired, or even prosecuted for it?" I asked.

"Sure I am," he told me. "But there's an old saying in our unit: better to be tried by twelve than carried by six. And the more gang bangers you piss off while you're here, the more you'll understand that saying."

In the gang unit, we had to worry much more about our witnesses' safety than our own. It was suicidal for a witness living in gang territory to testify and then return to his or her old neighborhood with nothing but our thanks for performing a civic duty. We put the witness's family in a protection program frequently, which could involve moving them to another neighborhood or even another state and getting them new identities.

Most of my colleagues and I ignored job-related death threats; sometimes we even *incited* them. If an *eyeball* (eyewitness) fearing gang retaliation looked ready to "go wobbly" in his testimony for fear of reprisal, I needed an immediate demonstration to calm the terrified witness. I tried signaling that I wasn't afraid of the gang banger and that he wasn't going free—and if he ever did, I'd be the one he'd be looking to kill. I learned from Terry Green how to treat a killer in court like a piece of trash: Nobody was better than Terry at using a sneer, a smirk, or an inflection to taunt some murderous punk into making a slip. Although this bravado helped defang some defendants' reputations in the eyes of our witnesses, it also made us incur the hatred of some dangerous criminals.

After receiving and ignoring (with sufficient office machismo) my latest death threat, as I worked at home one night at the kitchen table I heard the telephone ring. I walked into my darkened den to answer; it was my investigating officer calling to say he found my missing witness. I scratched down the witness's phone number, and then placed the call. While sitting in the dim room and talking with the witness, I glanced over to the living room window. Through the gauzy, sheer draperies I saw the outline of two men climb the steps and approach my porch. They stood at my front door huddled in quiet conversation for some time before one of them knocked. Because this phone call was important, I ignored what I assumed were two peddlers; I got annoyed when they knocked a second, louder time. Suddenly, a sound caused my heart to race: One of the men tried to turn the locked doorknob. The two dark figures still huddled, and one of them pointed something toward my door; again they tried the knob.

My earlier blasé attitude about death threats turned to sudden, cold fear: I cursed myself for not taking the latest one seriously. Not wanting to scare an already shaky witness, I said calmly that I had to take care of something and would call right back. Hanging up the phone, I dropped to the ground and crawled on my stomach to the bedroom to get my gun as I ran through my options mentally. If I didn't confront or catch the killers now, the next time they came gunning for me it might be from a bush or in a drive-by. There might be no future chance for self-defense. I had no choice.

Cocking my snub-nose revolver, I approached the front door stealthily as the men still fidgeted with the doorknob; from outside I heard muffled conversation. I flipped the lock quietly, and then flung open the door, dropped into a shooter's crouch, and leveled my gun at their silhouettes, shouting "Freeze, you fuckin' bastards!" I heard the thud of something hard hit the concrete as they raised their hands. "Make one move and I'll fuckin' kill you," I warned, flicking on the porch light.

With illumination came confusion. My assassins wore no hairnets, tattoos, baggy pants, leather jackets, or other gang-banging paraphernalia: They were two older men wearing short-sleeve white shirts, neckties, and slacks. At the feet of one man was a lumpy orange plastic bag, like the kind used by the paperboy to protect newspapers on a rainy day; the other man held a similar bag in his raised hand. Something was wrong with this picture.

The man with the bag took a big gulp, and then said in a quivering voice, "Please don't shoot, mister—we're Jack and Ralph from Calvary Bible Church in Burbank. We only wanted to leave this Jesus video for you!" With that, he offered the orange bag in his hand; it shook so violently that I had a hard time taking it from him.

It turned out that Jack and Ralph belonged to the local Christian outreach team who canvassed the neighborhood with bags of Jesus videos. If they found nobody at home, they hung the video from the doorknob in an orange plastic bag, along with a note of invitation to church services. Because my oversized doorknob was too big to fit through the small, reinforced hole punched into the plastic bag, they had been trying to squeeze it over the knob when I "greeted" them.

I breathed a huge sigh of relief as I lowered the gun. "Whew! Sorry, guys!" I said. "Come on in and have a glass of water so I can explain all of this." Ralph's voice still trembled as he replied to someone he presumed to be an armed lunatic: "Oh, that's all right, mister—we don't want to bother you none."

"No, really, come in," I insisted, waving them through the door with the gun barrel. "Besides," I told them, "I'd like to hear what you have to tell me about Jesus." Jack and Ralph looked at each other, and then Ralph stammered:

"Oh, there really ain't much to tell!"

• • •

The toughest part of trying gang murder cases lay in getting the witnesses to show up and testify, not in solving the "whodunit" of the murder puzzle. In college, the big man on campus is either the guy with a high grade-point average or a football letter, or some other indicia of scholastic achievement. Gang members don't brag about their GPAs; they brag about their viciousness. In a backward way, that's good: This trait helps police identify the killers, since in the gang culture the killer won't get tough-guy points for snuffing a rival anonymously. The gang *wants* credit for the killing, and they even paint their boast on the wall through the hieroglyphics of graffiti. It doesn't always take much investigation to identify the triggerman.

When traditional methods failed, some gang detectives had their own ways of finding out who killed Chuker or Sad Boy or Little Stupid (younger brother of Big Stupid)—each a dead gang banger who (recalling a saying of the late Judge Jack Tso) probably needed killing, but not fatally. If the late Mr. Chuker was a member of the Crips (sworn enemy of the Bloods), the homicide dicks might cruise around the neighborhood until they found a local Bloods member. Saying they wanted to talk to him, they'd toss the banger into the rear seat, and then drive around town. They'd keep asking their passenger, "Who killed Chuker?" knowing the gang member would never finger a fellow *homey*. Gang culture demands that the gang, not the police, get revenge for Chuker's untimely loss.

At some point, the detained gang witness would say the magic words: "I don't have nothin' to say, so let me out of the car."

"Well, if you can't help us, I guess that's all the questions we have," the cops would reply. Pulling over to the curb, they'd smile and say, "Okay, you're free to go."

Only when the car stopped would the distracted gang member recognize where he was: The detectives had driven him into rival gang territory and circled it during questioning, stopping right in the heart of blood-thirsty enemy turf. The now-panicked gang member knew that if the police let him out here, he'd be dead before he ran to the next corner: "You can't drop me here! I'll get whacked!"

"Sorry," the police would say, grabbing him by the ankles and prying him from the back seat, "You don't have any information, and you asked to be let out. So we're letting you out. Bye!" It didn't take long for the gang banger to turn canary and sing like a bird, providing the name, address, description, and other pertinent information about Chuker's killer.

Another obstacle to dealing effectively with gang murderers and their enforcers cropped up during trial. If we got a witness off the streets and into protective custody (to be relocated from the neighborhood after testifying), it was a safe bet that the gang would try to intimidate the witness in the courtroom. Often, a horde of them showed up early and filled the spectator seats, hoping to glare down the witness with threatening looks and signals. Whenever I saw that drill about to occur, I kept my witness sequestered in the jury room (where they couldn't see the gang member–filled courtroom) while my detectives and I went to work.

First, I'd have one cop go FI (field identify) each gang member, asking his name, date of birth, residence address, and so forth. I'd have another cop start taking individual Polaroid photographs of the gang members. This usually made most of them disperse before the police ran arrest warrant checks on them. As for those who remained, I followed behind the cops, scribbling their names on the stack of blank subpoenas I carried in my briefcase for such occasions. Then I'd walk down their line, smiling and introducing myself as I stuffed a piece of paper into each of their pockets:

"Good morning. I'm James Rogan, Deputy District Attorney. Here's your subpoena. Congratulations. You're now my witness. Take your seat; please don't leave this courtroom until the judge takes the bench and I give you further instructions." The befuddled punks clustered and cursed, trying to figure out what was up my sleeve. They didn't have to wait long; Once the judge took the bench, I made a routine motion to have all witnesses excluded from court, knowing the judge would grant it. Judges grant witness exclusion requests to prevent one witness's testimony from being tainted by another. This got all the gang members kicked out of the courtroom under the witness exclusion order, so when my witness came in she could testify without intimidation.

• • •

Although being a prosecutor had its thrills (and sometimes laughs), much of the time one felt distinctly sobered by the job. Dealing with crime victims or their next of kin on a daily basis could be heartbreaking; watching a shy four-year-old use anatomically correct dolls to show how her father or uncle molested her repeatedly was a crushing experience, and it grew worse with the realization that, because of her infancy or the risk of greater psychological damage, she couldn't testify. Under California law, a witness unable to understand the significance of the oath is not allowed to testify in court. It could be just as retching holding the hand of a sobbing mother while explaining to her why the judge just freed her daughter's grinning killer due to a technicality.

The parade of battered spouses and girlfriends cutting a swath to the courthouse never ended. Their stories sounded familiar: the battered wife who, after having her face fractured one too many times, finally had the bum arrested, only to be visited a few days later by his attorney to hear what Walt Lewis called "the speech":

"You know, poor old Joe is sitting in jail right now crying his eyes out. He sobbed like a baby to me for two straight hours when I visited him last night. For the first time, he admits he needs help. I made him promise he'll start going to AA meetings, and to counseling for his anger, and to church with you. He wants to put his life together. You want him to do those things, don't you? Well, the cops and the DA just want to put him in prison for his mistake. How are you going to pay the rent if they send him away for a couple of years? What will become of your kids? Who will help you feed them? Do you have any money in the bank to cover the bills? He needs help, not jail, doesn't he? If you could just hear him now, if you could see his tears, you'd know he's a different person. Please help me get him back on his feet—let me help get both of you back on your feet. He loves you. He loves the kids. Please do this—for the sake of your family."

By preliminary hearing day, when the swelling around her eyes had gone down and the bruising faded (with the help of heavy makeup), she developed sudden memory problems. Of course, without the accountability of a conviction and strict conditions of probation to force Joe into counseling and AA meetings, he went back to the house, back to the bottle, and back to beating her—until the next arrest, the next lawyer visit, the next speech, and the next memory lapse. Too bad: When a battered woman stuck to her guns and testified (or showed up *prepared* to testify), the defendant often pled guilty. If there was nothing else in his "jacket" (prior record) and the injuries were minor, he'd usually get probation with strict terms, including counseling and substance abuse rehab. If he abided by those terms religiously and showed a life-changing pattern of civility, at the end of probation the DA could recommend that he be allowed to withdraw his guilty plea, enter a plea of not guilty, and have the case dismissed to clear his record. Battered women never heard about that option when listening to "the speech," nor did most think ahead to what was the best course for both victim and abuser.

I learned early that in court, there's no such thing as a slam-dunk winner or loser case. One never knew what a jury would do with the evidence. The case of *People v. Harles Hamilton* illustrates the point perfectly. Prosecutors charged the defendant with robbing and murdering David Goldman, the former president of the Pasadena Bar Association, and his wife Bertha in their Altadena home. It was a horrible case: The evidence showed that after robbing and tying up the victims in their living room and putting pillowcases over their heads, Hamilton and his crime partner Calvin Dean allegedly bludgeoned the old couple with wrought-iron fireplace tongs until the tongs bent; then they used a hatchet until it broke off the handle; then they used a hammer to smash what was left of the victims' skulls until the hammerhead also snapped off the handle, shot across the room, and broke a window. The coroner told me it was the worst bludgeoning case he ever saw. And what did the killers get as booty for their carnage? Some inexpensive jewelry, random household items, and the few dollars Mr. Goldman carried in his wallet.

When Altadena sheriffs surrounded Calvin Dean at gunpoint and ordered him to surrender, the miserable killer did society a favor and shot himself in the head. Hamilton preferred giving up, and after supplying police with a couple of confessions, he then backtracked and claimed the dead man was the culprit. Hamilton's last story had himself as the unwitting "fence" helping his crime partner sell the stolen loot afterward.

Brent Riggs prosecuted the first Hamilton murder trial; it ended in a hung jury, with the panel voting 8-to-4 favoring not guilty. Brent brought me on as his second chair (junior prosecutor) for the next go-round. At the retrial, with pretty much the same evidence, the jury again hung, only this time the vote was 8-to-4 for guilty. Deputy DA William Holliman replaced Brent; Billy and I tried the same case two more times, getting a hung jury in each. In Hamilton III, they voted 11-to-1 for guilty; in Hamilton IV, they voted 10-to-2 for not guilty. After four unsuccessful trials, the judge declared a final mistrial and Hamilton walked out a free man.

The worst part of the experience? Learning that potential juror misconduct tainted two of the three Hamilton trials I helped prosecute. In my first Hamilton trial (Hamilton II), seven of the twelve jurors impaneled were black. All four jurors voting "not guilty" were black; the three remaining black jurors voted to convict. I gave no thought to the vote's racial breakdown until the trial ended, when the three black jurors voting "guilty" pulled me aside. Pointing to the other four blacks who hung the jury, one of them told me angrily: "Do you know why they voted 'not guilty'? They went into the jury room, folded their arms across their chests, and said, 'Listen, we aren't voting to convict some poor young black man for killing two old rich Jews. Look at the nice house those old Jews lived in. Do you think that poor Harles ever lived in a nice house like that? Those old people were in their eighties—they had a good life. What kind of life do you think that poor Harles had?' "

Stunned by this revelation, I looked over at the four "hangers," who were standing close enough to overhear this conversation. They never looked at the Goldman family members who'd just heard the sickening tale, or at me. Their apparent misconduct was all the more troubling because the acquitters were pillars in the community. If true, it was another grotesque travesty of justice.

After Hamilton III, excused jurors again alleged misconduct against one of their own. The one black woman on the jury acted as the sole holdout for acquittal. Unlike the previous jurors, she gave no reason for her vote. Her fellow jurors later told me that she walked into the jury room for deliberations, declared up front she was voting 'not guilty,' and spent the rest of her sequestered jury time refusing to discuss the case. Her motivation remains unknown.

Too bad we didn't learn about these stories until after the trials ended. Under California law, if the court uncovers misconduct or a refusal to deliberate, the judge can kick off the lawbreaking jurors and replace them with alternates. However, once a mistrial is declared and the judge releases the jury panel, it is too late to do anything. Unfortunately, in both cases we didn't learn about the allegations until the judge excused the jury panels.

Would substituting misbehaving jurors with alternates have made a difference in the outcome of the Hamilton case? Who knows? In the last trial—the one that swung 10-to-2 for not guilty—the evidence was the same, but there was no known juror misconduct. Hamilton's lawyers in all four trials, Ray Fountain and Bill Turner, just made a more compelling case in the eyes of that particular jury pool mix than we did.

That's the way it works in the courtroom: One never knows what will happen or why. Betting on the collective judgment of twelve ordinary citizens answering a summons is the ultimate crapshoot. If you like uncertainty, you'll love jury trials. They remind me of Winston Churchill's description of democracy: It's the worst form of government, except for all the others that have been tried.

I think a little courtroom uncertainty is a positive thing: "Certainty," when wrong, can have profound consequences. In one particular gang murder case I handled, I learned to be a little less cocksure and a little more respectful of the presumption of innocence. Although my memory may be a little faulty on the details, these are the essential elements:

It was New Year's Day on bustling Wilshire Boulevard in Los Angeles. The suspect (a gang member) quarreled with another man; the suspect pulled out a gun. The victim raised his hands in surrender and walked backward from the sidewalk into the street, causing cars to screech to a halt as the suspect followed. Once the suspect backed the victim into the middle of the street, he shot and killed him. A dozen or more witnesses had a clear view of the crime. As soon as the shot was fired, the suspect fled. A patrol car was around the corner. At the sound of the gunshot, the officer sped to the location and arrived seconds later. All the witnesses described the killer as a black male, eighteen years old, six feet tall, large round mole on his cheek, and wearing a red and blue Fila jogging suit with a white diagonal stripe across the middle. They pointed around the corner to show where the killer fled. The officer gave chase. After driving a few blocks, he saw a man running and perspiring heavily who matched the killer's description: black male, eighteen years old, six feet tall, large round mole on his cheek, and wearing a red and blue Fila jogging suit with a white diagonal stripe across the midsection. When the suspect saw the police car, he ran faster and refused all demands to stop. The officer jumped from the car, tackled the suspect and handcuffed him. After a proper reading of his Miranda rights, the suspect waived his right against self-incrimination and answered these questions:

Q: Why were you running?
A: I don't know.
Q: Why didn't you stop when I told you to stop?
A: I don't know.
Q: Where were you coming from?
A: I don't know.
Q: Have you shot a gun today?
A: No.
Q: Have you shot a gun lately?
A: No.

Every eyewitness identified the suspect as the killer, and the officer arrested him for murder. The suspect had no gun on him, but since the officer didn't see the suspect for the first few minutes after the shooting, there was plenty of time to ditch the weapon (a later search of the area failed to find it). Before leaving the scene, the officer wrapped plastic bags around the suspect's hands to preserve any gunshot residue (GSR) evidence. Microscopic GSR gets on the shooter's hand when a gun is fired. Back at the police station, the suspect tested positive for GSR—he had fired a gun recently. When asked how he got GSR on his hand, the suspect said he didn't know, and denied shooting a gun.

In reviewing the case before filing charges, I wanted to double-check the field identifications made by the witnesses. I ordered that a jail lineup be held with five other inmates who matched the general description of the killer (we even put fake moles on the other five men). We had all six men stand on the line; none wore the Fila jogging suit. Each witness at the live, in-custody lineup identified positively the suspect as the murderer. Based on these facts, I knew we had the shooter. With no reasonable doubt about his guilt, I filed murder charges against the defendant.

Three months later, I dismissed all charges and the defendant walked out of court a free man. There was something wrong with the case. Can any of you armchair whodunit solvers guess why? I'll give you a few clues:

- The missing gun was never a problem. Remember, in the L. Ewing Scott case, the police never found a murder weapon *or the corpse.*
- There was no problem with the arrest or interrogation of the defendant: The officer read him his *Miranda* rights properly.
- There was no problem with the at-the-scene witness identifications or the police lineup. The police didn't do anything to "taint" the witnesses before they identified the suspect. Each witness expressed independently his or her total confidence in fingering the killer.
- The GSR test was administered properly.

Give up? Don't feel stupid: It's a trick question. *Nothing was wrong with the evidence.* The direct and circumstantial evidence was as solid as it comes, short of having a detailed confession or a videotape of the murder thrown in for good measure. So why did the defendant go free?

He went free because he didn't commit the crime. It was the wrong guy. After I filed the case, my IO received an anonymous tip that the real killer looked exactly like our suspect, right down to the cheek mole. The tipster gave the killer's name as Lyndon and said he had fled to Belize. I thought the information worthless, but my LAPD homicide detectives wanted to check. They gathered as much information as possible, flew to Belize, hacked their way through some jungle until they found a hut, and knocked on the door. When they identified themselves to the eighteen-year-old black male with a cheek mole, the young man shrugged: "I guess this is about that murder on Wilshire Boulevard," he said. "Okay, you got me." Lyndon gave a full, detailed confession, and turned over the jogging suit he'd worn on New Year's Day, as well as the murder weapon. Ballistics tests confirmed that Lyndon's gun had killed the victim.

When my IO showed me the side by side mug shots of Lyndon and our suspect, it looked like the photos could be superimposed. No two un-related people could look so similar. The chances of two guys fitting this profile at that exact place and time would drive any statistician crazy.

Yes, I know—there are some unanswered questions:

Why was the original suspect fleeing?

Maybe he feared cops. Maybe he had just pulled an unreported crime. Maybe he likes to jog. Who knows?

How did the first suspect get GSR on his hand?

Again, who knows? Maybe he shot someone else. Maybe he shook hands with the real killer as he ran by. I don't know how he got it. I only know he didn't shoot the Wilshire Boulevard victim. Some things in the law, in court, and in life never get explained satisfactorily.

I gleaned two important lessons from this case. The LAPD's thor-oughness taught me the first lesson. Their follow-up investigation, espe-cially when everyone was convinced we had the real killer, went above and beyond the call of duty.

The second lesson remains the most important: From then on, every time I *knew* we had "the right guy," I remembered this million-to-one case of mistaken identity. The law presumes an accused is innocent until proven guilty beyond a reasonable doubt, and it does so for a reason.

Prosecuting an innocent man for murder helped me to never forget it.

• • •

I never needed to worry about the defendants' guilt in the notorious Lamb Funeral Home caper. Walt Lewis, the original prosecutor on the case, filed more than seventy charges against the Sconce family, a father–mother–son combination of Pasadena funeral home operators. To the outside world, the Sconces looked freshly plucked from Ozzie and Harriet's neighborhood: Mother Laurianne sang in the church choir and salted her conversation liberally with Scripture verses; father Jerry worked as a football coach at a local Bible college; and son David was a blond, blue-eyed college football player. The All-American Sconces looked wholesome, but behind their Scripture quotes, soft eyes, and pleasant smiles lurked a Jekyll and Hyde grave-robbing family business.

The case Walt Lewis filed against the Sconce family painted a gruesome picture. If you entrusted Grandma's remains to the Lamb Funeral Home for dignified burial or cremation, then you got the full treatment: Laurianne and Jerry comforted you and your family in the parlor with Bible readings and prayer. Meanwhile, son David sweated in the basement busting Grandma's jaw with a crowbar to get to her gold teeth, which he ripped out of her mouth for later sale. Then he'd dissect Grandma without permission, removing her bones, corneas, eyes, heart, brain, lungs, skin, and other organs, and sell her body parts to tissue banks. After picking clean Granny's corpse, her burial clothes were stolen and sold to second-hand stores. David stacked whatever was left of Grandma inside a truckload of other stripped corpses and hauled them off to the crematorium. David used a long fishing gaffe on a pole to hook Grandma through the throat and drag her naked body across the crematorium floor, and used a two-by-four to stuff her into the oven, along with a dozen or so other bodies. After finishing the mass cremation, he swept the commingled ashes into large trash bins. When you returned to the funeral parlor to claim Grandma's remains, you got back an urn filled with random ashes scooped from the trash bins, along with more prayers and sympathy. Meanwhile, money from customers' prepaid funeral accounts disappeared; corpses rotted in storage racks months after urns filled with cremated remains were delivered to families, and organ donor consent forms were forged.

When other funeral home operators grew suspicious about the Lamb Funeral Home, David Sconce hired goons to beat and rob his skeptics. In the most chilling aspect of the case, Neptune Society competitor Tim Waters refused to keep quiet, despite the savage mugging Sconce's thugs unleashed on him. Soon thereafter, twenty-five-year-old Waters developed food poisoning symptoms; he climbed into bed, went into convulsions, and died inexplicably. The coroner performing the autopsy found no obvious cause of premature death, so he assumed Waters died from obesity and natural causes.

Two years later, David Sconce wound up in jail awaiting trial on charges of conducting illegal multiple cremations and other funeral home crimes. According to a cellmate, Sconce bragged that he had pulled off the perfect crime when he murdered Tim Waters. Sconce allegedly claimed he tricked Waters into meeting him for lunch; he had Waters paged to a telephone, and then sprinkled highly toxic oleander leaves into Waters's drink. That night Waters got sick; he died a few days later. After Sconce's cellmate snitched on him, the police again searched Sconce's home. There they found a copy of *The Anarchist's Cookbook*, describing various ways to murder people, including the use of the odorless and tasteless oleander plant—a plant so toxic that one or two leaves can kill a man.

Here's the rub: When Waters died in 1985, the unsuspecting coroner performing his autopsy removed Waters's tissue samples for toxicological testing as a matter of standard procedure. However, the coroner forgot to order the test, so the lab technicians left the tissue samples undisturbed in the morgue refrigerator. Had the coroner tested the samples, he'd have found nothing suspicious, because when Waters died, no test existed to isolate oleandrin extract—even if the coroner had known to look for it. The evidence was preserved accidentally because the samples were never tested and discarded.

Later, when Walt got wind of Sconce's reported jailhouse confession, he discovered that Waters's tissue samples still existed. By then, modern science had developed the means to identify oleandrin in the tissue samples. A couple of renowned labs examined the samples; both reported finding traces of oleandrin in Waters's system. The original coroner changed Waters's death certificate from natural causes to homicide, and Walt filed a death penalty–eligible charge of murder by poisoning against David Sconce.

Walt also charged David Sconce with hiring thugs and ex-cons to murder the owner of a rival cremation business in a convoluted plot to collect the victim's life insurance proceeds, and with trying to have his own grandparents killed so he'd inherit their money. In the meantime, Sconce also solicited Walt's murder as revenge. Under Sconce's plan, killers would follow Walt home after work, kidnap him, and take him to the crematorium, where they planned to beat Walt and then burn him alive in the cremation oven. Once the murder plot against Walt was uncovered, Walt recused himself from the case and I inherited the lead prosecutor's chair.[12]

Another jailhouse snitch claimed that Sconce planned to pay for Walt's hit man by making and cashing in counterfeit gaming chips from Nevada casinos. As I pored through the thousands of pages of exhibits obtained by earlier search warrants, I found a small scrap of paper that had been overlooked many times before—because, until the threat against Walt came to light, it had no apparent evidentiary meaning. On a sheet of paper was a chart listing things like "Harveys" and "Sam's Club," and alongside each listing were measurements in millimeters and grams. I flew to Nevada (the Sconces had a home near Laughlin, a casino resort) and met with all the casino security chiefs. I passed out copies of the sheet of paper and asked if it meant anything to them. They agreed unanimously: The numbers on the paper represented the weights, grams, and diameters of their respective gaming tokens. It was clear to the security chiefs that Sconce was "slugging" (counterfeiting) casino chips.

---

[12]Later, when my appointment to the bench appeared imminent, Deputy DA (later Judge) Harvey Giss became lead prosecutor on the case.

At the end of the meeting, one of the casino security chiefs pulled me aside to share a private observation. A towering, thick, no-neck man with gold rings on every finger and gold chains around his neck, he looked and sounded like Hollywood's typecast retired Mafia killer. Peering at me through cold eyes, he snarled, "Hey Mr. Rogan, you know what the difference is between you and me? You want to put this Sconce asshole *in* the jailhouse; I want to put him *under* the jailhouse."

David Sconce later pleaded guilty to the solicitation of Walt's murder, along with soliciting the murder of his grandparents, soliciting the murder of the cremation company rival, and some twenty other crimes related to the funeral home scandal. Long after I left the DA's office, a jury convicted his parents of funeral home–related charges, and all three went to state prison. Another court dismissed the Tim Waters murder charge against Sconce: The prosecutors who succeeded me felt unsure about proving it because of conflicting expert witness problems and the age of the case.

The Lamb Funeral Home case was so macabre and labyrinthine that it spawned at least three true-crime books while the case was still pending: *Chop Shop* by Kathy Braidhill, *A Family Business* by Ken Englade, and *Ashes: The Most Shocking True Crime of Our Time* by James Joseph. Of the trio, Kathy Braidhill's treatment is superior for two reasons. First, as the scrappy reporter who broke the story originally and covered it from start to finish, she knew more about it than anyone else. Second, how could I not favor the book that described me as a DA with "fresh scrubbed looks [that] fit a movie producer's idea of a good-guy prosecutor who tangles with the bad guys and walks away with his tie on straight and a razor sharp crease down the front of his pants. The well-tailored suits on his health-club physique belied his upbringing in the tough neighborhoods of San Francisco."[13]

Any book containing such gifted prose about me, no matter how exaggerated or unwarranted, is worthy of a plug.

---

[13]Kathy Braidhill, *Chop Shop*, p. 259. New York: Pinnacle Books, Windsor Publishing Corp., 1993.

13

PULLING THREE Gs (GOD, THE GIPPER, AND THE GIRL)

Horace Mann said, "Be ashamed to die until you have won some victory for humanity." Under his recipe, my job as a prosecutor guaranteed me a shame-free death. Being a deputy district attorney gave me a deep-seated sense of worth because it let me help win some victories for humanity, at least locally. Just as politics attracted me because it mattered in people's lives, the law also hooked me for the same reason. Ironically, I set out thinking of the law as a precursor to politics; now I knew it was the other way around: Politics was the precursor of law.

Since fourth grade, I had cast my political lot with the Democrats because I believed they would make the best laws—the ones that looked out for the little guy. For over two decades, Democratic platitudes and my sentiments made for a good fit. I worked on scores of campaigns and served on my local Democratic county committees. I was a member of the California Democratic State Central Committee, and attended their conventions as a delegate. I spent years learning the ropes, making friends, and getting noticed. I lived in Glendale, a promising district from the Democratic perspective. Although nominally Republican for now, Glendale's population hung in the balance owing to migration trends from contiguous Los Angeles. Older, conservative, home-owning Republicans were moving out of Glendale, while younger renters and immigrants from Los Angeles moved in. As Democrats rubbed their hands happily, longtime Republican Assemblyman Pat Nolan grew alarmed that his district was "turning to yogurt." Local Democratic leaders started mentioning a young prosecutor with a compelling personal story as a good prospect to groom for office one day.

There was just one problem: After toiling for years in the Democratic vineyards, I felt more like a squatter than an occupant. My original party identification came from believing what I heard: Democrats were the party of the downtrodden. As I grew older, studied issues more closely, and became more active in the party, my romanticized notions about the Democrats changed. Personal experiences now colored my early assumptions. Coming from a single mother on welfare and food stamps, I cared about the poor. Raised by old people on fixed incomes, I cared about the elderly. Owing everything to a good education, I cared about public schools. Yet the more I focused on these and other issues, the more disenchanted I became with the Democratic Party's overall direction.

No issue ginned me up more than welfare reform. I kept asking: If we Democrats are the party of the poor, then why don't our policies move people from welfare to independence, and why do so few bother trying? The more I talked with welfare recipients I knew, the more obvious seemed the answer: They didn't leave welfare because they didn't have to. Inch by inch, we Democrats institutionalized, and then defended, welfare addiction. Waving the compassion banner, we produced a freakish system that kept single mothers on welfare (like my mom) from breaking free:

- Out-of-wedlock births generate off-the-chart school dropout rates, alcoholism, drug abuse, gang memberships, low self-esteem, and other social pathologies for children. Still, Democratic policies told a single mother that if she married the father to stabilize her baby's life, we cut or terminate her benefits. If she kept her baby fatherless, we reward her with indefinite welfare.
- If a single welfare mother took a low-paying job to improve her lot in life, or to develop employable skills and independence, Democratic policies cut or ended her benefits. If she remained

dependent on welfare for her needs, she could draw food stamps and relief checks indefinitely.

- If a single welfare mother moved back into her parents' home to get some mature direction, Democratic policies cut or ended her benefits. If she stayed on the streets where she first got into trouble, we rewarded her with more welfare benefits.

Year after year, decade after decade, Democratic leaders expanded welfare, balked at imposing meaningful welfare-to-work programs, and rejected time limits for welfare eligibility. As a result, we ended up with rules that took money away from people who did work, and gave it indiscriminately to people who didn't work—or to people who *wouldn't* work. This hurt millions of working poor and middle-class families: Government reached deeper into their pockets to pass out their money to the idle. Creating and funding programs that kept people poor from one generation to the next was not compassionate; it built up a crippling hurdle to self-sufficiency.

When I discussed this situation at Democratic gatherings, colleagues greeted my arguments with rolling eyeballs or hisses. A local leader pulled me aside following one of my ill-received commentaries and said, "Don't you understand? As long as these people depend on government for their livelihood, we can depend on their votes." I discounted the local leader's cynicism as an exception, and assumed (as I still do) nobler motives of most other Democratic leaders. Still, the manifest results of intergenerational welfare dependency existed nonetheless.

Miserably failing inner city public schools destroy the lives of poor and minority kids. My Democratic Party fought tooth and nail against charter schools and school choice proposals because the powerful teacher unions gave us tens of millions of campaign dollars to defend the status quo. Social Security and Medicare spiraled toward bankruptcy, but my Democratic Party fought every commonsense reform, preferring to scare seniors into voting for us and leaving the fix for another day. Lawsuit abuse, which erases millions of jobs and hurts economic growth, also was untouchable: The trial lawyers gave us almost every penny of their millions of campaign dollars; just like the teacher unions, they too liked the status quo. My Democratic Party preferred taxpayer-funded abortion on demand—including late-term abortions—over reasonable restrictions. They preferred the companionship of ACLU lawyers to victims' rights advocates. They preferred quotas to merit. They preferred higher taxes to support impersonal bureaucracies instead of leaving the money with the workers who'd earned it to support their families.

There was a voice in politics agreeing with me, only it belonged to an ex-Democrat: Ronald Reagan. There was a political party sharing my values, only it was the Republicans. One day I stopped mocking them and started listening to them. Reagan and the GOP wanted to help people in need; they hated what I hated—a broken system trapping people in poverty. Reagan's party wanted to bounce from the welfare rolls the able-bodied loafers preferring welfare to work (whose greed, by the way, made less help available to the truly needy). To many Democrats, lazy indolents hanging out in the Mission District and on Pinole Valley Road were victims needing swift relief; to the Republicans and me, they were bums needing a swift kick.

I'm not sure what stunned me more: that I was wrong for so long, or that Ronald Reagan and the Republicans were so right. From welfare to school choice to protecting retirement savings, the Republicans offered hope to minorities, the elderly, and the poor. It took me a long time to see it, mostly because of my desire to believe otherwise, and also because the Republicans have always failed at their own PR. Film producer Robert Evans, whose credits include *The Godfather* and *Rosemary's Baby*, is one of the rare admitted Republicans in Hollywood. He said it best recently: "I am a Republican for one reason. Ever since I was twelve, I worked and paid Social Security and income taxes, and I always took home more money in my pocket during Republican administrations. They really are the party of the workingman, but people don't know it [because] the Republicans just have the worst sales pitch."

Despite this frustration, I gave no thought to changing parties. Ronald Reagan used to say about his switch to the Republicans, "I didn't leave the Democratic Party. The Democratic Party left me." I didn't feel the Democrats left me; it was more a case of mutual estrangement. As my bearings tacked toward conservatism, the Democrats shifted further left, making it a less comfortable fit for either. That became clear the night I made yet another unwelcome policy suggestion at a Los Angeles County Democratic Central Committee meeting. A few grumbling committeemen walked by me; with a snort of disgust over my latest heresy, one of them offered this reminder:

"You know, there *is* another party."

I sensed a personal itchiness beyond my growing political frustrations. By now, I knew academic and professional success, and felt self-congratulatory over conquering many hurdles along the way. Switching from a civil law firm to the District Attorney's office brought me great career satisfaction. Still, there was a lingering sense that despite all this, something was missing.

I learned to shrug off that feeling long ago: Something *always* was missing in my life. As a kid on welfare and a high school dropout, I was sure that getting back in school and being self-sufficient would mean I'd "made it." When I made it back to school and had a job, a new self-imposed hurdle replaced the earlier one: "If I could just earn my community college degree, that's when I'll know I've *really* made it." When I pocketed that diploma, the next test, and the next one after that, dwarfed each victory: "If I can just get admitted to a good university . . . If I can just get my bachelor's degree . . . If I can just get into a top law school . . . If I can just become a member of the Law Review . . . If I can just earn my law degree . . . If I can just pass the bar examination . . . If I can just land that first big law firm job . . . If I can just get into the DA's office. . . ."

And so it went. I met each accomplishment with a new and greater ambition, keeping the fiction always before me that achieving my latest triumph would be the hallmark of "making it." Whenever I hit the target, the anticipated gratification never came or passed quickly. After riding out so many of these waves, I concluded that everlasting restlessness is the byproduct of people needing a challenge.

In matters of the heart, though, I felt no impatience. Having arrived at an age when most young men think about marriage and family, my instincts ran in the opposite direction. With one broken engagement already under my belt, and having gotten used to making my own way, I came and went as the wind blew—and I liked it that way. Winging from one casual relationship to the next, I had no yearning for anyone permanently. When some woman suggested the alternative, I was gone.

Katie James furnished the sole exception to this longtime serial indifference. I met her at my Lillick farewell party; she was a charming, pretty blonde who managed a downtown law firm, and we became an instant item. Over the next year, we dated seriously and exclusively. A few years older (and light-years ahead of me in maturity), Katie was ready for and entitled to a commitment. My public defender pal Lenny Read lobbied me to marry her: "Listen," he said, "after a couple of divorces and some years on you, let me give you some advice. Katie has the most important quality you'll ever find in any woman. She's the rare one who'll greet you each night with a big smile on her face. Nothing is more important. You love her, don't you?"

Sure, I loved Katie. What was not to love? She was independent, funny, and bright, and she loved me. I knew she'd make a great wife; I just didn't want to be anyone's husband—great or otherwise. After exhausting her patience, I let Katie slip through my fingers. "What a jackass," Lenny sputtered when he heard the news, shaking his head in disgust. "If you didn't marry Katie, you'll never marry anybody."

You got it, buddy.

Homicide detective Jan Stewart, a longtime veteran of the Los Angeles County Sheriff's Department, served as my investigating officer when I prosecuted the Harles Hamilton double murder case. In between tracking witnesses, poring through exhibits, and trying to figure out how to put our killer in the gas chamber, Jan and I sometimes turned to personal matters over unending cups of coffee.

One day Jan mentioned that she became a first-time bride while in her forties. When I asked why she waited so long to marry, she smiled and said her mother told her long ago: "Don't marry a man until you find one you can't live without."

"Over the years, I dated lots of guys, and lots of them wanted to marry me," Jan said. "Whenever I was asked, I remembered what my mother said, and I realized I could live without the guy. And since I could live without him, I always turned down the proposal. It wasn't until I was older that Ed came along. We dated, fell in love, and he proposed. For the first time in my life, my answer to Mother's advice was different. I couldn't live without him. Now I'm glad I waited."

Mother Stewart's advice to her daughter set a noble standard; it also offered me a great excuse to remain forever unencumbered by commitment. No matter who the woman was, I knew I could always live without her.

My apartment manager, Marguerite, wanted no young people living in her building. The hand-stenciled placard on her office window warned prospective tenants that "90% of the occupants of this building are seniors over age 70. We expect and *require* quiet." Marguerite and her husband George enforced the rule, patrolling the building at all hours making sure "no noise" reigned. Because I was so young, Marguerite tried to discourage me from renting one of her units, and I had a tough time convincing her that I'd fit in with her other tenants. I explained that elderly relatives raised me, and then closed the deal by showing her two boxes on my rear car seat: My cheap stereo with big headphones (indicative of quiet) filled one box, and in the other she could see my stack of Al Jolson and Bing Crosby albums. Satisfied she wouldn't hear loud music blaring from my unit, and if she did, it would be from the generation of her tenants, she handed me a lease agreement. Two years after moving into her building at 245 West Loraine in Glendale, Marguerite's rental standards remained very much in force. The only young people I ever saw in our complex were grandchildren visiting the other tenants.

A few weeks before Christmas 1986, as I went through police reports at home about yet another murder case, a growling stomach reminded me I hadn't eaten dinner, so I set out for a quick bite. The ratty baseball cap I wore suited the rest of my ensemble: mismatched socks, old dirty topsiders, old dirty jeans, and an old dirty sweatshirt (with the hole in the front stitched shut by me with unmatched colored thread). I looked like Lenny Read at the start of a jury trial! Although bachelor comfortable, I hardly presented the picture of elegance.

I stepped into our slow-moving apartment elevator and pushed the "down" button. When the elevator started creaking up, I looked and saw the third floor light illuminated. "Goddamn it," I mumbled, slumping against the corner wall. With lots of work still to do tonight, I was in a hurry and didn't want to wait through five unnecessary floors in a snail-paced elevator, only to end up holding the door for (and getting stuck walking behind) some unhurried senior citizen.

When the doors opened on the third floor, my attitude changed abruptly. A beautiful woman in a red knit dress glided in to join me. She smiled and offered a reserved greeting; my slumped posture uncurled in-stinctively as I started brushing away the big mustard stain on the front of my sweatshirt.

"Here to visit your grandmother?" I asked.

"No," she replied. "I live here."

Surprised that someone from my generation also lived in the complex (or from my mother's generation, for that matter), I asked if she'd just moved in. She shook her head: "No, I've been here over a year."

"How did I ever miss you?" I wondered silently. Now I was in no hurry for the elevator to reach its parking-level destination. Groping for con-versation as our ride neared its end, I complimented her dress. Her mouth opened to speak, and then she stopped: It was as if she wanted to return the compliment, but realized its pointlessness.

"You must be hitting the clubs for some dancing tonight, right?"

"Actually, no," she replied. "I sing in my church choir. Tonight's our dress rehearsal for the Christmas program. Our performance is next week."

"Oh, great," I thought. *"I ask if she's a bar-hopping disco queen and she*

turns out to be a church girl. She must think I'm an idiot, and judging from the way I'm dressed, a homeless idiot."

The doors opened. With a faint smile and a goodnight, she was gone.

Later I found it hard to concentrate on my case preparation. Who was that doll in the elevator, and how could she be living upstairs from me all this time without my meeting her? Now on the lookout for another red dress sighting, I rode the elevator up and down for days hoping to run into her again. About a week later, I saw her getting out of her car in the underground parking garage. Following her to the lobby mailboxes, I hid the mail I'd already picked up from the lobby and pretended to be going where she was. This time I struck up a more practiced line of small talk with the young lady, who introduced herself as Christine.

Right away, I was pleasantly surprised to learn we had something very much in common: When I asked what she did for a living, she told me she was a DA in Pasadena. "You're kidding!" I replied. "I'm a DA in Pasadena, too! What a coincidence! How come we never met there?" This was Fate. We worked together in the same DA's office and lived in the same apartment building. Now that our paths finally crossed, we needed to be better acquainted over lunch. She gave me her telephone number.

I took her to lunch at Ernie Jr.'s Taco House in Pasadena for our first date. As we talked about our lives, Christine's green eyes misted while telling the story of marrying her high school sweetheart and dutifully following all his multiple career and locale moves. Then he called home on their tenth wedding anniversary to tell her he was leaving. After the divorce, she moved to a one-room apartment in the building where I lived.

Christine didn't offer this story as idle table chatter: She wanted me to know the ground rules if we started dating. "The Bible says that God hates divorce, so if at any time my ex-husband wants to reconcile, I feel obliged to end whatever current relationship I'm in and take him back." Following this abrupt declaration, she sat back and awaited my reaction. She looked as though she expected me to summon our waiter to bring the check. After reflecting on her words, I said, "That's wonderful. If that's what you want, then I want it for you, too. If he comes back, I'll wish you well and fade into the shadows. But in case he doesn't call you tonight, what are you doing for dinner?"[14]

A committed Christian, Christine's faith gave her an inner calm and strength—qualities that intrigued me enormously. Dating a "religious girl" was a new experience: Most of my old girlfriends came from the clubs, not the choir. In the coming months we spent our free time together, whether shopping for Christmas trees, watching old movies, picnicking on balmy spring afternoons at the Santa Barbara Polo Grounds, attending outdoor concerts under the stars at the Hollywood Bowl, or taking sunset walks along the Malibu coastline. When I worked late prepping for trials, she'd come downstairs to keep me company or bring dinner. One night I sat munching on the burrito she brought me while I glued 8 × 10 color photographs to a large poster board.

"What are you working on?" she asked casually.

"I'm making an exhibit chart for my witness's testimony tomorrow."

"Here," she said, "let me glue the pictures so you can finish eating." She took the glue stick and photographs from my hand, and then she froze. Her face turned white as she dropped the pictures and rushed to my bathroom. I was so desensitized to murder trials by now that I forgot to mention these were coroner's autopsy photographs!

Always the DA, I kept warning Christine about safety concerns for a single woman living alone, but she brushed them aside. When I learned that she slept with her patio door and windows open at night, I blew a gasket. "Do you know how many rape and murder cases I've handled because stupid or careless women left their patio doors and windows open?" She told me to stop being paranoid, but the next morning, her cavalier crime attitude changed. I discovered that vandals had ripped open the sunroof of her car, busted the stereo out of the dash, and left be-

---

[14]Years later, Christine reminded me of my "fade into the shadows" speech and asked if it was sincere. "Get real!" I laughed. "Do you think I'd step aside after buying you a taco? I was thinking that after a couple of weeks, you'd be stew meat in the Rogan pot!" In as elegant a manner as the circumstance warranted, Christine hauled off and slugged me in the shoulder.

hind thousands of dollars in damage. I banged on her door to awaken her from a deep sleep; when she looked through the peephole and saw it was me, she refused to open the door: "Please go away," she begged. "My hair's not done; my makeup's not on. Call me on the phone and talk to me."

"Christine, open the door right now. I need to talk to you and I'm not leaving. I don't care what you look like."

She cracked open the door, standing there bleary-eyed, barefoot, disheveled, and wearing a long flannel nightgown. She tried shading her face with her hands. Ignoring social niceties, I pushed my way in, broke the bad news, and then called the police. Her countenance changed from sadness to interest as she listened to me report the theft over the phone:

"Sarge, between twenty-three hundred last night and oh-six hundred we had a 4-5-9-second, auto burg, on an '84 Peugeot, license Charlie-Alpha-Mary-Six-Three-Niner. VIN is Baker-Gordon-87659832-Xray-Zero. Subject vehicle was locked and loaded; suspect jimmied the hardtop and grifted the Kenwood. No wits; victim is R-O, Christine Anne Apffel, DOB 4-13-53, SWF, residing at this address. . . ."

When Christine inspected the damage, she started to cry: "I guess I won't be listening to any music for a while." I put my arm around her and said I'd take care of things. Later, as she left for work in her damaged car, she found a rose on her windshield and a portable tape player on the front seat; it had a sticker marked, "Play Me." When she did, she heard "music": a recording I made as a joke of me singing my favorite standards, all very loud and off key. It sounded more like a beating than a crooning. I didn't know it until years later, but my take-charge handling of the crime report, and my corny effort to cheer her up did more than make her laugh. Coming to her rescue that day made her decide that I was the man she loved.

Christine had old-world ideas about romance, and she wasn't shy in telling me to get with the program. Forget modern convention: When I parked the car, she waited in the passenger seat for me to cross over and open her door. She refused to pay for any restaurant meals: "As the man, it's your job to woo me, not the other way around." When I asked why she didn't follow modern notions of feminism, she smiled: "First, my mother raised me to be a lady, and to be treated like one. Second, as a woman, why should I try to be your equal when I'm already your better?"

Our pairing baffled friends and family. The more we dated, the less we seemed to have in common. Her family was well off; I came from welfare. She sang in the church choir; I wasn't very religious. She recoiled at profanity; I inherited the verbal repertoire of my longshoreman grandfather. She had no use for nightlife; I bartended on the Sunset Strip. She was a diehard USC fan and an ardent Republican; I was a UCLA grad and a member of the Democratic State Central Committee. Celebrity bored her; I loved the dazzling world of politics. She wanted to be a missionary in Africa; I wanted to be a congressman in Washington. She's Steak Dianne and the Three Tenors; I'm Quizno's Turkey Sub and the Three Stooges. Even our job coincidence fizzled: Soon after we met, we discovered what being a "DA in Pasadena" meant: to me, it referred to "district attorney"; to her, it was "dental assistant."

All these disparities masked one trumping factor: I fell for her the first time I saw her on that elevator. In Christine, I found the rare fusion of sophisticated but informal, serious but funny, vulnerable but tough—*very* tough. There was nothing syrupy or phony about this combine of femininity and tomboy. Besides, we had some shared traits: Like me, she was opinionated, stubborn, and wanted things her way.

I knew from our first date that I was going to marry Christine; after a couple more, I told her so. I expected her to be impressed that her notoriously elusive boyfriend hinted at commitment, but she treated my prediction with indifference: "Marry you? Let me explain something. As I see it, you've got two strikes right off the bat. First, you don't go to church, which makes me think you're a heathen. Second, I don't care how conservative you claim to be—you're still a registered Democrat. My parents raised me right: I might marry a heathen, *but I'll never marry a Democrat!*"

When we first started dating, Christine asked me to drive her to her sister's on an errand after church. I looked forward to my first chance to meet her family. I stuffed her into my banged up, paint-peeling-off

Chevy Impala (the same clunker I drove to Atlanta while in law school) and took off. As we headed to the freeway, I accelerated toward the on-ramp. The car to my left raced to match my speed; when I slowed down to let it pass, it also slowed, blocking me from merging. Furious, I looked at the driver and saw him laughing and pointing in my direction. "You son of a bitch," I yelled out the window at him. Christine turned and scolded me for unnecessary language and asked me what was wrong. "Oh, nothing," I lied. "I've got a touch of Tourette's syndrome. Just ignore it."

Wanting to let this rude bastard know how I felt about his maneuver, but not wanting Christine to catch me in the act just after leaving church, I raised my left arm out the window and out of her view, giving the driver a one-finger salute. When I looked her way to make sure I wasn't seen, I was puzzled to see her smiling and waving at the other car.

"I can't believe it!" Christine exclaimed. "That's my sister's husband Maurice and my little niece Elizabeth in that car! We're on our way to their house! What a coincidence. Just follow that car all the way back to Glendale." Inside the other car I now saw for the first time a dimple-cheeked, tow-headed little girl in the back seat: She stared out the window at me as if I were a troll. Later I learned Maurice hadn't cut me off intentionally: as my car approached, Elizabeth pointed to the ugly, merging car revving down the ramp and told her daddy that Aunt Chris was riding in it. "No, honey," Maurice replied to his five-year old, "Aunt Chris would never be riding around in a dirty car like that, or with such a scruffy-looking guy. Look, I'll show you it's not her." Maurice then sped up alongside to prove Aunt Chris had better taste than Elizabeth credited to her.

When we pulled in behind Maurice at his home, Christine introduced us. "We met back at the on-ramp," I said. "In fact, I was trying to let Maurice know his driving skills were 'number one.'"

Later that night, I watched Christine sing in the choir. When the service ended, I congratulated her and asked if she spotted me in the crowded church. "Sure, I saw you," she replied. "And so did everyone else in the choir. You were the only guy in church wearing dark sunglasses. Why on earth did you have those on?" I told her I didn't want anyone I knew spotting me in church; it would be bad for my roguish image.

She laughed as if I were joking.

A Catholic priest baptized me as an infant into the faith; years later, I figured that was all the holiness I needed. I viewed religion as a circumstance of birth, and gave little thought to it as a set of moral standards greater than one's own instincts. I tried living by the Golden Rule (well, most of the time). But Bible stories? Those were fables for the unsophisticated, not the streetwise. Guilt over sin? That's for people with hang-ups, not law degrees. As long as I didn't go through life knifing or cheating people, I expected no major problems with God when I hit the Pearly Gates. Mine was an easy, comfortable philosophy that let me live life as I pleased with no apparent consequences. Since I figured I could gab my way into Heaven anyway, why live under a bunch of killjoy rules that cramped my style?

Christine should have fled from that elevator.

Despite my cynicism, each Sunday I accompanied Christine to church. Our purposes crossed: She went to sing and worship Christ; I went to be with her. During the service I nodded off or kept checking my wristwatch for the liberating moment we could blow out of there and go to lunch. Hoping to get me more interested, she dropped me in a Sunday school class one morning. "I'll join you later after I sing in the first service," she promised, and then left me sitting in a room filled with people speaking Christian-eez to each other.

The old lady next to me sensed my discomfort. She patted my arm and welcomed me. "Is this your first time in Sunday school?" she asked. I said it was. "Well, we're so glad you joined us this morning, dear." She then spied Christine's Bible on my lap. "Oh, you brought your Bible with you! Wonderful! What kind did you bring?" Her question made me draw a blank. I didn't know that the Bible comes in different versions, like the King James Version, the New International Version, and so forth. Not wanting to look stupid, I glanced down at the black leather cover hoping the right answer might jump out at me. Thinking it had, I smiled and pointed to the title: "I brought the *Holy* Bible."

When Sunday school didn't work out, Christine tried supplementing church services by passing along Christian booklets, tracts, or cassette tapes. I humored her: "Sure, I'll read it . . . Sure, I'll listen to it . . . I promise I will."

I just never said when.

A sports doctor told me not to jog on city streets because of recurring knee pain. Taking his advice that I run on a softer high school track, I came to hate jogging as a form of exercise. Running in circles bored me numb, and listening to taped music while I ran was the only way to make it bearable. One day I laced up my running shoes, grabbed my tape player and a new music cassette, and drove to the Glendale High School track. Once there I realized that somehow I grabbed the wrong tape: Instead of music, I brought by accident one of those religious tapes Christine gave me. Irritated at my error, I turned on the AM/FM radio, but couldn't get reception on any station. Concluding that listening to nothing was better than listening to a preacher, I jogged in silence.

After a few laps, boredom overtook me. "I need to listen to *something—anything!*" I flipped on the tape and was pleasantly surprised. It wasn't a preacher; it was Chuck Colson, President Nixon's White House special counsel who went to prison during Watergate. Nicknamed the "hatchet man," an associate once described Colson as a guy willing to run over his own grandmother for Nixon. This tape was *politics*, not religion. This was Nixon and Watergate and hardball, not "gnashing of teeth" and endless genealogical *begattings*. I had lucked out.

Colson's story drew my attention because as he described himself, he described me. Growing up in a poor family, Colson thought a college degree would be his ticket to lifetime security. It wasn't. Later he joined the Marines and earned a commission, but satisfaction eluded him. He met later goals in succession: law school, starting a firm, financial success, and then politics. President Nixon appointed him at age thirty-nine to be Counsel to the President: "Here I was at the White House. After four years there, one day I looked out over the vast, beautiful manicured lawns and thought, 'I am sitting in the office next to the President. I have one of the most powerful jobs in the world. I have limousines waiting for me. Admirals and generals salute me. I have everything a person could want. Why do I still have an empty feeling inside?' "

As Watergate unfolded, Colson searched for God, and his efforts took on all the trappings of a litigator preparing for trial. He wanted to know if the Bible was true. To his astonishment, he found the Bible validated at every turn:

"I knew the Bible's truth turned on whether Jesus was raised from the dead. Despite all the miracles, the apostles denied or fled from Jesus at Calvary. After the resurrection, those twelve men traveled the Holy Land for forty years proclaiming His deity. Not one ever recanted, despite beatings, torture, jail, and executions. Would they have suffered if it weren't true? Think of Watergate: It took three weeks from starting a criminal conspiracy for John Dean to go cut a deal with prosecutors. When he did, so did everyone else. In Watergate, the twelve most powerful men in the world couldn't keep a lie for three weeks. Could all twelve apostles do it for forty years and suffer as they did if they hadn't seen what they claimed? People give their lives for things they know are true. They don't die for things they know are false."

After listening to Colson discuss the historical and archeological evidence of biblical truth, his conclusion made sense. By the time the tape ended, I had long abandoned my run. Seated in the bleachers listening to Colson, I considered seriously Christ's claims for the first time in my life. I went home and listened to another of Christine's tapes, featuring Caltech astrophysicist Dr. Hugh Ross. A religious skeptic, Ross set out to disprove Christianity. Opening the Bible, he was baffled to find on the first page, in the Creation account of Genesis, that Moses correctly named all eleven creation events *and* listed them in what science 3,000 years later determined was the proper order. Ross calculated the probability of Moses randomly accomplishing this feat to be one chance in 6 billion. Ross pored through the Bible and found its claims to check out scientifically, historically, and archeologically. The more he tested, the more convinced he became that the Bible was divinely inspired. Rather than publish a scientific rebuke of the Bible as he set out to do, Ross became an evangelical Christian. So did another former skeptic, Josh McDowell. I read his seminal book, *Evidence That Demands a Verdict*, which contained a treatise of historical and archaeological evidence supporting the Bible.

Chuck Colson, Hugh Ross, and Josh McDowell reached the same conclusion reached by Mother Teresa and Louis Pasteur; by Joan of Arc and Martin Luther King, Jr.; by Sir Isaac Newton and George Washington. For two thousand years, untold millions of people reached it; untold millions more will do the same until time ends. Now I added my name to the list. The seventeenth-century French philosopher Blaise Pascal said every man has a God-shaped hole in his heart that can't be filled with anything else. Speaking for myself, I discovered he was right.

During the 2000 presidential campaign, when Governor George W. Bush was asked to name his favorite philosopher, he answered without hesitation, "Jesus Christ, because He changed my heart. . . . When you accept Christ as your savior, it changes your heart, it changes your life." Like Bush's experience, God began changing my heart when I became a Christian, although in my case the change remains a laborious (and sometimes regressive) work in progress. I still cuss like a stable boy; I'm not particularly remorseful over every youthful indiscretion; I laugh at jokes not told in polite company; and by instinct I much prefer battling enemies to offering them a turned cheek. Each day I fail to uphold God's standards about as often as I breathe.

This being the case, one might ask, "Where's the change?" The change is that despite my failings, I now know certain things: I know that Jesus is who He claims to be. I know God is unimpressed with my resume, titles, or honors. He is impressed by my ability to show unconditional faith, love, humility, repentance, and forgiveness—all qualities that elude me most every time. I know that, despite all this, God created me and He loves me. I know there is eternal life after death, and I know where I'll be spending mine.

That's the real change: I know how the book ends.

• • •

I wanted to marry Christine someday, but getting us to the altar was harder than getting me to crack open a Bible. Our mutual stubbornness gave us some false starts. On the first anniversary of our dating, I took her to dinner at her favorite restaurant, Lawry's Prime Rib steakhouse in Hollywood. She'd been hinting this might be a good night for me to pop the question, and I decided to do it. With the ring in my pocket, off we went to dinner. Candlelight and strolling violins made the moment look right. Then the waiter wheeled a serving cart to our table. "Oh, you'll love this!" she declared as the waiter filled her plate with creamed spinach, and then tried to heap it on mine.

"No, thanks," I said, and waved him away.

"Oh, honey, just try it! It's delicious!"

"No thanks."

"Won't you just try it?"

"No thanks."

"For goodness' sake—just taste it."

"No thanks."

"You're so spoiled. My mother raised me to try everything. She told me it was rude not to taste good food prepared for me."

"I wasn't raised by your mother."

"What's wrong with my mother . . . ?"

As our banter escalated to bickering, the spinach went from being a food to a symbol. Christine was hell-bent on teaching an overgrown child table etiquette, and I was just as intent on not having some girlfriend tell me what to eat. We'd stopped speaking to each other by the time the entrée came. I got home that night and tossed the ring into my sock drawer.

My eventual proposal didn't exactly scale the heights of romance, but at least it had spontaneity. I dropped by Christine's apartment to raid her refrigerator after finishing a morning jog. Still sweating and wearing my running clothes and Sony Walkman headphones, I rummaged through her freezer when, as an afterthought, I mumbled, "Do you want to get married?" As soon as I spoke the words, I regretted it. Proposing with my head in the freezer looking for food was not the treatment she deserved. Don't worry, I thought to myself. I don't think she heard me.

She heard.

Although Christine didn't expect this sudden proposal, and the circumstances left much to be desired, she chose not to stand on formalities. A month or so had passed since our creamed spinach catastrophe, and I hadn't broached the subject since.

The lady said yes.

We announced our intentions, set a date in early May, and printed the invitations. Meanwhile, Pastor Laue gave us a standardized premarital counseling test. After he scored it, he returned to the counseling room carrying the results and shaking his head in dismay: He said my scores went straight off the charts in one direction, and hers in another. He rated us as opinionated, stubborn, having zero compatibility, and giving no middle ground. "According to these test results, you two should never marry. I'm not sure I feel comfortable performing this ceremony."

When we started reviewing each other's answers, it was creamed spinach redux. Soon we argued over the "foolish" or "wrong" answers the other offered in response to each question. The squabbling continued in the parking lot. By the time we got home, a tearful Christine yanked my ring from her finger and handed it back. The wedding was off, the invitations thrown away, and once again the ring rested in my sock drawer.

After we cooled off, it became clear that neither could get along without the other. Soon we got back together, and Christine didn't play coy about her expectations any longer: "I want back my engagement ring, and I want to get this show on the road."

"Not so fast," I said with feigned seriousness. "A man can't be rushed into these things."

Of course, I intended to give back the ring, but I wanted to string this out a while to make sure it didn't end up in my sock drawer for a third time. Meanwhile, her patience wore thin. One afternoon at her dad's company picnic, Chris's sister Caron introduced me to a longtime employee: "Jerry, I'd like you to meet Jim. Jim is Chris's . . . uh, I'm not sure what Jim is!"

Christine had heard enough. She stepped forward, grabbed my arm, and dug her fingers in deeply. *"He is my fiancé,"* she declared with defiance, and then stared me down with a tight-lipped seriousness, as if daring me to contradict her. With my mouth open and no sound coming out, people started congratulating me. Once again, here was that old maxim, "He who is silent gives consent," coming back to bite me.

Despite the statistical, biographical, empirical, and sociological mismatch of these two strong-willed firstborns, we put a November date on the calendar.

When we got engaged, I was still a member of the Los Angeles County Democratic Central Committee. Christine shook her head each time I explained why conservatives needed to remain as Democrats. She thought it was just a matter of time before the Democrats kicked me out. One night we went to my monthly central committee meeting. She sat reading her book as some left-wing debate raged around me. I kept disagreeing with idea after idea, and the members seated near me indicated their displeasure at increasingly higher decibels. Christine never looked up from her hardbound book (a conspicuous, pink-jacketed biography of Mrs. Richard Nixon by Julie Nixon Eisenhower), but a smile remained on her face throughout. Driving home, she kept grinning at me, saying finally, "Hey, nice meeting, Rogan! You really made a big impact tonight. Tell me again how conservative voices need to be heard by the Democrats."

"All right," I told her. "I know when I'm licked."

The next day I called my friend Bob Finch, the former GOP lieutenant governor of California under Ronald Reagan who had also served in President Nixon's first cabinet. I told Bob that I intended to resign from the Central Committee and change parties. Bob hailed the news, but he wanted to call his friends Vice President George Bush (now running to succeed Ronald Reagan) and U.S. Senator Pete Wilson and tell them about my plans: "If you're going to do this, I suggest you do it right. Don't do anything until you hear from me."

A week later, Bob called and said Senator Wilson wanted to make the announcement at the upcoming California Republican Party State Convention in San Diego. I submitted resignation letters to the California and Los Angeles County Democratic Central Committees. Later, in San Diego, Senator Wilson delivered the keynote convention speech, introduced me warmly to the convention, and then we held a press conference where he and State GOP Chairman Bob Naylor signed me up as a Republican. The first question I got was hostile. "So, Mr. Rogan," snarled a sarcastic reporter, "I guess now that you've endorsed Senator Wilson for reelection, I assume you agree with him on every issue, don't you?"

"No," I replied, "I don't agree with him on every issue."

"Then name one," the reporter shot back.

"Abortion," I replied.

At the rear of the room, I saw Pete's political consultant and press secretary exchange horrified expressions. They were sure their photo-op just flipped from coup to disaster. Meanwhile, I continued my answer: "The Senator and I disagree on abortion. He considers himself pro-choice, and I consider myself pro-life. That ability to disagree is one of the reasons I've become a Republican. This year, the Republicans drafted a platform opposing all abortions, but they nominated for president George Bush, who opposes most abortions. He'll campaign alongside Senator Pete Wilson, who is pro-choice. That's the difference: In the Republican Party, we can disagree on one issue and still work together, respect each other, and support each other. With the Democrats, the opposite is true. If you don't march lockstep on issues like abortion, you become irrelevant."

When I saw the campaign manager and press secretary smile, I knew I had ducked a beanball.

I wrote an op-ed about my party change for an election-eve local paper. The next year, former President Ronald Reagan (who knew of my switch) invited Christine and me to his Los Angeles office for a visit. Our friend Peggy Grande, who worked for Reagan, suggested I bring a copy of the article. "He'll love it," she said, "especially as a former Democrat himself." At the end of our visit, I handed Reagan an envelope with my article: "From one ex-Democrat to another," I said with a smile. As Christine and I walked out of his office, I looked back and saw Reagan sitting at his desk opening the envelope. To my surprise, the next day a letter arrived for me. Written entirely in Reagan's hand, it read in part:

August 3, 1989
Dear Jim:
I haven't the words to properly describe how impressed I am with your article. Thank you for giving such an account of what has actually happened to the political parties in our land in your article.

Like you, I left the Democrat Party, and like you I don't believe we changed. We still support the same beliefs we always held, but the party leadership set off on an entirely different course. It is this that you so eloquently explained in your article. It is the best and most complete exposition I have seen of the philosophical reversal of the Democrat Party.

Your essay should be the basis for freeing up Democrats who are discontented but still not aware of how far their party leadership has turned from what they as individuals believe. After dealing with a Democrat majority in the House of Representatives for eight years—a majority they've had for 55 of the last 59 years—I can't help but think our very safety requires that your exposition be widely distributed. I want you to know that I'll be quoting from your essay on my own mashed-potato circuit lectures.

My very best to Christine, and again, my thanks to you.
Sincerely,
Ronald Reagan

Dumbfounded by Reagan's generous comments, I showed the letter to Christine. As she read it, tears filled her eyes. I swelled with pride and said, "So! You like what the Gipper said about your old man, eh?"

"Well, truthfully, I wasn't paying attention to what he said about *you*!" she replied. "I'm crying because of this part right here—'*My very best to Christine.*' He remembered me!"

• • •

Now squared away with both God and Ronald Reagan, it was time to get right with Christine. On November 19, 1988, with family and a few friends assembled in her parents' backyard, I stood beside Pastor Laue and my best man, my stepfather, Jack Rogan. At the signal to begin the ceremony, my old UCLA roommate Mitch Hanlon played Christine's entrance music on the piano.

She didn't show up.

Once again Mitch banged out the entrance cue on the ivories; still no Christine. Her delayed entrance reminded Pastor Laue of our failed premarital compatibility test. Pastor had a pained look as he glanced at me and shook his head. Someone whispered that she was in the living room watching the last few seconds of the UCLA–USC football game, and she didn't want to come out until the final gun. We waited a while longer; when she emerged wearing a wedding dress and a beaming smile, I knew there were two winners today—USC and me.

I can't remember if the pastor earned his honorarium, which I told him privately he'd get only if he added to Christine's vows the conditions that she "love, honor, and *obey*" me. Although I knew it would take more than an honorarium to get my strong-willed wife to submit to authority, I needed all the leverage I could get.

My old Pinole buddy Frank Debrose was one of the few non-relatives at our wedding. After the ceremony, he claimed full credit for our marriage: "If I hadn't driven you crazy when you slept on my couch in Glendale a couple of years ago, none of this would have happened. It's because I brought over slutty girlfriends, smoked with the windows shut, and partied all night that you got fed up and found your apartment where you met her on the elevator. So remember: You got all this—a wife, a home in Glendale, and a new family—just because I'm a jackass to live with!"

"Frank, I couldn't have said it better myself."

Later that night, as we prepared to leave for our honeymoon, Pastor Laue revisited the compatibility test issue. Christine and I laughed at his parting words: *"God bless you both, and I sure hope this thing works out."*

Sixteen years later, we're still married—and we're still laughing.

14

GOODBYE, GOD

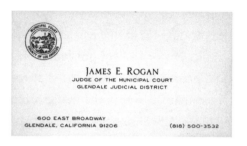

JAMES E. ROGAN
JUDGE OF THE MUNICIPAL COURT
GLENDALE JUDICIAL DISTRICT

600 EAST BROADWAY
GLENDALE, CALIFORNIA 91206   (818) 500-3532

If the 1980s opened for me in difficulty, they ended in promise. I went from bartender and struggling law student to successful prosecutor, handling thousands of cases during my years in the DA's office. One of my closing arguments in a homicide trial was so cutting-edge that the national *Trial Excellence* magazine highlighted it; my greatest honor came when, in a statewide poll of judges, prosecutors, and defense attorneys, *California Lawyer* magazine named me as one of the state's most effective prosecutors. At night I worked as an adjunct professor of both criminal law and trial advocacy at two law schools, and I lectured often on criminal justice and procedure at various law enforcement symposia. Each of these professional accomplishments tasted all the sweeter when I remembered my law school dean suggesting I drop out because "law school isn't for everyone."

By decade's end, many colleagues and judges urged me to apply to Governor George Deukmejian for appointment to the bench. I had serious doubts about trying: First, I was only thirty-one; most judges are well into middle age and legal careers when they assume the bench. Besides, I loved trying cases, and I saw what becoming a judge did to some guys: Salt-of-the-earth lawyers became tyrants once they got into that black robe. Walt Lewis had a theory: People couldn't listen all day to "Yes, Your

Honor," "No, Your Honor," and "Thank you, Your Honor" without it going to their heads. Given enough time, some judges start thinking the deference is due to them rather than to their position. Walt told me the story of "Jolly Ollie," a rotund, happy-go-lucky deputy DA who had a smile and a joke for everyone. When this office cutup made it to the bench, Walt thought he would be the one man immune to "judicial-itis." Wrong. After a year on the bench, someone sent Walt a transcript from Jolly Ollie's court. In a fit of pique, not-quite-so-Jolly Ollie held the air conditioning repair man in contempt because his chambers had gotten too warm!

My slow-growing interest in the bench came more from frustration than ambition. As a prosecutor, I tired of appearing before activist judges who interpreted the law as they wished it had been written, rather than as it was written. Many were liberal appointees of former California Governor Jerry Brown; they came to the bench with deep-seated antipathy toward police and prosecutors. Public safety suffered from judges on the lookout for hypertechnical reasons to let the defendant skate or to spend far less time in the pokey than he deserved. If I remained a prosecutor, I might spend decades asking these judges to make the right call; if I became a judge, I could make the call.

An incident during the Lamb Funeral Home case caused me to apply for a judgeship. Our trial court judge (a Brown appointee who once worked as counsel for the ACLU) allowed David Sconce to plead to charges of soliciting the murders of lead prosecutor Walt Lewis and Sconce's own grandparents. In exchange, and over my strenuous objection, the judge gave Sconce just five years in prison, with credit for time served; in addition, the judge dismissed on his own a conspiracy to commit murder charge that had been filed as a separate case. He also said he'd allow Sconce to plead guilty and receive "lifetime probation"—with no further jail time—if a higher court ever reversed his dismissal and reinstated the charges. In the end, that's what happened: the appellate court overturned the trial judge's actions. However, because Sconce had by then served the jail sentence, a federal court ordered the bizarre plea-bargain arrangement to stand.

The Sconce trial judge was a decent man, and I liked him personally, but I disliked it when judges ignored or bent the law because it gave them intellectual or philosophical heartburn. Judges take an oath to follow constitutional laws as the legislature intended them to be enforced. I decided I could make that happen most effectively if I became one.

I sought the counsel of my friend, GOP political veteran Bob Finch. When I called Finch and said I'd like advice about my future, he replied, "You must be psychic. I wanted to talk to you about the very same thing." We agreed to meet that afternoon for lunch at Beckham's Place in Pasadena.

At the restaurant, Finch started talking before we ordered food. He said an important fund-raising deadline loomed for the upcoming 1990 statewide elections. Everyone expected former Congressman Dan Lungren to seek the Republican nomination for state attorney general, but Lungren now balked. "The Republicans have no replacement if he doesn't run," Finch lamented, saying he spoke with U.S. Senator Pete Wilson (now the presumptive GOP nominee for governor) about the gap. "I've talked to Wilson about you," Finch said. "If Lungren doesn't do it, Wilson wants you to run with him on the ticket as our AG candidate." He said Wilson expected my boss, District Attorney Ira Reiner, to be the Democratic AG nominee: "Wilson likes the idea of having one of Reiner's deputies running against him."

Finch's words hit me like a ton of bricks. "You've got to be joking, Bob! I wanted to talk to you about applying for the bench, not running for attorney general of California!" Finch wasn't joking: "Don't get me wrong. Wilson wants Lungren to run, and has called him to say so, but all of Dan's signals indicate he's not running. He's making money in private practice, and I don't think his family wants him to do it. So my question is this: If Lungren doesn't run, will you?"

"I'm thirty-one years old," I replied. "People will think I'm too young; nobody would take my candidacy seriously."

"They will after we put together an exploratory committee of the big donors," Finch said. "With men from the Reagan and Bush kitchen cabinets, nobody will laugh. You've tried big felonies as a prosecutor. Wilson wants someone with your credentials to run against Reiner. He thinks it's a great idea, and so do I. Can I tell Pete you'll do it?"

The notion scared the daylights out of me, but not nearly enough. This unexpected twist made my heart race with excitement: I wanted to do it more than anything in the world. I said yes without thinking to run it by my new wife. With that, Finch declared lunch over before the waitress brought our entrees. "I need to get to work on this," he said.

Finch spent the next three weeks meeting with newspaper editors, potential supporters, contributors, and party leaders; he reported back to me that the meetings gave him increased optimism. He collected from me a pile of newspaper articles and biographical information to fax around the state. "People in the Republican Party are talking already about a young L.A. prosecutor as an alternate candidate for attorney general," he told me. "The feedback's all good."

The dizzying speculation and thrill ended abruptly when Finch called to say the Rogan Boom was over: "I just talked to Pete Wilson. At the last minute, Lungren changed his mind. He's going to run. He decided this would be his last chance at the brass ring, and he's going for it." That was that: My race for state attorney general ended before it began, but not without giving me a taste for it. Although Lungren was the far better candidate (with over a decade in Congress under his belt), I couldn't help but feel disappointed that politics, for me, must wait for another day.

"So, Bob," I asked, "now can we talk about my issue?"

With Finch's support, I filled out the lengthy application for a judicial appointment and returned it to the governor's office. Other local political leaders wrote Governor Deukmejian urging my appointment: Congressman Carlos Moorhead, State Senator Newt Russell, Assemblyman Pat Nolan, Supervisor Mike Antonovich, Los Angeles County Sheriff Sherman Block, and Los Angeles Police Chief Daryl Gates joined police organizations, victims' rights groups, defense attorneys, and judges weighing in for me. Soon I heard rumblings that the governor thought my record solid; with his term in office expiring soon, he wanted young, conservative prosecutors to carry on his judicial legacy.

The governor referred my name to the Judicial Nominee Evaluations Committee (the JNE, or "Jenny" Committee), asking them to investigate and rank my suitability for the bench on everything from ability to bias to judicial temperament. The JNE Committee mailed hundreds of evaluation questionnaires to local lawyers and judges, including every lawyer I ever opposed in trial and every judge before whom I ever appeared. One of my JNE commissioners, retired Judge Warren Ettinger, told me the committee had received over a hundred completed evaluations; not one contained a negative comment against me.

At my JNE interview, Judge Ettinger asked a question that I took to heart: "If you became a judge, and six months later I slipped into the back of your courtroom to watch Judge Rogan in action, what would I see?" I replied with a story, telling about the time as a teen that I'd gotten an undeserved traffic ticket. The cop said I'd done something that I hadn't, which made me determined to fight the unfair citation. When I showed up for court, my case was near the bottom of the docket. I found the courtroom scary: The black-robed judge sat on high, with the Great Seal hanging overhead and large flags bracketing him. The scene grew more intimidating when the judge opened his mouth: He was rude and sarcastic to each defendant ahead of me. When he called my case and snapped at me to enter my plea, I blurted out "guilty." My mind rebelled against my mouth: "This isn't fair!" I thought. "I didn't do it! Change the plea!" But I didn't change my plea. Fear, and a desire to get this ordeal over quickly, overwhelmed my desire to have my day in court.

"So," I concluded, "if in six months you slip into Judge Rogan's court, I hope you'd see a bench officer who remembers that lesson. I hope you'd see a courtroom where people are treated with respect and aren't too intimidated to tell their side of the story."

Just after Thanksgiving 1990, Christine and I were on the second day of our Carmel vacation when I called my office to check messages: There was one from Terry Flanigan, judicial appointments secretary to Governor Deukmejian. Holding my breath as I returned his call from a diner pay phone, I heard the magic words: "On behalf of Governor Deukmejian, I'm pleased to inform you that he appointed you as a judge of the Glendale Municipal Court today to fill the unexpired term of the late Judge Cheryl Krott. He knows you'll be an outstanding judge and will do a great job. Congratulations, and I suggest you think about getting sworn in." I looked across the restaurant to Christine; my smile and "thumbs up" signaled we were in for a career change.

News of my appointment ruined the rest of our vacation. I was too preoccupied with closing out my prosecutorial obligations and assuming my new responsibilities to enjoy the coastline. With her husband lost in a mental fog, Christine suggested we head home.

While driving back, I returned a call to the court administrator who wanted me to come by my new courthouse today to process some forms ASAP. Apologizing for my appearance in advance (added to my usual beat-up sweatshirt, jeans, and baseball cap was a few days' beard growth), I said I'd stop by that afternoon as soon as we pulled into Glendale.

When I arrived at the Glendale Courthouse, word spread among the employees that the new judge had dropped by. Donna Cheney, the assistant administrator, said that the court staff in Division Three (my new assignment) hoped I'd come by so they could meet me. I didn't want my first impression to be such a straggly one, but Donna insisted they'd be hurt if I didn't drop in.

Walking alone to Division Three, I entered just as the temporary commissioner called the last case before the noon recess. Nobody knew who I was, and I didn't want to disrupt the proceedings, so I took a seat in the rear of the courtroom to await the break. The bailiff lumbered over to me and mumbled something inaudible. "I'm sorry," I said, "I couldn't hear you."

"Are you deaf?" he snarled. "I said take off the fuckin' baseball cap."

"I beg your pardon?"

"Look, jackass, I said to take off the cap or I'll take it off for you."

"Of course I'll remove my cap. I'm sorry; I dropped by unexpectedly and forgot it was on. But your language is inappropriate and unwarranted, and I think you should know . . ."

"You don't like my language? Then just keep the fuckin' cap off your head when court's in session."

With that, the bailiff returned to his desk.

When court broke for lunch, the staff followed the commissioner out the back door while the bailiff barked to the audience that court was in recess until 1:30, and for everyone to return then. As the room emptied, I walked over to the bailiff's desk to introduce myself. There he sat, reading a copy of his *Guns and Ammo*; although he saw me approach through the corner of his eye, he refused to look up or acknowledge my presence. "Excuse me bailiff, but I wanted . . ."

"You really are deaf, aren't you?" he snapped. "Didn't I just say court is in recess until 1:30? Come back then and ask your question." He looked back at his magazine.

"Marshal, you don't understand. I'm trying to tell you . . ."

The bailiff stood: "*No, you don't understand.* Get your ass out of here and come back at 1:30."

"Okay," I smiled. "I'll be back at 1:30. And I promise I'll see you then."

When I returned to court at 1:30, Presiding Judge Barbara Lee Burke escorted me. Before we entered Division Three, I asked her to introduce me first to my new bailiff. When the bailiff saw me on Judge Burke's arm, he got a "what's wrong with this picture?" look on his face. "This is Judge Rogan," she said. "He'll be joining us next week when he is sworn in. He wanted to come by and greet his new court staff."

"Oh, we've met, haven't we, bailiff? You look familiar to me. Do I look familiar to you?"

The bailiff looked like he might wet his pants: His mouth dropped open, but no words came out. "Bailiff, I'm really looking forward to working closely with you—*very closely*—when I get here."

The bailiff later walked into the marshal's office, signed the requisite forms, and took a well-timed early retirement.

A reporter interviewed me on my last day in the DA's office. She told me she checked the records and found that, at age thirty-three, I'd be the youngest sitting judge in California. She asked if I had any regrets about going to the bench so young. "Just one," I replied. "I feel like I have one more big case left in me to try." A decade later, in the middle of my work on President Clinton's impeachment trial, someone mailed me the yellowed news clipping of this interview, with those words underlined in red.

On December 14, 1990, I cleaned out my desk in the Pasadena DA's office, the same office I had joined six years earlier without ever seeing a jury trial. I delivered my resignation letter to the District Attorney, and then walked across the street to the Pasadena City Hall. In the small anteroom behind the city council chambers, and with Christine holding the Bible, Judge Burke swore me in as a new judge. A few minutes later, Bob Finch repeated the oath ceremony with me before a large gathering of judges, colleagues, and friends in the council chamber. As I raised my hand to take the oath, my family occupied the front rows, watching in silent pride. In a private tribute to Grandpa, I carried the small Grace Lines pocketknife he used during his decades on the San Francisco waterfront. Following the oath, Christine slipped my new black robe over my shoulders. When people started congratulating "Judge Rogan," I felt like looking over my shoulder to see if they were talking to some guy behind me.

At the reception afterward, Pastor Laue (who offered the benediction at my enrobing ceremony) announced to the crowd, "Well, I've baptized Jim, I've married him, and now I've enrobed him. The only thing left for me to do is bury him!"

"Pastor, I want you to know that I look forward to that day," I called back amid the laughter.

"And that's because you know when that day comes, you'll be resting in the arms of our risen savior, Jesus Christ, right?" he asked.

"Wrong! It's because that'll be the one time I won't have to pay your honorarium!"

When I took the bench, Judge Ettinger offered the best advice anyone gave me for my new duties. He told about the time his law partner, retired California Supreme Court Justice Otto Kaus, called to congratulate a former law clerk just appointed to the bench. "What a coincidence," the new judge told Kaus. "In preparation for my first day, I'm reading your treatise right now on the proper way to hold lawyers in contempt."

"Contempt—shmempt," Kaus replied. "Forget everything I wrote in that article. You don't need to know how to hold lawyers in contempt. All you need to know about being a judge is this: Just be charming."

Just be charming. This was great counsel not just for the bench, but for life. I had the saying engraved on a small sign; it sat on the bench throughout my tenure as a state court judge; it sits on my desk today.

Although I agreed with Justice Kaus's preference for charm over contempt, I encountered an unavoidable situation during my first days as a judge. What's worse, it could have buried my judicial career, for all practical purposes, before it ever got started.

About the time I became a judge, voters enacted Proposition 115, which overhauled California criminal law. Prop 115 threw out the smorgasbord of liberal judge–invented criminal rights that went beyond rights guaranteed by the U.S. Constitution. One law revived by Prop 115 was "reciprocal discovery," which meant that both prosecutors and defense lawyers must disclose, before trial, their witness lists and their expected testimony. This encouraged, up front, the process of getting to the truth, instead of permitting last-minute perjured testimony with no time to investigate it. Before Prop 115, prosecutors gave all their police reports and witness statements to the defense attorneys as soon as we got them; the defense gave us nothing. When defense witnesses testified, we didn't know in advance who they were, what they'd say, or if they had criminal records. Judges didn't like crowding their dockets with continuances to investigate the testimony, so we had to cross-examine at the last minute by the seat of our pants. Often, we discovered perjury long after the case was over, the witness gone, and "double jeopardy" attached to the defendant, preventing him from being tried again for the same crime.

One of the few lawyers I held in awe was Wilbur Littlefield, a World War II hero serving as the much-respected Los Angeles County Public Defender. Bill Littlefield's office decided to test the constitutionality of Proposition 115's reciprocal discovery provision, but they did it in an awkward manner. Rather than seek an injunction against the provision, Littlefield instructed his deputies to refuse judicial orders providing reciprocal discovery. Occasional news reports surfaced of some deputy PD refusing an order somewhere in the county. When the judge scheduled a contempt hearing, Littlefield appeared personally to accept the punishment. The judgments all went about the same way: "The Court finds Mr.

Littlefield in contempt; however, the Court's respect for Mr. Littlefield is such that the fine is $10, and the Court stays the fine permanently."

I had an intellectual problem with this approach: If the PD's office wanted to challenge the law, they should do it through a proper appellate remedy, not through defying the courts. Although I felt their course undermined the system, I didn't worry about it. Very few prosecutors bothered to seek reciprocal discovery, and none had done so at my courthouse. Then one morning the DA assigned to my court demanded it under Proposition 115. I told the deputy public defender to comply; he refused on orders from his office, and I calendared his contempt hearing.

On the hearing date, all the PD's top brass packed my courtroom, along with reporters and lawyers wondering how the new judge would handle this delicate situation. Before taking the bench, I ran into a senior public defender in the hallway; we were old friends, and between us handled hundreds of cases in my time as a prosecutor. He gave me unsolicited but heartfelt advice: "I'm not talking to you now as lawyer to judge. I'm talking to you as friend to friend. You've just become a judge; you're brand new on the job, and everyone is watching you. Early impressions are the lasting ones. This is the kind of thing that can kill your career. Bill Littlefield's a war hero. He's one of the most respected lawyers in the state. Don't 'overreact' when he appears before you today. Take a pass; let the appellate courts sort this issue out. Don't stick your neck on the chopping block."

I admonished my old friend that private conversations about pending matters were inappropriate, but I appreciated his concern nonetheless. As for "overreacting," I had a simple philosophy: Every lawyer in my courtroom expected me to follow the law, and I expected them to do the same. Besides, the hearing was still against Littlefield's deputy; if Littlefield wanted to replace him, I'd deal with that request when it was made. With that, I went into chambers alone and closed the door.

Sitting at my desk, I couldn't shake loose my friend's warning. As much as I hated to admit it, my friend had a point. I'd been on the bench a couple of months only; so far I'd gotten good marks, but this Littlefield issue could change everything overnight. If I took a dive and looked the other way at his anticipated contempt, I'd be unworthy of the job. If I slammed Littlefield for contempt, the Public Defender's office would "paper" me off the criminal court bench. Under California law, any lawyer can file one challenge per case against a judge without giving a reason. When the public defender's office or the district attorney's office doesn't like a judge, they can "blanket affidavit" him, which means every lawyer in their office exercises a challenge against the judge on every single criminal case. In effect, the judge can't preside over any more criminal cases, which in Glendale made up about 95 percent of my court's docket. The judge is "papered" off the bench.

What to do?

I thought about my first day on the bench: Old friends and former colleagues appeared as prosecutors and defense lawyers on almost every case I called that day. I made scores of decisions, and in each, one friend won and another lost. At day's end, I slumped into my desk chair in chambers feeling drained mentally. Why was I so beat? It dawned on me eventually: I spent all day worrying about what my friends and former colleagues thought of my rulings—so much so that it affected my stamina. What kind of judging was that? A judge is supposed to make a call and move on; their job is to worry about the law, not their popularity. If I couldn't do that, then I wasn't cut out for the position. From that moment, I tried never to focus on what people thought of me for doing my duty. My task now appeared simple: Listen to the evidence, make an honest call, and let the chips fall where they may.

At the hearing, I granted Bill Littlefield's request for substitution, which made him the target of the contempt hearing. This began the two-hour proceeding, with both sides presenting argument and rebuttal. I telegraphed my intentions in advance, warning that this was not like most contempts, which are thoughtless acts committed in the heat of battle. This contempt was calculated; it was an intentional abrogation of a lawyer's duty to obey a lawful court order. I urged Littlefield to reconsider, warning that I'd treat this contempt with the maximum penalty if he continued refusing to follow my court order. In stalwart fashion, Littlefield thanked me for the advice but refused to yield. I sentenced him to the maximum punishment and then stayed execution of sentence so he could appeal.

The appellate courts kicked the Littlefield case around for a couple of years. Meanwhile, thanks to what I'm sure was Bill Littlefield's personal intercession, no deputy public defender "papered" me. I continued hearing criminal matters even after the appellate courts affirmed my Littlefield contempt order three times. Finally, the California Supreme Court took the case for review. On the day of oral argument, the lawyer defending my court order called me to report on how it went: "I knew it wasn't going to be good for us," he said, "when the Chief Justice took the bench and started the proceedings by wishing his good friend Bill Littlefield a happy birthday."

As it turned out, the court upheld my broad findings on Prop 115's constitutionality, thus validating the new law. The court tossed out my contempt citation against Littlefield on a technicality, which was fine with me. I wouldn't have thrown him in jail anyway. Although I disagreed with Bill's method, I knew what motivated him—not malice but a wish to test the law's constitutionality. Shortly after I found him in contempt, and well before the Supreme Court later vacated the order, I wrote the California State Bar and urged them to take no disciplinary action against Littlefield: "It is clear to any person present in the courtroom during the hearing, or who has read the transcript of the proceeding, that the purpose of Mr. Littlefield's conduct was an effort to raise a constitutional challenge to a statute as yet untested by the appellate courts. The ultimate result of the contempt hearing was largely symbolic."

A few years later, when Bill Littlefield retired from the Public Defender's office, I wrote him a note of congratulations: "Based upon the Supreme Court's decision in In re Littlefield, I have ordered that your retirement be commemorated in a special way. Since a pastry was named for Napoleon, a soft drink for Shirley Temple, and a life vest for Mae West, I have ordered that from now on all the dry bologna sandwiches served in the lockup be named 'The Wilbur.'" And how did Bill Littlefield respond to the judge who sentenced him to jail after a lifetime of public service? When I later sought election to the state legislature and to Congress, my friend Bill Littlefield served on all my campaign committees.

Lessons in life, like history, often repeat. A decade after signing Little-field's contempt order, I was a member of the House Judiciary Commit-tee during the impeachment investigation of President Clinton. The press and pundits speculated over what I'd do as a freshman Republican con-gressman from a Democratic district. Most thought I'd buckle to politi-cal pressure, vote "no" on impeachment, and save my political hide. I've always suspected that at least one person—a retired Los Angeles County public defender—knew in advance the answer to that speculation.

Not all defendants in contempt hearings brought the same dignity to my courtroom as did Bill Littlefield. And despite Justice Kaus's philosophy, *charm* only went so far. I knew no one more immune to it than Mr. Ner-sessian, a defendant I inherited from my late predecessor. A year earlier, Mr. Nersessian had gone to trial charged with damaging someone's prop-erty; the jury convicted him, and Judge Krott ordered him to pay restitu-tion. She had set his case far in advance so he could pay his debt as a condition of probation, and when the date arrived for him to show proof, I was the judge at the helm. Once again Mr. Nersessian was about to re-mind me that just because I'd gone up in the ranks of professional dig-nity, it didn't mean the nutty characters like the ones I grew up around in the Mission District would disappear forever.

Before court began that morning, Brian Jones came to my chambers and introduced himself as my new bailiff. I liked BJ from the start: A lay pastor, he exuded a gentle spirit, was unfailingly polite, and had a heart for service. I knew he'd fit in wonderfully, and I promised him that his first day with me would be a low-maintenance one.

When I took the bench, I called the first case up, one which should have been a routine matter—*People v. Nersessian*. The proceedings went something like this:

The Court: Mr. Nersessian, your case is here for proof of restitution. The court file shows that Judge Krott ordered you to pay $900 to the vic-tim. Do you have proof of restitution?

Nersessian: Fuck you and your fucking restitution!

The Court: [Turning to the court reporter, Verlaine Turner] Please read that back to me, Miss Turner. I'm sure I misunderstood Mr. Nersessian.

Reporter: There was no misunderstanding, Your Honor. [Verlaine read back the defendant's reply.]

The Court: Mr. Nersessian, am I to understand you have not paid your restitution?

Nersessian: I said fuck you and your fucking restitution! I am not *geelty*! I *weel* not pay for crime I *deed* not commit. *Theez* court *eez* like Iran! You are like Ayatollah Khomeini! I *weel* not pay! So fuck you and your fucking restitution!

BJ was out of his seat reaching for his handcuffs with Mr. Nersessian's first profanity, but I waved him away. Glancing down at my "Just Be Charming" sign, and remembering my promises to BJ and Judge Ettinger, I took another run at this idiot. Mustering a patient smile, I thought an explanation of the American system of law might make my defendant with the thick accent and defiant eyes understand the need to accept his obligation:

The Court: Mr. Nersessian—my dear Mr. Nersessian, if you feel an injustice has been done to you, please understand how the courts work. Under our legal system, a defendant is entitled to a public trial, a free lawyer if he cannot afford one, and a jury chosen from the community to hear the evidence. The defendant enjoys a presumption of innocence. When juries decide the facts, they do their best to get it right. Most of the time they do, but sometimes they don't. Their decision is not always perfect, but it is the best system we have been able to devise in a free society.

This may be one of those rare times the jury got it wrong. Maybe you are innocent. I don't know; I wasn't the judge who heard your case. Judge Krott heard it, and she died last year. So I never heard the evidence. All I know is what's in your file, and your file shows you were given a lawyer, a jury trial, and twelve people to hear the evidence. For whatever reason, they decided against you. By paying restitution you are not admitting guilt. You are recognizing that you submitted yourself to the process of law, and you did your best to explain your side of the story to the jury. By paying restitution you are not acknowledging the jury was right; you acknowledge your obligations of good citizenship—an obligation that must be respected if the rule of law is to prevail. It is the rule of law that keeps you and your family safe and protected. Enjoying the rule of law is a far greater benefit to you than the amount of your restitution. So, considering all I have just said, if you have not yet paid your restitution, I am prepared to give you a continuance so that you may begin to do so.

Nersessian: Do you have *sheet* in your ears? I said fuck you and your fucking restitution! I *weel* not pay! You are Khomeini!

I glanced into the audience at the wide-eyed spectators. Many looked worried, as if they expected a Nersessian-induced judicial foul mood to poison their case when I called them forward. Wanting to erase that impression, I grinned slightly and rolled my eyes to let them know I wasn't flipping out. The spectators smiled back, and then enjoyed the rest of the show Mr. Nersessian provided:

The Court: Mr. Nersessian, let me explain the consequences of your conduct. Your crime carries a maximum penalty of a year in the county jail and a $1,000 fine. In lieu of jail time and the fine, Judge Krott placed you on probation. As a condition of your probation, and to stay out of jail, you have certain obligations. One is to pay restitution. If you fail to pay willfully, you are in violation of probation, and you could go to jail. Your attitude leaves me with little alternative but to find you in violation. However, this is what I'm going to do: I'll continue your case for one week. You go home and think about what I said. When you come back, I'm sure you'll see things differently. This case is continued for one week.

Mr. Nersessian looked at me and shook his head in dismay: Surely this judge was one deaf jackass.

A week later, I took the bench and saw Mr. Nersessian seated in the front row. He was wearing jeans and a sweatshirt, and wore no jewelry. I knew before I called the matter that he was dressed for the hoosegow:

The Court: In the matter of *People v. Nersessian*, the defendant is present with counsel pursuant to the court's previous order. The defendant's case is on calendar to show proof of restitution. Mr. Nersessian, I hope you have reconsidered your position and thought about what I told you last week.

Nersessian: Fu-u-u-u-u . . .

Mr. Nersessian never got past the first two letters of his four-letter word. BJ had him face down on counsel table and handcuffed with lightning speed, and then escorted the profanity-spewing defendant out the back door and downstairs to the lockup. In this day's courtroom audience for Nersessian II was a fresh batch of defendants not present for the previous sideshow. Feeling they needed an explanation, I smiled and said, "Ladies and gentlemen, pay no mind to the disturbance just created in court. Last week I ordered Mr. Nersessian to show proof of restitution. I just sent him to jail because he failed to do so. I hope everyone will keep in mind this court takes its restitution orders seriously."

At least with that batch of defendants, we had no restitution collection problems.

I interfered with the random selection of the jury pool twice during my judicial career. On the first occasion, I received a personal summons for jury duty to my own courthouse. I knew it would make those lawyers who worked permanently in my court uncomfortable to see me in the jury box, so I asked the jury commissioner to withdraw my Glendale summons and send me to another county courtroom. The commissioner offered to excuse me from service, but I declined, thinking it important, at least symbolically, for a judge to honor the summons, too. However, once I had pinned on a juror's badge, I discovered that my notions of symbolism didn't play out as expected. Lawyers felt damned if they kept me on the jury and damned if they didn't. They worried that a judge would overwhelm lay jurors during deliberations if he remained; if they kicked him off, they worried about making an enemy of a judge before whom they might later appear. Each time I showed up on a jury panel, flustered lawyers went into the hallway and settled their cases rather than continue with me in the box. I began jury duty thinking a sitting judge's service was egalitarian; I ended thinking it was a waste of time.

I interfered a second time when my wife Christine got summoned for jury duty to my courtroom! Again I asked the commissioner for a reassignment, only now it was for my personal comfort more than it was for the comfort of my lawyers. I remembered hearing the story of what happened when Judge Younger's wife ended up in his court as a juror. She used her maiden name, and none of the other jurors knew she was the judge's wife. She took a seat in the back row of the jury box to answer questions from the judge about her impartiality. The light comical banter between the judge and his wife amused the other jurors, but they remained in the dark about the connection. When the time came to end the charade, Judge Younger concluded with a cute final question to reveal his wife's identity: "My last question is for the female jurors. Ladies, please remember that you're under oath. Here is the question: Is there any woman on the jury panel who'd like to go home and sleep with me tonight?"

Before Mrs. Younger could raise her hand to identify herself, another female juror seated directly in front of Mrs. Younger (and still oblivious to her identity) shrugged her shoulders. "Oh, well," she sighed, "I'm under oath," and raised her hand!

As Judge Younger found out, sometimes spouses and the law don't mix.

One of the obligations of a judge is to answer late-night phone calls from police who need an emergency search or arrest warrant. The cops are supposed to rotate these late-night requests among judges, but in reality they end up calling the ones who'll get out of bed without a fuss, and avoid those who gripe. I got my first late-night warrant request a few days after taking office. My good friend Don Meredith, a Glendale police sergeant, needed a warrant reviewed so his team could hit a heavily armed crack house to seize drugs and guns. "Give me about ten minutes, Don," I replied groggily. I hung up and stumbled out of bed; as I splashed cold water on my face trying to wake up, Christine put on her bathrobe and followed me. "Honey, is everything all right?" she asked.

"Everything's fine. Don Meredith and his coppers need to come over and have me review a search warrant. This may take a while, so why don't you go back to bed." Christine disappeared; a few minutes later, a piercing noise broke the midnight silence with all the placidness of an ice pick through my eardrum. Rushing to the living room to see what was causing the cacophony, I found Christine vacuuming the carpets. "What the hell are you doing?" I snapped. "It's 3 A.M.!"

"Company's coming over," she replied.

"They're cops, not company!"

Vacuuming in the dead of night wasn't so bad, but when she offered a plateful of homemade cookies to Don's crew, I knew it meant trouble. After signing the warrant and sending the squad on their way, I told her what her hospitality now would cost us: "Once the cops hear which judge on warrant duty serves food in the middle of the night, guess who they'll all be calling?" Sure enough, the word spread on the G-man grapevine: Judge Rogan doesn't squawk when you awaken him for a warrant, and his nice wife feeds you! Soon I began to get more than my share of countywide warrant requests; some cops became regulars and asked in advance what Christine would serve. When the warrant requests started trickling in from hungry cops outside my jurisdiction, it was time to shut down the commissary or give up uninterrupted sleep for the rest of my career.

On another night, a cop awoke me with a complex arrest warrant question. "Judge, let's just say I have a hypothetical question." He asked me to assume that someone "hypothetically" summoned him in the middle of the night to a residence where the spouses were going through a bitter divorce. Each spouse had called the police, accusing the other of physical abuse. When the cop arrived, he hypothetically found fresh red "slap" marks on each spouse's cheek. Here's the kicker: The spouses were *judges!* One was a superior court judge, and the other a municipal court judge. Both demanded that the cop arrest the other for assault.

As I tried to absorb this midnight melodrama, the cop continued: "Now assume hypothetically that the superior court judge is telling me that since the municipal court is constitutionally inferior to the superior court, the arrest order of the superior court judge supersedes the order of a municipal court judge. What do you recommend I do, hypothetically?"

I didn't need a splash of cold water on my face to figure this one out: "Officer, hypothetically speaking, here's what you should tell any married judges found in this situation. Tell them Judge Rogan had a bad dream tonight. Tell them Judge Rogan dreamed that two very smart and very capable judges were about to create mutually assured career destruction. Tell them if this dream ever revisits Judge Rogan again, he will dream he told you to arrest them both. Tell them Judge Rogan's dream will become their nightmare if you ever need to call Judge Rogan with any more hypothetical questions."

Later I "dreamed" that the marauding magistrates retreated to their neutral corners without further incident. In time, the hypothetical municipal spouse was elevated to the superior court, giving the formerly inferior-jurisdiction judge both career advancement and arrest warrant equality.

Each afternoon I handled "the custodies," people picked up on the arrest warrants I issued after they failed to appear for their court date. The cops often pinched such people during routine traffic stops. When they got to the courthouse, the bailiffs manacled them at the wrist to a long chain and led them into my courtroom, where they conferred with their public defender, usually admitted their violation, offered their excuse, and took their medicine.

One custody hollered all afternoon from the downstairs lockup, "You got the wrong guy! How many times do I gotta tell you? You're lookin' for my brother, not me! I gotta get back to work! I got my obligations!" When he entered my court, I admonished him to be quiet while I handled other matters. As each minute ticked by, he grew more irate. Finally, it was his turn: In a blistering verbal assault on cops and the courts, he insisted this was an outrageous case of mistaken identity. According to the defendant, police stopped his younger unlicensed brother for speeding; the brother gave police the name of his sibling (my current defendant). The defendant claimed the warrants should be for his brother, not him. "This is the third time this has happened to me! I'm gonna lose my job over this! You bastards better get your records straight! I got my obligations!"

This guy was the most convincing defendant I ever saw—a little too convincing. I listened until he ran out of gas, and then (remembering the Ettinger/Kaus "charming" prescription), it was my turn:

"You know, I've got a kid brother who once tried to pull that same trick on me when I was young, so I know how you feel. In this country, a man's word should be good. You've appeared before me, you've given me your word, you look sincere, and I have little reason to doubt you."

My formerly incensed defendant's eyes widened at my apparent willingness to buy his story at face value: "Well, Your Honor, I'm sorry if I got out of line. I'm just upset, you know? It's because I got my obligations. . . ."

"Yes, I'm sure you do," I replied. When I suggested we needed to release our innocent defendant and send him on his way, my bailiff appeared dazed. Meanwhile, the other custodies looked like they were mentally hatching their own "wrong man" defenses to exploit my gullibility. "There's just one small detail we need to handle before we release the defendant," I said as the bailiff reached for his handcuff keys. "When you get home, please tell your brother to clear up these tickets. Tell him not to get tickets and throw them away, okay? If he needs time to pay them, we can always work something out with him." The overjoyed defendant promised to send his brother to court to iron out these troubles the next day. "Great," I said, and told the bailiff to uncuff his right hand.

"How come only my right hand?" the defendant asked.

"Well," I replied, "even though you've convinced me that you're who you say you are, there's the slight possibility that you're lying to me. So just to play it safe, I'm going to have you raise your right hand and I'll put you under oath. I'm going to have you swear to your story. I'm not worried about you lying under oath; who'd be stupid enough to commit felony perjury, punishable by up to four years in the state penitentiary, for a pile of nothing traffic tickets? So, bailiff, go ahead and uncuff his hand so I can administer the oath."

My defendant's eyes darted furiously over the courtroom. "So, let me get this straight," he asked nervously. "If I take the oath and lie, I could go to prison? But if I take the oath, you'll let me go right now?" The other custodies snickered at his backpedaling.

"If you take the oath, I'll weigh that in my decision whether to release you. But if you lie to me under oath, I can just about guarantee you'll go to the pen for a long time. But why talk about it? Nobody would be so stupid as to commit felony perjury over a bunch of nothing traffic tickets."

After a few more silent moments of staring at his shuffling feet, the defendant piped up: "Okay, I lied. It's really me, not my brother. Sorry."

"Sir," I replied with a still-charming smile, "remember when I told you not showing up in my court for bench warrants on a bunch of traffic tickets was no big deal?"

"Yeah."

"I lied, too."

A good trial judge learns to trust instinct. The same feeling I had about Mr. "I Got My Obligations" came to me when Miss Johnson wanted to interview me for her newspaper. There was nothing unusual about the request of a reporter from a legal paper wanting to ask a judge some routine questions. However, after the interview was confirmed, this reporter's request went beyond routine: "I've heard so much about you, judge. This is going to be a thrill for me to meet you. I was thinking that instead of doing the interview in your chambers, where it's so stiff and formal, we could meet for a drink at the Hungry Tiger in Burbank." I told her the interview would occur at the courthouse.

Later, I told the bailiff about the call; in an abundance of cautious propriety, I told him to leave my chambers door open when she showed for the interview. A day or so later, Miss Johnson called my clerk, who let her cancel the chambers interview unwittingly and reschedule it at the bar. When I found out, I was furious as well as suspicious. I called the paper and asked if a Miss Johnson really worked there. When told she did, I had them transfer me to her direct line. All I got was her voice mail, so I left a firm message telling her we'd not be meeting at the Hungry Tiger bar or any other location. I canceled the interview.

Soon Miss Johnson returned my call: "Judge Rogan, I got your message. I'm sorry, but I don't know what to make of it. I never called you for an interview. I never asked you to meet me at some bar."

My bailiff called the Judicial Protection Unit (JPU). They feared this was a setup for a kidnap or assassination. During my decade as a gang murder DA and judge, death threats came with the job. More than once Christine found plain-clothes detectives at the front door: "Mrs Rogan, there's no cause for alarm. Judge Rogan is fine. But we'll be stationed around your house for the next few days. Pretend we're not here. We'll try not to get in your way."

JPU brought the Glendale Police Department into the investigation. The group met in my chambers discussing the best way to handle the situation. My insisting on going to the location as a decoy was more practical than valiant: I'd rather smoke out the threat with police around than wait for another day when trouble could happen without warning. JPU opposed my idea adamantly: "If there's a sniper on the roof or in a bush, you'll never make it out of your car in the parking lot. We have to protect you. We can't guarantee your safety if you go to the location." Glendale police felt like I did: If I didn't show up, we'd probably miss our chance to catch whoever was behind this.

In the end, the decision was mine: I chose to show up for the "interview." I turned down JPU's request that I wear body armor; again, this wasn't bravado. Wearing a bulky bulletproof vest might tip a savvy assailant that police lurked nearby. I decided to trust my safety to the Lord, the JPU, and the Glendale Police. I went without any weapons or body armor.

The plan was set: I'd drive myself to the restaurant and take a seat in the bar area. To show I was unarmed and without protective gear, I'd walk in coatless and in shirtsleeves. The police stuck a "body wire" under my shirt with a hidden microphone to intercept and record any conversations.

When it was time to go I made a last-minute call to Christine. She knew nothing about the threat. I told her in a cheery voice, "Just a busy day today, that's all. I'll tell you about it at dinner tonight. I've got to run to a meeting now, so I'll check in later. I just wanted to call and tell you I love you—and I always will."

I got in my car and drove to the Hungry Tiger. Both in front and behind my automobile were undercover cars with plain-clothes detectives; hovering overhead and out of sound range sat a sharpshooter in a police helicopter. I parked in the lot and got out of my car. It was an eerie feeling knowing that I might be in a sniper's crosshairs that very moment, and the breath I was drawing might be my last. Grateful to God, I made it inside the restaurant without incident.

The bar seemed quiet as I took a seat at a rear table (with my back to the wall). I spotted a well-dressed couple (two undercover police) cooing romantically in a booth across the room. The scruffy guy at the bar looking like he had one drink too many was an undercover cop, too; a third posed as the bartender. Five minutes, ten minutes, twenty minutes went by. Nothing happened. Then a woman walked into the lounge without looking around, took a seat at the bar, and ordered a drink. As soon as I saw her, I walked to the restroom, made sure it was empty, and then spoke into the body wire: "I recognize the woman who just walked in. She's one of my defendants. I sentenced her to county jail a few months ago for drugs. She's an addict with a record. I remember telling her that if she violated probation or came up with a dirty drug test, I'd revoke her probation and max out her jail time. I think her last name is Prodan."

I returned to my table in time to see the "drunk" at the bar sidle up to Sonja Prodan and ask to buy her a drink; in so doing he pretended to stumble, bumping her purse atop the bar with the back of his hand. When he did so, he felt a hard, metal, bulky object inside. Prodan rebuffed his overture; the cop returned to his bar stool and slipped his right hand inside his loose coat. Fearing the bulky object in Prodan's purse was a gun, the cop aimed his unseen pistol under the bar at Prodan's stomach.

Pretending not to notice her, I kept watch on the front door as if awaiting someone's arrival impatiently. When I glanced over, she acted surprised to see me, and then smiled and waved; she asked the bartender to send me a drink. An undercover cop gave me a prearranged signal to get up and leave. I walked out of the bar, entered my car, and drove away.

I listened to the police voice-traffic coming from the radio receiver in my car. Prodan grew nervous in the bar; she left right behind me and drove off. Suspecting a police tail, she led undercover cops on a two-hour evasive drive. When her car ran out of gas, police ordered her out at gunpoint. They searched her and took her to jail; she had no weapons. A detective read Prodan her Miranda rights, and she agreed to talk. When asked why she wanted to kill Judge Rogan, she burst into sobs: "Kill him? Are you crazy? I'm not trying to kill him! I just wanted to [seduce] him."

It turned out that Miss Prodan failed her last random drug test. Remembering my promise to revoke probation and jail her if that happened, she plotted to "accidentally" run into me in the bar, buy me a few drinks, take me to her home, and help me forget about her dirty drug test. When the press got wind of the story, I thought my daring escapade might earn me a headline like "Brave Judge Laughs at Death." Instead it read something like, "Female Drug Addict Tries to Seduce Local Judge." Not exactly my first choice, and one that didn't amuse Christine (already mad at me for showing recklessness in going to the bar). Everyone else seemed to think the story was funny: The jokes and ribbing I took blocked out any hint of personal gallantry. My buddy Pat Nolan, our state assemblyman, clipped the article and sent it to me with this scribbled note: "To Jim Rogan, A man obviously seduced only by good government."

There was at least one case in which I'm glad I trusted the instincts of others. Of the thousands of defendants I dealt with during a decade in the courtroom, the one I remember most is the one whose name I forgot long ago. I remember everything else about him: his smell; his matted hair and beard; his filthy clothes; his unending rap sheet of dope arrests; and his dozen failed probation chances. Mostly, I remember the near-dead look in his eyes.

When the bailiff brought the manacled defendant into my courtroom on a new drug charge, and on multiple probation violations pending against him, his very able public defender, Dwight Corum, asked for an in-chambers conference. Joined in my office by Dwight and the prosecutor, Dwight asked me for an indicated sentence if his client pleaded guilty and admitted the violations. "Well, Dwight, it's just a matter of how much time in the bucket he's going to get. . . ."

"Your Honor," Dwight interrupted, "would you consider reinstating probation?"

The notion was so ridiculous that I laughed, thinking either Dwight was making a sarcastic joke or the request was a formality. Instead of surrendering the issue, Dwight renewed his request. "Forget it, Dwight. Probation's a waste of time. He's got dozens of arrests and convictions. He's not a candidate for probation. If I gave him probation, it would be judicial malpractice. And, frankly, you're risking your credibility for even asking."

That last statement was a bluff: During my years as a prosecutor, I handled tons of cases against Dwight. He was a friend as well as a colleague; I respected him greatly. If I hadn't, I wouldn't have spent more than two seconds on the cockamamie suggestion. But the more I said no, the more Dwight pleaded, telling me repeatedly, "Judge, I just have a feeling about this one. The guy tells me he's ready to clean up his life. Don't ask me why I believe him, but I do." I must have been feeling soft-headed that day; against every fiber of common sense, I said yes, but with extreme conditions: "He has to plead to the new case, and he has to admit the truth of every probation violation before me. Then I'm going to add up the total number of years I can give him on each case, and I'm going to sentence him *consecutively* on each one. I'll stay execution of the sentence and grant him five years' probation. Then I'm going to impose such draconian conditions of probation that he's all but guaranteed to fail them. And when he does fail, I'll lift the suspended sentence and he goes straight to prison for the maximum sentence. If he has any common sense, he'll turn down the offer, take his lesser jail time, and be on his way until his next case."

Back on the bench, I shook my head in dismay when Dwight announced that his client accepted my conditions. I tried hinting that his client should reconsider, warning that I would warehouse him for years if he had the slightest violation. The vacant-eyed defendant said he wanted to try.

In Los Angeles County superior courts, most drug defendants placed on probation are ordered to do anywhere from 30 to 180 Alcoholics Anonymous meetings over a three-year period. I ordered the defendant to do *two a day for five years*, and bring me weekly proof. I ordered him to go to the police station *each morning* and submit to a drug test. I piled condition upon condition on him, but as I did, he accepted each. I was dismayed that the capable Dwight Corum got his foolish defendant a devil's bargain.

At the end of the first week, the defendant appeared with his proof of AA meetings and drug tests. He still looked like Charles Manson on a bad day, but he showed up as ordered. He was there the next week, and the next, and the next. I was so sure he was forging his AA proof of attendance meetings that one night I went to the meeting just to see if he really was there. He was, and he stayed until the end.

The defendant still looked and smelled homeless, but he reported regularly and without fail to my court. After six months I lowered his obligation to one AA meeting a day, and required him to bring in proof each month instead of each week. When he shuffled back in for his monthly court appearances, he brought proof of two meetings each day. "It's helping me," he said, "so I'll keep going to the extra meeting each day if it's all right with you."

This went on for a year. I was so impressed that I told the defendant if he kept up his faithfulness for another year, and if the DA agreed, I'd consider advancing his cases and dismissing the charges.

A few months later, my heart sank the day his case was on calendar for monthly review. When I didn't see him in the courtroom, I held off calling his matter until the end of the day, hoping he'd get here. When day's end came, I called his case in sadness: "The defendant has failed to appear as ordered. The Court orders probation revoked in all cases. A no-bail bench warrant is issued for the defendant's arrest." Just then I heard a tentative voice from the audience: "Excuse me, judge, but I'm here." Walking toward counsel table was a gaunt but clean-shaven man with a haircut. There stood my defendant, wearing a second-hand suit and necktie. "I know I look a little different," he said with some embarrassment. "But I got a job now."

The year went by, and the defendant fulfilled all his probation conditions. As promised, and with the DA's blessing, I advanced all the cases and dismissed them. Dwight hugged his smiling client and congratulated him. Just then a tired-looking, frightened woman in the audience stood. Her voice cracked as she whispered, "Judge, can I say something? It's about this case." When I invited her forward, a little girl in a faded dress with long blond ringlets followed behind, clutching her mother's hand. The humble woman trembled so much that I invited her to have a seat. Drawing a breath, she said, "I just wanted to say that I'm his wife. We've been apart for years. His drugs destroyed our life. I wanted you to know we're back together now. This is our little girl; for the first time she has a daddy. We're a family again thanks to you. I just wanted to tell you, that's all."

I told the little girl seated on her mother's lap that heroes come in all shapes and sizes. When she grew older, I hoped she'd remember her father was a hero who loved her enough to overcome huge hurdles for her sake. The defendant thanked me again, picked up his daughter, and left the courtroom. As he carried the girl toward the exit, she peered over his shoulder and called out to me, "Goodbye, God."

With tears in his eyes, Dwight asked if he could approach the bench.

"Do you know why she called you God?" he asked.

"No, why?"

"For as long as she can remember, she's been praying that God would bring her daddy home to her. You're the one who answered her prayer, so she thinks you're the one she's been praying to."

I called a recess and went alone into my chambers. Closing the door, it took more than a few minutes before I was composed enough to go out and call the next case.

15

THINGS THAT MATTER

Judge and Mrs. James E. Rogan
Announce the birth of their daughters

Claire Christine & Dana Alice

July 31, 1992

"You need to know something about me. . . ."

A dewy-eyed Christine spoke these words when we first discussed getting married. I coaxed from her what she feared might be a deal-breaker: As a young woman she underwent emergency abdominal surgery; complications and infection set in that created a shattering by-product: "I don't think I can have children," she said as tears rolled down her cheeks. Sighing relief, I admonished her: "Don't scare me like that. I thought you were gonna tell me it was something bad, like you don't shave your legs."

"This is serious," she said. "Don't you want children?"

"Sure," I shrugged. "But if we can't, that's what adoption is for."

These weren't noble words spoken to ease her hurt. It *didn't* matter to me. My personal circumstances defused aspirations to "carry on" the family name. I never used the surname of the man who impregnated and abandoned my mother; I had no contact with Jack Barone beyond that one time while I was in law school. My stepfather's surname would survive without my help: My kid brothers were populating the world with heaps of hereditary Rogans. When I married Christine, children, but not childbearing, mattered.

That's what adoption is for.

A couple of years into our marriage, Christine and I revisited the pregnancy subject. We explored *in vitro* fertilization, but that idea proved a bust. When we met with the doctor running the clinic, I didn't know how scientists fertilized female eggs in a Petri dish: "How do you get the sperm for it?" I asked innocently. "Do you use a hypodermic needle, or some medical device?"

"Uh, no," the doctor replied, looking at me like I was a dork. "We still do some things around here the old-fashioned way."

"What's the old-fashioned way?"

"Well," he said sarcastically, "we send you into a private room with a glass beaker and a magazine, if you know what I mean. We have you extract the sample yourself."

Now I understood: "Hey, doc, unless you're sending me into that private room with the *American Political Items Collector* magazine, you may not get what you're looking for!" The humorless doctor stared at me until I shifted in my chair uncomfortably, signaling I'd shut up and pay attention.

Changing topics, the doctor said he'd fertilize three or four of Christine's eggs, and implant all of them in her womb for maximum effectiveness. "Of course, that presents a problem," he continued. "Often the woman becomes pregnant with twins, triplets, or even quads. But if that happens, we recommend a process we call selective termination. I assume you know what we mean by that." Unfortunately, I did. His comment antagonized me: We came seeking professional help to have a baby, and in ten minutes this guy was offering his services as our abortionist, and did it without probing our sensitivity to the subject.

"Gee, doctor, I'm not sure. *Selective termination*: Does that mean you kill my mother's grandkids randomly?" Christine pushed me back in my seat, apologized for my bluntness, and then offered more diplomatic words: We came to pursue having babies; a multiple pregnancy would be fine. Observing my wife's unspoken wishes, I sat back in my chair and shut up, again, for about a minute.

"Now let's discuss the costs," he said. "The fee is $10,000, and of course there are no guarantees. But you should know that we enjoy a 50 percent pregnancy rate on the first try, and a 70 percent pregnancy rate on the second try. Plus, the second try is only an extra $1,000." Christine nodded approvingly, but I blanched at the cost. "Babe, that's a lot of money," I whispered to her. "It would wipe out our entire savings on a mere gamble."

"How do you put a price on a baby?" she pleaded. "If risking it would give us a 70 percent chance of holding a baby in our arms. . . ." As Christine spoke those words, my peripheral vision caught the doctor in motion. Now it was his turn to shift in a chair uncomfortably; his countenance looked different. My old DA radar beeped: Something was up with this guy. I turned toward him: "Is that right, doctor? For $11,000 we have a 70 percent chance of bringing home a newborn baby?" The doctor grew evasive; it didn't take much cross-examination to squeeze the truth from him. In the doctor's vocabulary, "pregnancy" was a medical term of art. If the reimplanted egg remained fertilized in the womb, even for a second, he counted that as a "pregnancy." Delivery of a live baby had nothing to do with his statistic. This guy was a thief in a lab coat, stealing money from couples who misinterpreted his figures and left the office with inflated expectations.

"Let's just cut to the chase," I demanded. "What's your live birth success rate from in vitro fertilization on a couple's first attempt?" The red-faced doctor looked down. "About 15 percent," he replied.

"Okay, I've got the picture," I said angrily. "You quacks collect $11,000, tell your patient to go jack off in a glass beaker, and then you offer to abort their babies that won't be conceived under your 70 percent phony pregnancy rate. . . ." Christine grabbed my arm and yanked me out the door as I dropped a string of F-bombs on the enemy.

The next day, we called an adoption agency.

Friends at church recommended we try Bethany Christian Services, an organization dedicated to helping young pregnant women. Over the next few months, Christine and I waded through mounds of paperwork; being a prosecutor and judge didn't short-circuit the mechanics of fingerprinting, background checks, counseling sessions, and home visits. We jumped through these hoops knowing it might be for nothing.

When Bethany "cleared" a family for adoption, they placed the family's profile in an adoption book, along with thousands of other profiles. A pregnant mother choosing adoption pores through these books and selects the parents she wants for her baby. Bethany counselors told us we wouldn't know if a mother picked us until the baby was born and the legal releases signed. "Once we clear you for adoption and your profile goes in the book, you should get the basic things you might need for a baby in advance," a counselor said. "But don't go overboard doing things like setting up a nursery. Walking by an empty nursery each day can be depressing. Remember, once you're placed in the adoption book, you might get picked tomorrow, or you might get picked never." They didn't want heartbreak added to uncertainty if the birth mother changed her mind.

As we neared completion of the application process, we attended yet another counseling session where they quizzed us on the kind of baby we would accept. My standards were minimal ("A live one would be nice"), but Christine chimed in with something she kept to herself until now: "I'm almost forty, so I'm getting a late start. If you want to know the desire of my heart, it would be newborn twin girls. Although we're open to different options, you asked what I wanted, and that's my ideal: newborn twin girls." The counselors shared a sideward glance before one said not to get our hopes up for twins. She explained that with the rise of lawyer-negotiated private adoptions, pregnant women carrying twins command a premium in the attorney bidding wars. She read of a woman pregnant with twins wanting to give up her babies for adoption; two families vied for the babies through their lawyers. After the mother agreed to give them to one couple, the second couple's lawyer called: "My clients will match their offer, and throw in a new Mercedes." The twins went to the Mercedes. "That's why we haven't seen twins come through here in maybe ten years. The chance of getting twins is small, and twin girls smaller than that, and you being picked for them even smaller. We don't want to discourage you, but we don't want you to have unrealistic hopes."

I shrugged my shoulders, thinking that ended that. Christine had a different outlook: "Just because you haven't gotten twin girls in ten years doesn't mean I can't pray for them." Each night for months afterward, that's what she did.

Although we came to love the Bethany counselors as an extension of our family, we hit a couple of rough spots in the process. In preparing our profile for the adoption book, Bethany asked for a selection of photographs: "Give us formal, casual, serious, even fun photos—a mix that tells a birth mom about all the sides of the real you." I included one in our packet showing Christine and me with President Ronald Reagan. I felt this choice appropriate, given my lifelong political passion. Later, when I saw the completed profile ready for the adoption book, I noticed that they had cropped Reagan from the picture. "What the hell happened to Ronald Reagan?" I thundered at the unfortunate staffer tasked with showing me the finished product.

"We were afraid that if a birth mother was inclined to pick you, she might see that picture and change her mind if she didn't like Ronald Reagan. We thought it best for your adoption chances to cut him out."

"Listen," I replied, "if some woman doesn't like Ronald Reagan to the point where it would change her adoption decision, then I don't like her gene pool. She can keep her dumbbell kid." The next day, The Gipper was back in the photo.

When another Bethany counselor came over for a final home inspection, she went through her checklist for baby-proofing a house. Christine anticipated everything in the inventory: safety lock on the refrigerator: check; knife and utensil drawers locked: check; medicine cabinet secured: check; plug covers on all wall outlets: check; no frayed electric cords: check and double check.

"Now, one more thing," The counselor said before leaving, "I *assume* you have no firearms in your house."

I didn't like the inflection in her voice; if she was a closet anti–Second Amendment type, then I needed to stand for my constitutional right to keep and bear arms. "You assume wrong," I replied.

"*Real* guns?" she asked with an air of incredulity. Christine knew me too well: I couldn't keep from needling a pacifist. Ignoring my wife's silent, head-shaking plea to shut my trap, I had a little fun with her.

"Of course they're all real—you can't shoot people with fake ones."

The counselor's eyes bugged: "You said *they* are *all* real. Does that mean you have more than one gun?"

"Yeah."

"How many?"

"I never counted."

"Why do you have so many guns?"

"How else you gonna hold off the Commies dropping from black helicopters?"

"Well, if you get a baby, have you thought about how you'll store all these guns?"

"Yeah, I probably won't leave them cocked under my pillow anymore when I go to sleep. That might not be safe with a nosy little brat running around the house. . . ." The counselor began scribbling furiously in her notebook until Christine elbowed me out of the way. Assuring her that I was joking, Christine made me show that my few guns were stored safely.

Christine said it every night without fail: "Dear Lord, I pray for the health of the woman who might be carrying our baby; and Lord, you know the desire of my heart. If it is your will, please think about bringing us newborn twin girls." Only once did I see her otherwise immovable faith fade.

As a last step, we had to clear the fingerprint hurdle before our profiles made it into the adoption book. When we submitted our print exemplars for processing, we saw light at the end of the adoption tunnel at last. The Department of Justice cleared my prints in a couple of weeks; two months later, they told us to redo Christine's exemplar. Gardening had worn down some of her fingerprint ridges, making the exemplar insufficient for checking. The next day we mailed in a new card. Another couple of months went by, and again they kicked back her prints. "Let's forget it," she cried in frustration. "I don't want to go through this disappointment anymore."

Putting my arm around Christine, I reminded her of her nightly prayer: "We said we'd trust God, didn't we? Maybe your fingerprints haven't cleared because He knows the mother carrying our twin girls isn't ready to look through the adoption book. If we're put in the book prematurely, some woman outside of God's perfect plan might pick us." Christine smiled at my demonstration of spiritual maturity; too bad that I then opened my mouth and ruined the moment. "So let's try again," I said. "Hey, it's better to wait than to have some anti-Reagan woman pick us, and then we get stuck raising her dip-shit kid."

A few weeks later came the happy news: Christine's prints cleared. That afternoon, Bethany placed our profile in the adoption book. Now came the hard part: waiting.

When Bena Rollo and her contractor-husband returned from their honeymoon on that 1930 morning, he carried her over the threshold of the little house he built for her at 1215 Graynold Avenue in Glendale. Although it was cramped, she loved what would be the only house in which she ever lived. Three children and half a century later, the old widow lived there alone, resisting pleas from her kids to sell the place. She wouldn't budge, not even after a burglar broke in and victimized her. She caulked shut the windows as her remedy: That kept out the thieves, along with circulation in a home without air conditioning. The summer heat magnified in Mrs. Rollo's home, but she didn't care: She preferred sweltering to surrendering.

On the day Christine and I returned from our honeymoon in 1988, I carried her over that same threshold. We had bought Mrs. Rollo's house in her probate sale a few weeks earlier. The old widow won her battle, hanging on to her beloved home until the end. Like her, we loved the house; like her, we couldn't afford to install new windows or air conditioning, so we also inherited Mrs. Rollo's uncomfortable climate.

Friday, August 7, 1992, was one of those blistering days. As the afternoon wore on, Christine debated whether to bake cookies for the expected late-night cop visits. Cooking would make the place much hotter, if that was possible. Deciding to place hospitality over comfort, she cranked on Mrs. Rollo's old gas oven and started making the dough. An electric kitchen fan offered small relief: Perspiration ran down her face and back as she stirred the ingredients with a big wooden spoon. The telephone ring created an unwanted intrusion on her haste to get out of that miserable kitchen. Picking up the receiver, Christine gave an uncharacteristically brusque greeting. She didn't mean to; she just wanted to finish her chore without disruption.

"Hello, Christine, this is Susan from Bethany Christian Services."

Christine's heart sank. "There must be another problem with my fingerprints," she thought. When she noticed Susan's voice sounded hollow, like she was using a speakerphone, she wondered why Susan would use the speakerphone to tell about fingerprints.

The call wasn't about fingerprints.

"Christine, I'm calling to share with you some wonderful news: you have a daughter . . ."

Nothing distracts like discomfort. Christine cradled the telephone between her shoulder and ear; her hands held the mixing bowl. She was soaked with sweat; the oppressive temperatures dulled her reflexes. What did Susan just say? Before she could ask Susan to repeat the sentence, Susan *completed* the sentence: *". . . You not only have one daughter, but you have two—she has a twin sister!"*

The thermometer no longer mattered. Whether in shock or just a superb actress, Christine put down the mixing bowl, excused herself to fetch pencil and paper, and then calmly jotted down the details: twin girls born July 31 two minutes apart; blond hair, blue eyes, English-Irish ancestry, born prematurely and in incubators, but doing satisfactorily. While a montage of anonymous voices around the speakerphone chirped congratulations, Christine asked if she could call Susan back in a few minutes; she needed to do something right away. Hanging up the phone, Christine put down the mixing bowl, shed the most consuming tears of joy she ever knew, and gave thanks to God for answered prayer.

I was in my chambers signing last-minute arrest warrants when the telephone rang on my private line. *Probably Annie* [my sometime nickname for Christine] *calling to see when I'll be home for dinner,* I thought. When I answered, a hysterical woman on the other end screamed something about my being the father of her twins. At first, I thought it was a wrong number until she called me by name. A moment of sudden dread hit: Was this some old bartending-era indiscretion parachuting onto my doorstep? I interrupted the diatribe with a question:

"Who is this?"

What were the odds?

The ultrasound showed that Kristy, the young pregnant girl, carried twins. When Kristy told her boyfriend, he took a walk. Frightened and alone, she turned to her grandmother, a Christian woman intent on protecting these unborn babies, who in turn called Bethany Christian Services. After receiving counseling, Kristy agreed to bring her babies into the world and place them for adoption. There would be no aborting these little girls.

As Kristy's time approached, she thumbed through hundreds of profiles in the Bethany adoption books. Then she stopped at one page, read and reread the information, and studied the photographs for a long time. When she was done, she pointed to the profile: "I choose them," she told the counselors quietly. Ironically, this profile was placed in the adoption book that very morning. There had been an extraordinary delay—something about a problem with clearing the woman's fingerprints.

The Bethany counselors were flabbergasted; remembering Christine's unwavering, prayerful intervention for newborn twin daughters, they never mentioned that detail to the young mother before she picked us. "Before I tell you something special about this family you've chosen," Bonnie DeJong (the local Bethany director) said to her, "I have a question: Why did you choose them?" The shy teen shook her head: "I don't know. There was just something inside that told me to pick them."

Some people believe there is no God. Some people believe prayer is a waste of time. Some people believe that miracles can be explained as random acts of chance.

Some people need to look into the blue eyes of my twin daughters.

• • •

Christine remembers her baby brother Dana vaguely; she was little more than a toddler when the newborn came home from the hospital. Tragically, he'd lived but a month. The same was true for my little sister Christie, who also died at four weeks when I was a child. It wasn't hard for us to come up with names for our new daughters: Claire Christine and Dana Alice. Christine's mom wept when she heard who we had named the babies after: "What a beautiful bouquet you have handed back to their grandmothers," she said with a smile.

Christine had considered infertility a curse. The moment we walked into the neonatal care unit of Sylmar County Hospital and looked into two cribs labeled "Twin A" and "Twin B," we viewed it as our greatest blessing. The moment we held them, the power of love trumped the science of genetics. We wouldn't have traded them for all the biological children in the world.

Dana and Claire taught me that no experience tops fatherhood. As the girls grew and our bond deepened, I pitied men who dealt themselves out of life's greatest experience. The face of Jack Barone, my biological father, often attached to those thoughts. My initial anger after meeting him had long ago turned to indifference. Now when I thought of him, I felt sorrow for the aging man who would miss out on a second generation of his family. But that was ancient history. When I held Dana and Claire, I focused on the kind of father I was, not the kind of father others were.

The girls were about eighteen months old the night a ringing telephone interrupted our playtime:

"Hello, Jim? This is Jack Barone."

It had been almost fifteen years since the one and only time I heard from him. I was taken aback by his call; after we exchanged awkward pleasantries, he got to the point. He had suffered a major heart attack recently, one that almost killed him. Though now on the road to recovery, his brush with death made him think about many things. He wasn't sure how much longer he had to live: "I need to know before I die," he said. At his request, I agreed to meet him a few weeks later at Irwin Memorial Blood Bank in San Francisco for the paternity test. At his request, I also agreed to split the cost.

The lab wanted my mother to participate in the test; they said having both parents guaranteed a foolproof result. Mom agreed to do it; she and I drove to the blood bank together. I wondered how she would react seeing Jack for the first time since he told her to abort me. When we entered the lobby and found him pacing alone inside, Mom was unfazed: "Hey, Jack! How the hell are you? You haven't changed. You look great!" They hugged; he and I shook hands. I handed him an envelope with $250 cash—my half of the test fee.

A haggish old nurse entered the room and bellowed out my name. "Come with me," she commanded. "You're first. I'm drawing your blood." I followed her to the doorway where she stopped suddenly. "This is a paternity test, right?" she barked as she checked multiple boxes on the hospital form stuck to her clipboard. I told her it was. She looked perplexed as her eyes scanned the room occupied only by Mom and Jack.

"So, where's the child?" she demanded.

I couldn't contain a grin: "That would be me."

"Mom, are you *sure* you're sure?"

From that day as a boy when I first learned about Jack Barone, Mom told me he was my father. When I met him years later, I indicted him with the charge. Now we were going to find out, and a horrible thought came to me: As an ex-cocktail waitress and a dancer, maybe Mom had been a bit wilder in her youth than she let on. After all, *wildness* got her pregnant in the first place. Following our visit to the blood bank, as we drove back to Mom's house alone, I wanted hard confirmation that there was no margin of error on this one.

"So you're absolutely sure? There's no possibility of mistake here?"

"Jimmy, of course I'm sure . . . well, pretty sure . . . I mean, you know, hey, that was so damned long ago. . . ."

I buried my face in my hand. Suddenly, this "paternity test" idea didn't seem like such a good one.

In the coming weeks, as we awaited the results of the test, Jack called often, and always under the pretense of wanting to know if I had gotten any results. I could tell he just wanted to talk. His voice sounded far different from the suspicious and defensive one I had encountered years earlier. Sometimes he couldn't contain his giddiness with the prospect of having fathered a biological son (his other child was Beverly's adopted son from her first marriage). As the weeks wore on, Christine told me, "Can't you see? He *wants* that test to come back positive."

About five weeks after we took the test, Jack called me one morning. His voice felt different: It was heavy and sorrowful. A wave of panic shot through as my mind raced: *"Oh, no—he just got the results. I can tell from his voice. I've put this guy and his family through decades of hell with a false accusation. What can I now say to him to make it right? It's all Mom's fault—she lied to me. Why did I ever believe her? I should have known. . . ."*

Jack said he just received his copy of the test results: "I couldn't make heads or tails of the scientific stuff on this form, so I called the blood bank and asked them to explain it. They said their conclusion came back with a 99.99 percent certainty. I asked if there was any chance for error. The doctor told me that in science, there's no such thing as 100 percent. He said the closest result they ever report is 99.99 percent sure. That means they're as sure as modern science can make it. . . ."

While he spoke, my head dropped and I closed my eyes, feeling overcome with embarrassment and shame. What could I say, almost forty years later, to this falsely accused man? Oblivious to my humiliation, Jack continued:

"So the doctor tells me there is no mistake. He says that unless I had a clone running around with your Mom back in those days, then I'm your father. I don't know what to say to you, kid. I'm not sure how you're gonna feel about this news, or how you feel about having a dad like me. I wish I knew what to tell you to make it okay. You probably don't feel too good about this. . . ." He started to cry on the telephone.

Now I understood why I heard such stress in his voice. He had been agonizing over how I'd feel knowing that he was my father, and here I sat worried about how *he'd* feel toward a guy who fingered him unjustly all these years. I don't think I ever drew a deeper breath of relief.

As the months passed, Jack and I spoke often on the telephone, got together occasionally, and tried to cram all we could learn about each other into those infrequent contacts. Our reconciliation was sincere, but by now we lived a continent apart, and family-raising and professional obligations consumed my time. It was a shame: Jack had wasted all those years with no contact when I had nothing but time. Now there was almost no time—for either of us.

A couple of years after our blood test, Jack called me one night. "I went in for a routine heart checkup," he told me in a breaking voice. "My heart's fine, but they discovered leukemia. It looks pretty bad." He underwent a bombardment of chemotherapy and radiation that left him miserably sick. After a brief remission, the cancer flared vengefully. There was no hope.

I thought a lot about Jack as he was dying, and what might have been had he married Mom. Grandpa, Grandma, and Aunt Della might have been nothing more than holiday-visiting kinfolk. What if their profound influence had bypassed me? There might have been far fewer hardships throughout my life, but all those tests and trials brought growth. Maybe, as a father, Jack could have made my days easier; I'm not sure how he could have made my life experiences much richer. I guess it all worked out the way God meant for it to happen. Funny, but in the end, I wasn't mad at Jack. I felt obliged to him.

I flew cross-country to see him one last time. He was so weak that he couldn't sit up. We sat alone in his room and he cried as he expressed bitter sorrow for the lost years. I brushed it off, telling him, "The Bible says that once you're forgiven, you don't need to ask again." Sitting at his bedside, I read to him passages of Scripture as he slipped in and out of consciousness. When it was time for me to go, I leaned forward, kissed the dying man on the forehead, and whispered in his ear: "We didn't spend much time together on earth, but hold tight to God's hand, and He promises we'll get better acquainted some day in Heaven."

"Wait for me there, Dad."

16

THE MAN IN
THE ARENA

CALIFORNIA LEGISLATURE
James E. Rogan
1957 | M | 6'0" | Hzl
Year Born | Sex | Height | Eyes
Assemblyman
43rd. District
1995 - 96

It is not the critic who counts, not the man who points out how the strong man stumbled, or where the doer of deeds could have done better. The credit belongs to the man in the arena; whose face is marred by dust and sweat and blood; who strives valiantly; who errs and comes short again and again; who knows the great enthusiasms, the great devotions, and spends himself in a worthy cause; who at the best knows in the end the triumph of high achievement, and who, at worst, if he fails, at least fails while daring greatly; so that his place shall never be with those cold and timid souls who know neither victory or defeat.

—THEODORE ROOSEVELT

California State Assemblyman Pat Nolan was a

bear of a guy. When it came to his love of politics, the 280-pound legislator's brain possessed no "off" switch. In plying his trade, he evoked old-school Irish charm mixed with intense patriotism; he called hundreds of constituents by their first names, and they returned the informality. He was sentimental, a loving husband and father, and as solid a conservative as ever was minted. Although affable by nature, Pat was a warrior in political battles. Playing to win, he could be overbearing, tireless, and devastatingly persuasive. Pat Nolan had many sides, but dishonesty was never among them.

Sent by the Glendale–Burbank voters to Sacramento in 1978, the young firebrand proved quickly that his political instincts rated among the sharpest in town. Soon his senior Republican colleagues made him their leader, and Pat set his sights on winning a Republican Assembly majority for the first time in a generation. Cobbling together his united caucus with a rump band of five dissident Democrats, Pat secured the 41 votes needed to send longtime Democratic Speaker Willie Brown to the showers. On the night before the historic vote, one of Pat's colleagues died unexpectedly. The moment to strike against Willie Brown passed, and for Pat it never returned.

About this time, law enforcement authorities started a sting operation on possible Sacramento corruption. Facing prosecution, one of Pat's staffers implicated her boss. For five years, prosecutors tried digging up evidence to corroborate the staffer's statements. Pickings were slim: Pat Nolan never pocketed one corrupt cent during his sixteen years of service. Yet newspaper reporters and columnists padded their circulation figures by ginning up doubt. Through this half-decade of hell, Pat lived under an asphyxiating cloud. Although his constituents returned him to Sacramento every two years during the ongoing investigation, the one-time future governor's statewide prospects were dead.

On the eve of the statute of limitations expiring, a federal prosecutor filed six counts of racketeering, extortion, conspiracy, and money laundering against Pat, who pleaded not guilty and declared for reelection in 1994. His trial was set for early March, a few months before the primary. This gave Pat a chance to clear his name before facing the voters again. Either way, the primary would be a tough one: Several candidates had already lined up to challenge the wounded warrior.

Each political season, as my resume and experience blossomed, friends suggested I think about running for office. My appointment to the bench in 1990 did much to increase my visibility and prestige in the community, but being on the bench also removed me by law from partisan activities. Further, my new family responsibilities made politics far less likely. Christine enjoyed having me settled into the comfortable, dignified life of a jurist. Although I never stopped thinking about entering the political arena one day, there's a large gulf between thinking and doing.

Now in my fourth year on the bench, I was about to get my political "fix." In 1994, I was required to stand for election to the court in my own right, and I felt hopeful that my record would commend me for retention. Having just completed a successful year as presiding judge, my colleagues (two gifted and distinguished judges, Barbara Lee Burke and Joe De Vanon) and I refunded to the taxpayers almost $700,000 from our $4 million budget. We drafted a court consolidation plan that became a model for the entire state, resulting in a multimillion-dollar savings of tax dollars. I implemented a vigorous plan to reduce delays in my own courtroom: When I first started, it took many criminal cases two years to come to trial. Near the end of my term, the waiting period for almost all such cases had gone down to under 90 days. Although the threat of a challenger always existed, no serious opponent loomed in the wings. I held my breath during the filing period and was pleased when no rival materialized. This made my judicial post safe for the next six years. With California Governor Pete Wilson as a friend and mentor, my future prospects for elevation to a higher court looked bright. Christine and I went to dinner to celebrate the close of filing and my unopposed reelection. When the conversation drifted to the future, she told me she hoped I'd never enter politics. "My dream," she said, "is one day seeing you on the Supreme Court."

"The bench is a great career," I told her, "but it leaves me unfulfilled in one way. When I was a prosecutor, I asked other judges to make what I thought was the right call. Now that I'm a judge, I make the call, but I'm limited to the laws written by others. As a legislator, I'd write the laws. That makes all the difference."

"But don't you see that God has another plan for you?" she said. "He steered you in another direction when you became a judge. The opportunity for the legislature or Congress never came your way. Maybe God wants you to surrender your desires to His."

Here again was that huge obstacle of faith for me: the notion of surrender. True, I loved my work on the bench, and it added stability to my life. Perhaps God indeed signaled another plan for me—one that didn't include politics. I felt a strange peace as I told Christine that, for the first time, I was ready to surrender my lifelong ambition for Congress and accept God's will.

I came home from work exhausted the next evening; a busy court calendar had kept me jumping all day. Christine appeared shaken when she greeted me at the door: "I just heard on the news that Pat Nolan is resigning from the Assembly," she said somberly. "He's accepted a plea bargain." The revelation stunned me. Only last week at his reelection kickoff rally, Pat renewed the vow to clear his name. The abject pain I felt for Pat and his family increased with each televised news report I watched.

Later, as Christine and I talked about the tragedy, I lamented, "This is just terrible. It's also devastating for the Republicans. The primary election is only weeks away. Who will they find to run for Pat's seat?"

The telephone rang as I finished my sentence; Christine answered it in the kitchen. I returned to watching the news broadcasts, paying no attention to her muffled conversation. A few minutes later, she called to me. Entering the kitchen, I found her looking different, as if laden with some sudden, invisible burden.

"It's for you."

Allen Brandstater was a longtime local Republican activist, political consultant, newspaper columnist, and friend. He was an even better friend to Pat Nolan, whom he'd known since their college Young Republican days at USC. Now Allen was on the telephone, fighting back tears as he confirmed the resignation and plea story. "Pat resigned today; tomorrow he'll enter a plea bargain in federal court," Allen said. He told me the feds pressured Pat into taking the deal. If Pat threw the dice with the jury and lost on just one charge, he would have faced a minimum of nine years in federal prison, and many more if convicted on additional charges. Pat had three small children; he wouldn't see his babies until they were in high school or college. "After five years of battling these guys, his money's gone and he's tired," Allen lamented. "The government's resources are limitless. If he takes the risk and gambles wrong, his young family would be devastated."

Switching gears, Allen got to his main point: "Jim, as painful as this is, political life must go on." He said the Republicans were in a fix: The Democrats moved a former federal prosecutor into our district to run against Pat, hoping to exploit his legal problems. The district shifted in registration to one favoring the Democrats, so even an incumbent like Pat would have had a tough time holding it. "We don't have a strong candidate for the 43rd Assembly seat. We need someone with your background and record to hold the seat for the Republicans. Are you interested?"

Was I interested?

"Allen, this is crazy," I replied, running through all the reasons why I shouldn't consider running:

- I just won a full term to the bench without opposition. To run for the Assembly, I'd have to withdraw my judicial election papers and vacate my safe judgeship. I'd sacrifice virtual lifetime security on the bench for a crowded field and begin an underdog Assembly campaign. If I lost the race, I'd no longer be a judge.
- An assemblyman's term is only two years, with a six-year maximum term limit and a lifetime ban from ever returning. There aren't even pension benefits. A judge has no term limits, and my pension rights from the court would vest in eighteen more months. I would have no vested pension if I left the bench.
- Under California law, I'd have to leave the bench without pay during the campaign. I'd be a candidate with no outside income, and the law precluded me from lawyering. A judge, even one on an unpaid leave of absence, cannot practice law. Chris-

tine and I had no savings: We emptied our account to pay the adoption agency fee for Dana and Claire.

- Assuming I won, the job change would mean a massive $30,000 pay cut, which we couldn't afford.

- Almost overnight, I'd have to come up to speed on a truckload of complex local and state issues that a candidate must be prepared to discuss. This would put me at a tactical disadvantage against those who had been campaigning and studying for months.

- Politicians are viewed with disdain and are trashed by their opponents and the media at will, and their families are exposed to extreme ugliness. The career of a judge is dignified and respectful. I'd have to be crazy to make the switch.

"Allen, there's no logical reason why I should be a candidate," I concluded. "Besides, I had a little talk with God last night that involved surrendering certain notions."

"With all due respect to God, maybe you didn't hear my question," Allen replied. "I didn't ask if you *should* be a candidate. I asked if you were *interested* in being a candidate."

I was interested.

Over the next ten days, my telephone rang off the hook from friends and supporters urging me to make the race. One call came from Pat Nolan, who hoped I'd run: "After spending a lifetime building our party in the district, it would mean a lot to know a solid, honest conservative took my place," he told me. Pat added that he'd spoken with Republican legislative leaders in Sacramento and asked them to weigh in for me. "I told them you are our only hope for the district," he added, "but beware. You'd be up against a dirty machine that recruited a U.S. Attorney to challenge me. Isn't that something? The U.S. Attorney fields a candidate from their own ranks to run against me while they're investigating me. The whole thing stinks."

I asked Pat a pointed question: "If you knew before you first ran that you'd later pay with thirty-three months of your freedom in exchange for your sixteen years of service in the legislature, would you have done it? Was it worth it?" Pat paused at length, and then answered: "It was worth it."

Not everyone whose opinion I respected was enthusiastic about my running. Former California Lieutenant Governor Bob Finch, who was Richard Nixon's 1960 national campaign manager and later cabinet member, was concerned about my jumping into the race: "Do you know how tough a political life can be on you and your family? I know you can handle it, but other than ego gratification, being a legislator isn't much of a job. Being a judge is a great calling, and you'll move up the ranks. You could have a distinguished career on the bench."

"Bob, I get called 'Your Honor' all day long," I told him. "I wouldn't give that up if ego gratification was a factor. I just want to serve wherever I can make a bigger difference, and I think this is the place."

Former Governor George Deukmejian, the man to whom I owed my judgeship, echoed this ambivalence. "Politics can be a terrible life," he told me. "The bench is such a better world, and you'll go far there." The governor confessed to a personal bias: He hoped his younger appointees would spend decades on the bench, extending his judicial legacy long past his term. When I asked if he ever had the chance to be a judge during his legislative career, he recounted the multiple times then-Governor Reagan offered him an appointment. I asked why he remained in the legislature. Clearing his throat, the governor replied, "Well, that's where the action is." After contemplating his own answer for a moment, he added with a chuckle, "Okay, I see your point." Governor Deukmejian ended the conversation by endorsing my prospective candidacy.

The 43rd Assembly District Republican Central Committee announced the formation of a "Committee of 100," a gathering of local GOP opinion leaders. The committee would assemble and hear presentations from the candidates, then choose their preference for a successor to Pat. The vote was advisory and wouldn't be a formal endorsement; the committee would disband after they discharged their mission. However, the vote would signal the Party's favorite to the press, business leaders, donors, and activists. On March 2, Republican Central Committee Chairman Don Meredith wrote and invited me to serve as one of the 100 members of the committee, which would meet the night of March 9 at the Glendale Public Library's main branch. Don appended a caveat to the end of his letter: "You cannot be both a member of the Committee of 100 and a candidate."

I declined his invitation to serve on the committee.

Assemblyman Curt Pringle, a longtime Pat Nolan ally and Assistant Republican Leader, asked me to fly to Sacramento and meet with Assembly and Senate Republican leaders. My meetings were positive, and everyone with whom I spoke urged me to make the race. While shuttling me between meetings, Curt admitted it would be tough, especially since the Democrats had a big lead in voter registration since reapportionment. "We need a strong law-and-order candidate to blunt the guy Willie Brown hand-picked to run against Pat," he added. "We think you'd be perfect." Curt did his homework for me in advance: By the time I flew home that night, I found on my fax machine a letter signed by twenty-four Assembly Republicans, urging the Committee of 100 to select me as Pat's replacement.

Torn between security and her husband's dreams, Christine hoped this cup might pass. As the Committee of 100 approached, we talked long into the night; she asked why I couldn't be happy as a judge. "I love being a judge," I replied, "but all my life I've wanted to give politics a shot, and this is my chance. Better to try and lose than to spend the rest of my life wondering what might have happened if I tried." The final decision, she said, was mine to make. She'd support whatever I did.

That night I couldn't sleep; the Committee would meet the next day. At 3:00 A.M., while still pacing the floor, I reached for a book to occupy my mind—it was Richard Nixon's *In the Arena*. Flipping the pages, I landed on a chapter entitled "Risks":

"In politics more than in any other profession," Nixon wrote, "the risks worth taking are those where the odds are great. The more you risk if you lose, the more you stand to gain if you win. Nothing great can be accomplished without taking great risks. In determining what risks to take, you must never be obsessed by what you might lose. You must always keep front and center what you might gain."[15] Nixon also wrote, "Those who choose politics as a career are embarking on a perilous voyage. But they should always remember the words of St. Thomas Aquinas seven centuries ago: 'If the highest aim of a captain were to preserve his ship, he would keep it in port forever.'"[16] I felt Nixon's words spoke to me directly. When I closed the book and returned it to the shelf, I had my answer.

At court that afternoon, I called my last calendared case of the day. Retiring to my chambers, I called Christine to check with her one last time. With her blessing, I told my colleagues I was stepping down. Withdrawing my judicial election papers, I took Nixon's advice: Risk it all and don't look back.

At the Committee of 100, I declared my candidacy for the California State Assembly. After each candidate made a presentation, the committee members voted for their preference in a secret ballot. I garnered 83 percent of the total votes; Peter Musurlian, the candidate who received all but one of the remaining votes, withdrew and endorsed me.

After a lifetime on the periphery, I had gotten my wish—I was in the political arena.

My makeshift campaign office was in the Glendale storefront occupied by political consultants Sheila McNichols and Natalie Blanning. When I arrived on my first day as a candidate, I expected Sheila and Natalie to send me out giving speeches, walking precincts, shaking hands, and kissing babies. "You don't do those things," Natalie said. "We do those things for you. You raise money." With that, Natalie handed me a list of names

---

[15]Richard Nixon, *In the Arena: A Memoir of Victory, Defeat, and Renewal*, p. 197. Norwalk, CT: Easton Press, 1990.
[16]Ibid.

and phone numbers, and showed me to a metal desk with nothing on it but a pencil and a telephone. "I bet they didn't tell you about this in your college classes," she said with a grin. "Welcome to politics."

Over the next few weeks, I felt chained to that damned telephone. Looking for shortcuts, I spoke again with Governor Deukmejian and with Governor Pete Wilson, Attorney General Dan Lungren, Los Angeles County District Attorney Gil Garcetti, and former DAs John Van de Kamp, Bob Philibosian, and Ira Reiner. Each told me that I had no alternative: Full-time fundraising was a big part of a candidate's job, and all saw it as the worst part of the experience. Bruce Herschensohn, the 1992 GOP nominee for U.S. Senate, told me that when he ran, he made most of his fundraising calls between noon and 2:00. "That way, the person I was calling would be out to lunch," Bruce said. "I'd leave a recorded message, and tell my manager I made the call." When I told Bruce that sounded like a great way to "dial for dollars" without having the unpleasantness of asking for money, Bruce agreed: "Sure, it's a great way to avoid asking. But remember one detail: I lost."

To make it worse, I soon learned the fundraising chore didn't end on Election Day. Once we counted the votes, a new cycle began to assemble a war chest for the next election. As one veteran legislator told me, "If you have a big cash-on-hand war chest, your enemies will look for opportunities elsewhere. If your coffers look bleak, they'll come in with guns blazing to bury you. Perpetual fundraising is a matter of political survival."

Governor Wilson called the special election to fill Pat Nolan's unexpired term for May 3, and thirteen candidates filed for the seat. Under the election rules, if no candidate received 50 percent of the total votes cast, the runoff between the top vote getters of each party would be on June 28. Meanwhile, I also had to run in the regular Republican primary on June 7 to be the nominee for the general election on November 8. A few weeks earlier, I lamented that God intervened to prevent me from running. Now it looked like I'd be running in four separate elections in the space of six months. As the old saying goes, be careful what you pray for.

After the Committee of 100, my Republican opponents didn't fade away. Two well-financed challengers, Julia Wu and Peter Repovich, intended to continue the fight. Under the laws regulating special elections, the campaign contribution limit was $1,000 per person. This excluded Repovich from the May 3 special election, because most of his $350,000 campaign war chest came from a single-source loan. Repovich skipped the special election to focus his efforts against me in the June primary. Wu went on the immediate attack against me. The scenario worried my campaign consultant, Jim Nygren. He foresaw a situation where Wu spent heavily against me for the May 3 special election: She would lose, probably, but siphon off enough votes to push me into a runoff on June 28. Meanwhile, Repovich would weigh in with a $350,000 blast for the June 7 primary. The Democratic candidate was unopposed in his primary, so he could sit back while the Republicans savaged me, and save his resources for the general election. Nygren warned, "You stand a good chance of winning the special election for the remainder of Pat's term, and then losing the primary in June, or winning the primary and losing the November general election. You will have been the Assemblyman for only a few months, so you'll spend all your resources defending yourself against opponents lined up to take turns attacking you." Nygren's analysis made me feel like a political piñata.

Meanwhile, the Democrats cleared the field for Adam Schiff,[17] who earlier quit his job as an Assistant United States Attorney to run against Pat. They expected Schiff to wield a law-and-order hammer against a Republican under federal indictment; instead, they drew a former gang-murder prosecutor and judge. Clearly, Pat's resignation disappointed local Democratic activists.

Nobody expected any candidate to win the May 3 special election outright: The field was too crowded, and my managers believed that the barrage of hit mail directed at me from opponents would "drive down my numbers." The smart money was on a June 28 runoff between Schiff and

---

[17]This was the first of three times Adam Schiff and I faced each other as opponents over the next six years; I beat him twice for the State Assembly; in 2000 he defeated me for reelection to Congress.

me. On election eve, the *Glendale News-Press*'s headline read, "No Clinch Expected in 43rd Assembly Election." It was a safe bet. Assembly Republican Leader Jim Brulte called me on Election Day with this request: "Just come in first and get 40 percent of the vote, and you'll make my life much easier."

"What if I win outright?" I asked jokingly.

"You'll save about $300,000 for my caucus," Jim said, "and I'll kiss your ass."

Jim Nygren thought I had a decent chance to get 40 percent. "Expect the early absentees to bring you in around 60 percent," he predicted. "You'll then do a free fall into the 30 percent range when the Democratic precincts in Los Angeles and Burbank come in. Hopefully, Glendale's precincts will bring you up to 40 percent and a first place position for the runoff."

When the polls closed that night, our family attended an election party at the home of family friends John and JoAnn Gantus, where 200 supporters gathered to await the returns and wish us luck. The absentee ballots were reporting just as we arrived. Jim Nygren's prediction was close: I had 58.2 percent of the absentees. The next three hours showed those numbers decline, but not in the free fall Nygren predicted. My totals crept down to 58 percent, 56.5 percent, and then, with half of all precincts reporting, 53.6 percent. The excitement of a possible upset victory grew with each new tally. Reporters who'd left the party earlier started reappearing, sensing an unexpected story brewing. With 70 percent of the precincts reporting, I held at 53 percent of the vote. A wave of cheers filled the room when Nygren called to predict victory; I still rejected his optimism—it was too close. At 11:30 P.M., Natalie posted a new tally sheet. With 91 percent of the precincts reporting, our vote totals *increased!* I was back at 53.6 percent of the vote, and I thought the Gantuses' roof might cave in from the noise. Nygren again called: "Almost all of the precincts are reporting, and there are 2,000 uncounted absentee ballots. Most of those ballots will be yours. Congratulations, Mr. Assemblyman." Dan Bolton, the *Glendale News-Press* editor, called in his story from the party: "Give Rogan the headline," he said, "and declare him the winner."

Christine and I slipped out the back door for a few moments of privacy as Natalie posted the final vote tally. The cheers blaring from the Gantus home told us the result. We walked alone outside, holding hands and collecting our thoughts. Neither of us expected this result, and we had not prepared for an immediate transition to Sacramento. Amid the dizzying and exciting prospect, we said a quick prayer asking for guidance. It's a good thing it was quick—a campaign volunteer rushed outside looking for us. "Get back in here!" he called. "The governor's on the phone for you!" We went back inside; someone thrust roses into Christine's arms while I took the congratulatory call from Governor Wilson. Assembly GOP Leader Jim Brulte interrupted his late-night poker game in the Sacramento hotel suite of Senator Rob Hurtt to call and congratulate me. Jim passed the telephone around the card table so my new colleagues (and future poker buddies) could welcome me to their ranks. Later that morning, Christine scooped up souvenir copies of the *Glendale News-Press* and its banner headline, "Rogan Wins Assembly Seat in Landslide." When all the precincts reported, I won 54 percent of the total vote; Democrat Adam Schiff won 25 percent, and Julia Wu, my nearest GOP rival, who attacked me aggressively and outspent me, received only 10 percent.

Christine and I flew to Sacramento that weekend, where we toured the Capitol and inspected my new office in preparation for Monday's swearing-in ceremony. As the junior member of the minority party, Speaker Willie Brown consigned me to Room 6017, nicknamed the "broom closet." It was the worst office in the building, but I didn't mind: it was bigger than my first DA office, which lacked windows and was shared with three other DAs (two of whom smoked). On my new desk was a note from fellow Republican Assemblyman Larry Bowler, himself a former Room 6017 resident. "Just remember," Larry wrote, "that this office is a Republican badge of honor!"

On Monday morning, May 9, 1994, I left my hotel room and walked across the street to the Capitol for a meeting with Jim Brulte. As I approached the east steps and looked at the beautiful grounds and impressive dome, I felt overwhelmed by my rapidly altered circumstances. I knew I'd need God's guidance for these new responsibilities.

Jim gave me a quick tour of the grounds and a procedural overview, and then escorted me to a ceremonial meeting with Willie Brown, the longest serving Assembly Speaker in state history. To California Republicans, Willie Brown was the Great Satan. Love him or despise him, nobody dared underestimate him. Born into poverty in the racially segregated town of Mineola, Texas, this young African-American got his education while working as a shoeshine boy, janitor, and crop picker. Moving west to California with his belongings in a cardboard suitcase, he worked his way through college and law school, and then began a successful San Francisco practice. Elected to the Assembly when I was seven years old, Willie served there for over three decades and held the longevity record (fifteen years) as speaker. He was the "most" of everything: the most charming, the most savvy, the most successful, the most cunning, the most skilled orator, and (when he wanted to be) the most ruthless. He had a reputation for enjoying the exercise of raw political power, once calling himself the "Ayatollah of the Assembly." His legislative might matched his penchant for flashy cars and expensive suits. Forever amused by rumors of corruption surrounding his lavish lifestyle on a legislator's modest salary, Willie wasn't crooked and didn't need to be: He maintained a lucrative law practice on the side. Republican candidates for years ran against Willie Brown as much as they ran against taxes and big government. I was no different, but privately I couldn't wait to serve with him. To me he was the most fascinating man on the American political scene.

When Jim escorted me to Willie's office, he rose from his desk and greeted me warmly. The broad smile on his face looked a tad suspicious. Wrapping his arm around my shoulder, he walked me to the rear of his conference room: "Come, Judge, I'd like to show you something." He opened a door leading directly to the Assembly floor. Pointing to the members now collecting at their desks for the start of session, he asked, "Do you know what most of those people are?"

"Assemblymen?"

"Very good," Willie responded. "Do you know what most of them did before coming here? They were lawyers. Do you know why lawyers come here? To get to know a governor who will appoint them to the bench. In this room, we have many assemblymen wanting to be judges; until now, I never met a judge wanting to be an assemblyman. So, Judge Rogan, I'm curious: What made you give up the bench to come here?"

Assuming this was an esoteric question, I gave an esoteric answer: "Well, the legislature is where our laws are written. Although I loved the bench, I thought this opportunity would give me a chance to serve in a different venue. I wanted to have a hand in drafting laws to make our state a better place for my children."

Like a cat playing with his mouse before eating it, Willie toyed with me before pouncing for the kill: "Judge, let me share with you some arithmetic: There are 80 members in this body. I lead 47 Democrats; Jim Brulte leads 33 Republicans. I have what we call *a majority*; you have what we call *a minority*. 'Passing laws'—we do those things. On rare occasions, when a bill requires a two-thirds vote, I may consult with a few members of your caucus."

"Of course," Willie added, "don't feel you gave up the bench for nothing. You have an important role to play. Please show up on time, which helps my majority to make a quorum, so *we* can pass those laws that make better the lives of *your* children. And don't forget to collect your salary and per diem check."

"Judge Rogan," the Speaker concluded with a wide grin, "welcome to the California State Assembly!" As we shook hands, I couldn't help but smile. The schoolmaster had just tutored his new assembly-boy with a verbal hickory switch. This was my introduction to a man I came to respect, like, and fear in equal measure. Say what you will about Willie Brown: For my money, each day I wished he was on our side.

Speaker Brown called the house to order at 10:30. After the preliminaries, he appointed an escort committee to lead my family and me to the rostrum for the oath of office. As we walked down the center aisle of the chamber, my new colleagues rose graciously to greet me. Standing at the dais, I remembered my first visit to the chamber as a young boy. Looking up, I now saw a young boy watching from the same seat I occupied that day. Despite Willie's earlier math lesson, it was a great feeling.

Using the same Bible Christine gave me before we were married, Speaker Brown swore me in as a new member of the Assembly. After I made brief remarks, the escort committee led me to Pat Nolan's old desk in the chamber. My seatmate, Assemblywoman Andrea Seastrand, helped me navigate through the remainder of the fifty or so bills on the daily calendar for debate and vote. Later, when the session ended, my afternoon and evening were crammed with meetings, interviews, and appointments. Christine and the twins kissed me goodbye and flew home, leaving me to my new duties. For the time being, they'd stay in the district while I remained in Sacramento for legislative business.

I worked in my Capitol office late into the night, reviewing mounds of briefing papers and bills scheduled for tomorrow's session. Still feeling overwhelmed by it all, it was pushing 1:00 A.M. before I realized I had eaten no lunch or dinner, nor did I have a place to sleep. In the post-election bustle, I'd forgotten to secure Sacramento lodgings! Scouring the Yellow Pages for a nearby motel with a vacancy, I started reflecting on what these changes had wrought. My family was 400 miles away; I was lonesome, hungry, and temporarily homeless with no job security, a big pay cut, and a brutal campaign season ahead. From now until my political run ended, I could expect daily attacks from opponents, mudslingers, cynics, and opportunists. Meanwhile, I'd have to fight like hell just to hang onto my job by my fingernails.

A rare twinge of doubt hovered over me. Had I made the right choice? "Maybe Willie Brown was right," I thought. "Maybe leaving the bench and coming here wasn't such a good idea after all." I shook off the feeling: I was just tired, I told myself. It had been a long day.

Just then, the telephone rang in my Capitol office. "It must be Christine," I thought. "Who else would be calling me at one in the morning?" When I answered, an unfamiliar baritone asked to speak with Assemblyman Rogan. After I identified myself, I took my first constituent call:

"Listen," the man said. "I was just sitting here at home thinking about how all you bastards have it made up there. You live high off the hog with your fancy lifestyles, big offices, and chauffeured limousines, while us little guys work hard to scratch out a living. So I just wanted to call and say screw you, you bastard!" He slammed down the receiver in my ear.

All my life I wanted to be in politics. This man's call reminded me how very much I had gotten my wish.

Epilogue

MY AMERICAN DREAM

When you fight for what you believe in, you've already won. The end result doesn't matter.

—CAROLE LOMBARD

"The Chair recognizes Mr. Manager Rogan."

Four short years after winning my race for the California State Assembly, I sat in another legislative chamber 3,000 miles away—the United States Senate. When the Chief Justice summoned me to begin my opening statement in President Clinton's impeachment trial before the Senate and a live, worldwide television audience, I saw a man watching me in the back row: It was Senator Edward M. Kennedy. That moment transported me back in memory almost thirty years; I remembered being a kid with dreams of serving in Congress and waiting outside that San Francisco TV studio to get his autograph. Looking at Kennedy now, I felt overwhelmed by how our country gives each of us a shot at our dreams. When Chief Justice Rehnquist beckoned, the walk from my chair to the lectern was but a few feet; the walk from the Mission District to that lectern was immeasurable.

"Mr. Chief Justice and members of the United States Senate, my name

is Congressman James E. Rogan. On behalf of the House of Representatives,
and in the name of the people of the United States, I will present the evi-
dence against the president to show he committed perjury before a federal
grand jury. . . ."

On display in my office today is a yellowing Styrofoam stand holding
those thirty-six little five-for-a-dollar toy statues of U.S. presidents my
mother gave me when I was in the fourth grade. Who could have known
back then that a grocery store promotional gimmick would trigger such a
profound influence in a young life? I look at those statues today and see
something far greater than nostalgic kitsch; I see a symbolic reminder that
the American Dream thrives. How else do you explain the journey to Congress of an illegitimate welfare kid who went from high school dropout
and bartender to prosecutor, judge, and legislator? There is but one explanation: The American Dream exists for all who bother to seek it.

How did my American Dream play out? I'll give you the *Cliffs Notes*
version for now: Six months after I won that special election to the California State Assembly, I won a full term in my own right and became Assembly Majority Leader. In a *California Journal* poll of Capitol
journalists, legislators, and staff, they named me "number one in in-
tegrity" and "number one in effectiveness," beating out even the mighty
Willie Brown in that latter category. Even if those polled grossly overesti-
mated my abilities (or grossly underestimated Willie's), the designations
remain the most meaningful of tributes from my public service.

In 1996 my longtime congressman, Carlos Moorhead, announced his
retirement. Thirty years after assembling that collection of presidential
statues, my time had arrived. Running as a Republican in a Democratic
congressional district, my grueling eighteen-month campaign ended
with my eking out 50.1 percent of the vote to win a seat in the United
States House of Representatives. Two years later, I won reelection just as
narrowly. Within days of the election, my duties as a member of the
House Judiciary Committee thrust me in the national spotlight, when my
colleagues selected me to serve as one of the prosecutors in the Clinton

impeachment trial. With many of the Hollywood movie studios located in my district (and the president enjoying phenomenal popularity there), my participation in his impeachment had the expected result: It incurred the wrath of my constituents, and at the next election they bounced me out of Congress. This was their right, and they exercised it by a healthy margin.

Ending sixteen years of government service, I was back in private life, but not for long. A few months after leaving Congress, President George W. Bush nominated me to be the United States Under Secretary of Commerce for Intellectual Property and Director of the United States Patent and Trademark Office. The U.S. Senate confirmed me unanimously for the position in late 2001, and I served in the Bush administration until 2004. Now I'm back at Venable LLP in Washington, D.C., my old law firm where I became a partner soon after leaving Congress. This summer of 2004, Christine, the twins, and I look forward to two things: the publication of this book, and moving home to Southern California, where I'll set up Venable's West Coast office.

If you've stuck with this book, you know we Irish hate to rush what we think is a good story. But since my editor wants this memoir kept to a single volume, I'll reserve my account of life in Congress and the statehouse for another day. When I do take pen in hand for those tales, I'll share them with a blessed and grateful heart.

"Wait a minute!" I hear you say. "How can Jim Rogan feel blessed and grateful? Didn't I just read a whole book about a guy who spent his life clearing hurdles to get to Congress, only to get kicked out soon after getting there?" If that's your first-blush impression, let me invite you to a different perspective.

First, there's no mystery to incumbency: You just convince a majority of voters that you agree with them on most everything, even if you really don't. The real trick is to be *worthy* of incumbency. Worthiness comes from leadership, and leadership means getting beyond the preoccupation of job security and doing what you believe is right, even when the sentiment proves unpopular. Only then can metamorphosis change the politician caterpillar into the statesman butterfly.

I wasn't in Congress long enough to leave a legacy that comes anywhere near qualifying for statesmanship, but for the time God and the voters gave me to serve there, I did my best to apply an honorable standard. Richard Nixon once wrote that politics separates the men from the boys in one way: He said the boys want to *be* something; the men want to *do* something. If my grandfather, Jimmy Kleupfer, had lived to see me in politics, he would have wanted to see a man on that stage, not a boy. I did my best to make Grandpa proud of what he might have witnessed.

The morning after I lost my reelection battle, a reporter asked me if I still had the political bug. When I told her I did, she asked if there was any cure for it. "Yes," I replied, "it's called embalming fluid." I don't know, and it matters little, whether I will again have the privilege of holding elective office. Today, at age forty-six, I look back on a pretty full public life. People reading my resume see impressive titles: gang-murder prosecutor, presiding judge, state assemblyman, majority leader, Member of Congress, Under Secretary of Commerce, Director of the U.S. Patent and Trademark Office. I say it matters little because I know God reads my resume and sees only one title: sinner. The hired spin of media consultants and pollsters doesn't impress Him. Where man sees accomplishment, God sees spiritual immaturity, foolishness, pride, and lack of contrition. All those maladies (and many more) apply to me. Despite the bulkheads I've constructed between my Maker and me, God remains. His hands keep smoothing the rough edges while whispering—always whispering—that He catches the falling sparrow. That's His promise from Jeremiah 29:11: "For I know the plans I have for you, declares the Lord, plans to prosper you and not to harm you, plans to give you hope and a future."

So that's why my congressional defeat left no bitterness. Why should it? In Congress, I had a job with predecessors named Jefferson, Webster, and Lincoln; as a bartender, my predecessors were named Zonko, Chi-Chi, and Filthy. When one views one's life through the appropriate prism, gratitude comes easily. Besides, I've learned the only permanent defeats in life are the self-imposed ones.

As a young boy growing up, one of my favorite political figures was that Democratic Party icon, Hubert Humphrey. Forever the ebullient idealist, Humphrey's dream was to be president: Three times he ran; three times he lost. Yet throughout his long political career, Humphrey never lost sight of how far *his* American Dream carried him: a young Walgreen's druggist from Huron, South Dakota, went on to City Hall, Congress, and the vice presidency of the United States, and came within a whisker of the Oval Office.

A quarter-century ago, with only a few months to live before a ravaging cancer claimed his life, Hubert Humphrey penned his final letter to me. In it he discussed his own political defeats, and shared with me an important perspective: "Bitterness is not a political asset—in fact, it is not an asset in any profession. It preys on one's mind and consumes time and energies which should be directed toward resolving problems and meeting the challenges with which one is faced in government and politics."

Then, in a final paragraph, Humphrey closed with parting words to his young admirer who, like he, spent his youth hoping to tread in mighty political footsteps. His simple words of advice are a fitting valedictory for anyone daring dreams of public service:

"We need good, progressive, honorable young people in government and politics. So, go to it! Work hard; study hard; fight the good fight; and, my friend, be of good cheer!"

Appendix A

THEN AND NOW

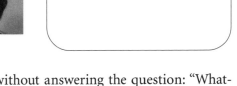

No autobiography is complete without answering the question: "Whatever became of . . ."

MY FAMILY

My grandfather, James G. Kleupfer, died at age fifty-eight on December 20, 1964. My grandmother, Helen, died at age sixty on October 13, 1966.

My great aunt, Della Glover, died at age sixty-nine on March 15, 1971. Her beloved beau, "Uncle Ralf" Olson, died December 4, 1968.

My mother, Alice Rogan, is a grandmother who baby-sits far more than fairness dictates. She lives quietly and tries her best to stay out of trouble—when she can help it!

My stepfather, Jack Rogan, is a retired engineer with the San Francisco Unified School District. He spends his time fishing, diving, digging for arrowheads, and writing checks to needy children and grandchildren.

My biological father, Jack Barone, died at age sixty-eight on September 12, 1999.

My sister, Teri, is a sometimes-waitress who enjoys life on a houseboat; my brother Pat is the operations manager at SBC Baseball Stadium in San Francisco; and my brother Johnny is a chief engineer for Wells Fargo Bank in San Francisco.

John Kleupfer, my legendary Uncle Jack, retired from the Army in 1969 and became a deputy sheriff in Brevard County, Florida. He died of a heart attack at age fifty-seven in 1984.

Lynn Coffee Manning, the cousin raised with me by my grandparents, grew to love me despite my unending childhood torments of her and her boyfriends. She became a librarian in Pacifica, California, where she died tragically of Lou Gehrig's disease at age fifty in 1998.

MY BUDDIES GROWING UP

Dan Swanson is an internationally recognized antitrust lawyer and a partner in the law firm of Gibson Dunn and Crutcher in Los Angeles.

Roger Mahan is a senior staff member for the Budget Committee of the U.S. House of Representatives in Washington, D.C.

Clint Bolick is co-founder of the public interest law firm *The Institute for Justice*. A respected author and lecturer, Clint is one of America's foremost lawyers protecting individual liberty and challenging the regulatory welfare state.

Frank Debrose, the Pinole buddy with whom I have shared so many adventures, was a special services officer for the Sergeant at Arms, California State Senate.

Rocky Iaukea, the other member of our Pinole mafia, became a professional wrestler. He fought for many years under the name of Abu Deen, the Mad Libyan, playing the fan-hated bad guy who always cheated to win. Today, he is owner and skipper of a catamaran on the beach at Waikiki, taking tourists on pleasure outings.

Eldon Jernigan, who taught all of us as teenagers that it's okay to be good friends with a gay guy, became a sales manager for Radio Shack. Sadly, he died of AIDS at age thirty-five in 1992.

Bob Wyatt, my fellow Straw Hat Pizza cook who moved with me to Los Angeles, earned his undergraduate degree at UCLA. Later he served as my assistant district director in the California State Assembly and the United States Congress. Today he is completing his master's degree in public administration; I'm the proud godfather of his son Joe.

Bret Muncy, the Straw Hat Pizza buddy who hid in the attic so we could swipe pizzas and beers during our unapproved midnight crew poker games, is now a sergeant with the San Jose Police Department.

Mitch Hanlon, my UCLA roommate, never did make it to medical school. Instead, he followed his heart for music; today, he is the assistant conductor at the Hollywood Bowl. An accomplished musician and recording artist in his own right, he also leads the Mitch Hanlon Singers.

Raffi Kuredjian, my other UCLA roommate, is an engineer and successful entrepreneur in Michigan. Had I known he'd end up rich, I'd have been a hell of a lot nicer to him in the old days.

Before Christine came along, I had three early loves in my life: Terri Lemke, Gay Hahn, and Katie James Nesbitt. Terri and her husband own and operate a print shop on the West Coast; Gay still ice skates and travels the world; and Kate is a marriage and family therapist in Santa Monica, California. All are happily married; all remain beloved friends.

MY BOSSES AND MY BARS

Filthy and Wolfgang McNasty sold their nightclubs in Hollywood and got out of the bar business. Today, they are businessmen in Southern California.

Tommy Thomas, the longtime owner of The Palomino Club, died of a heart attack at age sixty-one in 1985.

Our Place bar is now a karate school.

The Tarzana Inn is now a dry cleaners.

The nightclub I opened with Joe Cocker is now a barbecue teriyaki house.

The Pussycat Theater is now a government office building for the City of Los Angeles. I'll avoid the temptation to joke about that irony!

Filthy McNasty's on the Sunset Strip is now the Viper Room nightclub. Filthy's North Hollywood after-hours nightclub is now a lounge catering to Mexican bands.

The Palomino Club in North Hollywood is now a banquet hall.

My Buddies in the Law and Politics

Walt Lewis, my first boss in the Los Angeles County District Attorney's office, retired in 2001 after almost thirty-five years as a prosecutor. He is now in private practice.

Terry Green, my other supervisor and role model in the DA's office, is now a judge of the Los Angeles County Superior Court. I was his best man when he married Leslie, a superb and respected lawyer in Los Angeles.

Lenny Read, the Los Angeles County Deputy Public Defender with whom I had lots of laughs (and who was the first one to beat me in a jury trial) is a criminal defense attorney in private practice in Hawaiian Gardens, California.

Pat Nolan, my friend and predecessor in the California State Assembly, spent thirty-three months in federal prison. He now serves as executive director of Justice Fellowship, a ministry of Chuck Colson's Prison Fellowship.

John L. Burton, the bartender who worked with my mother and biological father Jack Barone at the Cable Car Village in San Francisco, served as a member of the California State Assembly and the United States House of Representatives. Today, he is the president pro tempore of the California State Senate. In every phone conversation I have with Uncle Johnny, he still busts my chops for becoming a Republican.

And a Few Honorable Mentions

President Harry S Truman helped me twice: once with my homework, and once in settling a score with a nasty seventh-grade teacher. He died at age eighty-eight on December 26, 1972.

Vice President Hubert H. Humphrey, an early inspiration upon whom I inflicted terminal writer's cramp from all the autographs he signed for me, died of stomach cancer at age sixty-six in 1978.

Jim Dunbar, the longtime news anchor at KGO in San Francisco who helped me meet so many political leaders as a boy, was inducted into the Radio Hall of Fame in 1999. After forty years, he's still at KGO.

Sam, the dirty, bongo-carrying beatnik that showed up to date my cousin Lynn (until Grandpa tossed him down our stairs) later became a Nobel Laureate who served two terms as governor of Montana.

By the way, as for what became of Sam—don't be so gullible!

Appendix B

WHAT YOU CAN'T PUT IN YOUR FIRST BOOK

My book agent is Jillian Manus, the remarkable president of Manus & Associates Literary Agency in New York and California. I love Jillian; she's a solid pro who has been in the business for many years. Unlike me, when it comes to writing books, Jilly knows what she's doing.

As I cranked out chapter after chapter of the first draft over a two-year period, she remained enthusiastic. The only time she suffered a tinge of indigestion was when she read my original draft of a chapter I titled "Off the Reservation." This was my issue-by-issue analysis of why I changed parties from Democratic to Republican. Although she understood my desire to explain things, Jilly didn't think this chapter was a good idea, telling me to keep two things in mind: "First, this policy stuff interrupts your life story. Second, to get your book published, you'll need a publisher. Since many are liberal Democrats, this might not go over too well with them."

Jillian said take it out, so I took it out. Yet I remain convinced that (like Ronald Reagan and me) many registered Democrats are really conservative Republicans and just don't know it. So I crafted this short closed-book test and hid it in the appendix where Jillian won't find it (I'm told book agents never read the appendices!). This pop quiz will help you self-described liberals decide if you're really closet conservatives. Consider it my contribution to helping put you in touch with your true Jungian inner creature.

Only those scoring 90 percent or above are eligible to learn and use the secret handshake when greeting fellow conservatives. So good luck— *and no cheating!*

↓↓↓↓

CLOSED BOOK TEST

Part One: True or False

____ 1. John Lennon's song "Imagine" expresses my worldview completely.

____ 2. Senator Joe McCarthy got a raw deal.

____ 3. Whittaker Chambers got a raw deal.

____ 4. When proposing her plan to socialize America's health care delivery system, Hillary Clinton got a raw deal. (*Warning*: If you answered "true" to this question, you are disqualified automatically).

Part Two: Multiple Choice

5. Socialism is
   a) good, because everyone should be social.
   b) good, because I want other people to work and pay higher taxes so the government can support me.
   d) good, because when it comes to government programs run by out of touch Washington bureaucrats, bigger is better.
   e) bad, because it destroys my personal freedom.

6. Communism is
   a) good, because people should commune with each other.
   b) good, because 10,000 Hollywood movie activists can't be all wrong.
   c) good, because Lenin and Marx are, respectively, my favorite Beatle and comedy team.
   d) bad, because it destroys my personal freedom.

7. "One World" government is

    a) good, because it would make learning geography a lot easier.

    b) good, because I can only live in one world at a time.

    c) good, because then other countries with shattered economies and no understanding for the rule of law can have a say in how we live in the USA.

    d) bad, because it destroys my personal freedom.

8. The so-called "Campaign Finance Reform" that Congress passed, President George W. Bush signed, and the U.S. Supreme Court upheld is

    a) good, because then millionaires and billionaires can self-finance their campaigns, not be forced to live under artificial spending limits, and therefore will be the ones always winning elective office.

    b) good, because it's better to have the news media elite tell me what a candidate stands for instead of hearing it directly from the candidate.

    c) good, because I would rather see taxpayers' dollars going to producing TV commercials and campaign posters for politicians than seeing it spent on hospitals, police, highways, education, national defense, and other nonessential services.

    d) bad, because it destroys my personal freedom.

9. The United Nations is

    a) good, because having lots of third world countries taking our money and then dumping on us is proper penance for our capitalist greed.

    b) good, because we'd all be better off shedding the U.S. Constitution and letting places like Cuba, Iraq, and North Korea have a say in how we govern ourselves.

    c) good, because having a new world order would be so groovy and bitchin'.

    d) good, especially when American troops fight under the UN flag, because giving military commanders from countries that always get their ass kicked in wars the chance to order American soldiers into combat will be a great learning experience for them.

    e) a place where pontificating diplomats talk much, is of marginal

value, and often takes positions hostile to America's vision of freedom.

10. Washington politicians and bureaucrats should
    a) make all the decisions about how my child should be educated.
    b) make all the decisions about where my retirement money gets in-
       vested.
    c) make all the decisions about how my city should be zoned.
    d) tax me more and more, because they are wiser and more compas-
       sionate when it comes to spending the money I have earned.
    e) all of the above, and then some.
    f) leave me alone, and let more decisions be made on the local and state
       level, where my accountability on politicians is easier to maintain.

11. "Com-Symp" is
    a) a new cough syrup.
    b) a new Nintendo game.
    c) a new liqueur.
    d) a sniveling, whiny communist sympathizer.

Bonus Question

Some Parisians are rude to Americans tourists abroad because
    a) we Americans are artistic illiterates who watch movies like *True
       Grit* and *The Sands of Iwo Jima*; we don't quite get *La Cage Aux
       Folles.*
    b) we read inferior books.
    c) we eat inferior cheese.
    d) we drink inferior wine.
    e) we sleep on sheets with an inferior thread count.
    f) all of the above.
    g) some Parisians are jerks.

Check your score: If you answered

All 11 correct: You are a conservative *sensei.* Hail, brother! Hail, sister!

9 to 10 correct: You are a highly evolved thinker. Tune in more often to

Rush Limbaugh and Sean Hannity to achieve perfect oneness with the universe.

7 to 8 correct: You were a Rockefeller delegate to the 1968 Republican National Convention. Buy a six-month subscription to *Human Events* and then retest.

5 to 6 correct: You were a John McCain delegate to the 2000 Republican National Convention. Buy lifetime subscriptions to *Human Events,* the *Wall Street Journal, National Review,* and *The Weekly Standard,* and then retest.

4 correct: You are a registered Democrat; a faded McCain bumper sticker is still on your car, covering the remnants of your Reelect Clinton & Gore bumper sticker.

3 correct: You voted for Bill Bradley for president.

2 correct: You voted for Al Gore for president.

1 correct: You voted for Jesse Jackson for president.

0 correct: You voted for Nikita Khrushchev for president.

Acknowledgments

Two weeks after my defeat for reelection to Congress, former House Speaker Newt Gingrich took me to lunch. When I arrived at the restaurant, I found Newt seated in a booth. He'd already covered the table with scribbled notes, pagers, cell phones, two opened books, and other paraphernalia that occupies a brain never at rest. For the next couple of hours, Newt threw out helpful suggestions about my future. One of them involved the furthest thing from my mind. "You need to write two or three books," Newt said. "And *impeachment* is your second or third one."

"What's the first one?" I asked.

Newt ripped a piece of paper from his tablet, scribbled a quick note, and then passed it to me. It read, *From Welfare to Impeachment: Pursuing the American Dream and Pursuing the American Ideals—The Jim Rogan Story.*

"*That's* your first book," he replied. "It's a great story and very motivational." When I told him I didn't think anyone would buy a book about my life, he scoffed. "You have to sell 30,000 books for it to be considered a commercial success. You can walk into a publisher's office and tell them you have a list of 70,000 donors in fifty states who might buy it."

Newt called his agent, Jillian Manus, who met me for coffee a few weeks later. To my surprise, she was interested: "I'll set you up to interview ghostwriters; you pick one with whom you're comfortable, and we'll go from there." When I told Jillian I wanted to write the book myself and without a ghostwriter, she looked annoyed. Raising an eyebrow and shaking her head, Jillian said diplomatically that "lawyers write for other lawyers," which means we stink as authors. "In the publishing world, it takes a far different style to tell a story and write a successful book," Jillian explained. "I've never met a lawyer who could write for the public. So no offense, but I'll send over a few ghostwriter recommendations."

"But people tell me I'm a pretty good writer," I interrupted. "I've written a few things that I could show you. . . ."

"No thanks," Jillian interrupted. "I'm not interested in reading what you've written before. This is totally different."

Our debate continued until Jillian threw up her hands in frustration with my persistence. As if addressing a spoiled child, the gist of what she said was, *All right, little boy, go home and write your first chapter. Then send it to me, and after I read it we'll find you a ghostwriter.* Later that afternoon, I sat at a Wendy's hamburger stand with a large Coke and legal pad before me. After roughing through an outline, I started writing. A couple of weeks later, I e-mailed the finished prologue and first chapter drafts to Jillian. She read it, and told me to get cracking on chapter two. So began *Rough Edges: My Unlikely Road from Welfare to Washington.* Now that I'm done, I'm thinking maybe Jillian was right: With a ghostwriter, I'd have someone else to blame for the shortcomings.

Over the next few years, Jillian encouraged me with each chapter I sent, and she kept my spirits aloft with constant affirmation. When she read my almost 400-page, single-spaced completed first draft, Jillian told me it was so good that maybe next time I should try my hand at fiction. "Funny you should say that," I answered with a grin. "That's what my wife thinks I just wrote!"

Jillian shopped the manuscript to a dozen New York publishing houses. To my delight, we heard back with interest from several of them. After making the rounds in New York, I settled on ReganBooks, an imprint of HarperCollins. As soon as I met the fellow who became my editor, Cal Morgan, I knew he was the guy with whom I wanted to work. For the next year, Cal helped me take a fat, lethargic draft and pare it down to something leaner and meatier. Every suggestion he made was on the mark.

I never would have begun or continued this three-year marathon without Newt, Jillian, and Cal. To those three, and to Mark Jackson, Ian Lundy, Amy Baron, Judith Regan and all my other friends at ReganBooks and HarperCollins who believed in and helped with the project, I remain deeply grateful.

When my old friend Frank Debrose heard I had started this book, he asked what I was going to say about him. "I'm not sure, Frank," I replied. "I just know that whatever it is, it's going to make me look awfully good at your expense!" Thanks, Franko, for over thirty years of laughs.

Now and then I let a few close friends read selected chapters to get their input. Thanks to Denise Milinkovich, Mary Khayat, Patty Roe, Jim Nygren, Linda Bonar, Rocky Iaukea, Walt Lewis, Judge Terry Green, and Dru Gregory. Thanks also to my roadie-in-waiting, Alissa LeViness, for her handholding during editing. Love and thanks to my wonderful mother-in-law, Trudy Kruse, who's letting me stay married to her daughter despite the occasional bad language that pops up in the book. I tried to keep it clean throughout, Mom, but when describing my Hollywood bartending years notions of Chesterfieldian politeness just don't cut it. To Jason Roe: Your suggestions were *marginally* helpful; Wayne Paugh—yours were just *fair!* (Just kidding . . . thanks, guys!)

My mother and stepfather, Alice and Jack Rogan, are examples of overcoming the toughest adversities. I learned so much from them, and I appreciate deeply the lessons each imparted to their children. Growing up with my brothers Pat and John, and our sister Teri, we managed to have lots of fun and not kill each other in the process. I love you all, and I'm very proud of each of you.

Finally, to Christine, Dana, and Claire: For now, Dad's done hogging the family computer (at least until I start the next book). Thank you for your love and patience during this undertaking.

The final word goes to my young daughters, Dana and Claire. Girls, the story of your old man's life hasn't always been a pretty, but at least it's a true one. Your mother and I have tried to raise you to embrace the truth over the pretty or pleasing. Someday, when you're older, I hope you'll read this book with that spirit in mind.

Index